Presidential Lessons in Leadership

What Executives (and Everybody Else) Can Learn from Six Great American Presidents

Ron Felber

Hamilton Books
A division of
ROWMAN & LITTLEFIELD PUBLISHERS, INC.
Lanham • Boulder • New York • Toronto • Plymouth, UK

Copyright © 2011 by
Hamilton Books
4501 Forbes Boulevard
Suite 200
Lanham, Maryland 20706
Hamilton Books Acquisitions Department (301) 459-3366

Estover Road
Plymouth PL6 7PY
United Kingdom

British Library Cataloging in Publication Information Available

Library of Congress Control Number: 2010937799
ISBN: 978-0-7618-5352-7 (paperback : alk. paper)
eISBN: 978-0-7618-5353-4

Back cover photo by Christaan Felber

"This book is not just the stories of the past but a book of hope and confidence in the future. What happens to the country, to the world, depends on what we do with what others have left us."

John F. Kennedy
Profiles in Courage

Contents

Introduction:
Presidential Lessons in Leadership

These are changing times. Americans everywhere are working in a global economy full of new challenges that are testing the world's financial systems ranging from recession to the banking crisis to sweeping corporate re-structurings. As today's managers, sales reps, and just plain American citizens, we compete not only with the person at the next desk or our competitors across town, but also with Asians, Indians, Middle Easterners, and Europeans. And one thing is certain: globalization isn't going away, and the challenges we face are not going to be solved easily.

To get ahead and stay ahead, we need more than ever to lead, and lead effectively and with authority. As president of a manufacturing company in the United States, I—like most managers—understand that making profit numbers and productivity improvements are absolutely essential to short-term professional success. But numbers and quotas change all the time. So do jobs, bosses, corporate goals, and the external world around us. Some companies survive, while others go bankrupt. It's no longer our parents' time, and corporations don't always have our best interests at the forefront of their agendas. It's up to us to figure out how to advance in our careers and our lives in a way that's both effective and meaningful.

Being responsible for our own professional success and personal fulfillment means that we need to think ahead. Once we finish with a particular job and move on to rise to the next challenge, it's important to take with us the principles, concepts, and vision that paved the way for our past success and can move us toward future opportunities.

LEADERSHIP THAT ENDURES

The kind of leadership needed today is an enduring kind, one that can be applied across jobs, companies, and even country lines with the same kind of winning results. I feel fortunate to have found that kind of leadership style to emulate, although not where you might expect.

When I first started reading up on the subject of leadership for my own professional development, as well as that of my management team, it seemed logical to look to traditional leadership programs. So many people are disciples of these theories, surely they must have something important to teach. But as I delved into the various strategies, I began to realize that the "traditional" instruction offered by celebrity business authors like Jack Welch and Jim Collins, and consultancy firms like Hay Group, not only miss the mark, but, in the end, had little to do with "leadership" at all.

In place of true leadership, it seemed to me that each offered their own flawed management systems which ignored concepts central to leadership either in business, politics, or everyday life, such as *principles, belief, critical thinking*, and the *ability to act decisively*. Understanding the shortcomings of much of the leadership theory out there, I embarked on my own historical journey into the lives of those who have proved themselves to be the "best and brightest" leaders of our nation, America's six greatest presidents as identified year after year by both historians and the public alike, in polls ranging from Gallup to Zogby to Harris. Those presidents are Abraham Lincoln, John F. Kennedy, George Washington, Franklin D. Roosevelt, Theodore Roosevelt, and Ronald Reagan.

A JOURNEY INTO HISTORY

Afterward, when I began telling others about my leadership quest and the answers I'd found, many interrupted me to ask, What do American presidents have to teach today's hard-hitting, high-achieving managers about leadership?

Well, I'm not talking about just any U.S. presidents. Like everybody else, there are a few I might like to toss into a barrel and throw overboard. But then there are those men who faced incredible, daunting challenges in both their personal and professional lives, who triumphed and led our nation to its finest historical moments in the toughest of times. In studying those presidents, I found a treasure trove of accessible leadership lessons essential to business managers and just about anyone else interested in their own personal and professional development.

I'm not alone in thinking that the leadership lessons derived from the study of our great presidents can be applied to business. As early as September 1986, *Fortune* magazine ran a cover story on then President Ronald Reagan entitled "What Manager Reagan Can Teach Managers." Here was a man who triumphed in terms of Reaganomics and his peace-through-strength policies with the Soviet Union; during his second term, however, he made the mistake of relying too much on delegation, leading to the Iran-Contra affair, the greatest failure of his administration. Clearly, we can learn many valuable lessons from a leader like Reagan, including warnings about what leadership practices to avoid.

Make no mistake: the leaders I've selected are presidents, but more profoundly they are individuals, often courageous and sometimes flawed, who have stood in the eyes of historians, the media, and the public, head and shoulders above the rest. Each faced periods of devastating hardship and awesome challenge, both in their presidencies and in their personal lives, but ultimately rose to the occasion; today they call back from history for us to study and to learn the invaluable lessons we can gain from them.

In his classic *The Book of Five Rings*, Japan's greatest samurai, Miyamoto Musashi, makes the point that "personal victories precede public victories."[1] By that he means our greatest leaders, like these American presidents, didn't fake their way through the crises they faced. They became great leaders as a result of personal development, hard fought for and won by each of them during their lifetimes. Their strength of character was an internal victory over the natural vices all of us face as human beings: laziness, excessive pride, greed, egotism, rash behavior, and fear.

Yet the task of studying these six American presidents during the periods of their greatest challenge in order to garner the leadership lessons they can teach us is not easy. As the lives, and even the presidencies, of these individuals are quite expansive, I've narrowed the terrain to include only the background and biographical information pertinent to what I believe was the "greatest" challenge each faced during their lifetime (usually during their presidency).

The "challenging" period represents a time during which each acted in accordance with *character-driven* leadership. So, for example, if a case were to be made that Kennedy denied his character-driven instincts during the Bay of Pigs fiasco, the incident will be examined, but only in light of how it affected the leadership he exercised during the Cuban Missile Crisis, the period I will examine in detail.

Likewise, I've narrowed the chapter on Washington to cover his life leading to his role as commander of American forces immediately preceding the Revolutionary War. The chapter on Lincoln will focus on the leadership he

demonstrated during the controversy surrounding the Emancipation Proclamation. The period I've selected for Theodore Roosevelt is centered around
his "trust-busting" in 1901–2, when he took on Rockefeller, Morgan, Carnegie, and the most powerful monopolies that the United States has ever seen.

In the case of Franklin D. Roosevelt, I've chosen the fourteen months
immediately following the bombing of Pearl Harbor, when, through his
leadership, the U.S. manufacturing base was "miraculously" converted to the
world's most efficient manufacturer of weapons and military supplies. And
for the most current of the six presidents, Ronald Reagan, I will analyze the
character-driven leadership he demonstrated during the period leading up to
and including the collapse of the Soviet Union.

THE TRANSFORMATION

The transformation from "good" leaders to "great" leaders—for the presidents or for ourselves—is not a quick fix or a superficial solution. It's a
developmental process.

By going through it myself, I was able to move from a sales job to the
position of business manager, then VP of sales, on to CEO of a major U.S.
manufacturing company, and finally to my current position as president of
the Americas for a four-billion-dollar global corporation. During that same
time, I achieved my doctorate in arts and letters, authored nine books, and
have been a frequent guest speaker at conferences on the subject of presidential leadership, all while enjoying a happy marriage and raising three great
kids. The leadership skills I learned have been something I can take with me
in all my pursuits, both personal and professional. And now I'd like to share
them with you, our future business leaders and anyone interested in leading,
whether for their career or their own personal life.

The presidents I've selected have something to teach each one of us. Because
of my own hard-won experience, I feel confident that if you emulate the leadership lessons offered by America's greatest presidents and go through the critical developmental process they epitomize, you too will become a great leader
who endures, proud of who you are and of what you have become.

Chapter I

The Big Mistake: Substituting Management for Leadership

There are a multitude of business books, audiotapes, lectures, and training seminars available on the subject of leadership. They include *Leadership* by James J. Cribbin, *The Cycle of Leadership* by Noel M. Tichy, and John P. Kotter's *The Leadership Factor*, just to name a few.

Three of the most popular and influential proponents of leadership theory over the past decade are business icon Jack Welch, former CEO of General Electric and author of the best seller *Jack: Straight from the Gut*; Jim Collins, author of one of the all-time best-selling business books, *Good to Great*; and the Hay Group, a multimillion-dollar consortium that offers corporations worldwide "Leadership Development" training. Each of these widely accepted sources offers their own unique model that promises to enhance their students' leadership performance. These popular programs, however, are all based on one big mistake. They all teach management theory, not genuine leadership, with the result being that they overlook what truly characterizes great leadership: that it is *character-driven* as opposed to *situational*.

Character-driven leadership is founded on the belief that *adherence to universally accepted principles is what fosters great leaders*. From this platform, intelligence, education, and experience, along with other acquired skills, can transform a "good" person into a "great" leader.

Situational leadership—that is, the kind put forward by Welch, Collins's, and the Hay Group—puts management techniques and models at the core of their teaching. This approach makes the critical mistake of reversing the natural order of the learning process: it seeks to build leaders from the *outside in*, rather than from the *inside out*.

Let's examine more closely each of the three leadership programs.

HAY'S HAD ITS DAY

Consulting firms like the Hay Group teach managers not to lead, but to manipulate subordinates based on psychological profiling and situational management. In Hay's model, a combination of the executive's personality traits are measured in order to designate his or her leadership profile—for example, "Directive," "Visionary," "Affiliative," "Participative," "Pacesetting," and "Coaching."[1] A bar graph is developed from these scores and an interpretation given when weighed against three alternate models generated by answers supplied in identical testing, in which subordinates, peers, and superiors are each required to rate that same individual in an assessment process called a "360."

With the executive's leadership profile defined both by the individual and those who work with him or her, an ECI (Emotional Capacity Index) is administered, consisting of hundreds of questions. It is meant to gauge the individual's level of "Self-Awareness," "Self-Management," "Social Awareness," and "Relationship Management."[2] From that data, an EICM (Emotional Intelligence Competence Model) is developed. It maps out the executive's scores in areas like "Self-Confidence," "Empathy," "Achievement," "Emotional Self-Control," and "Adaptability."[3] These scores are then matched against a SUCCESS PROFILE, based on thousands of test scores that have been accumulated in the Hay Group's computer data bank over decades of testing.

Clearly, there are intrinsic ethical and privacy problems with this type of "scientific" model. One executive reports that his boss used the Hay Group Leadership Development Program as a method to "get even with him" for the firing of his best friend for nonperformance. With no corporate policy in place to restrict the sharing of results, the executive could not be certain who would see his "file" or how it would be used. Was this "punishment" going to be the basis for his own termination if his resulting profiles didn't match the Hay Group's SUCCESS PROFILE?[4] Or, if indeed he was suffering from low "Self-Esteem," for example, was this information going to be used to help develop him—or to manipulate him through knowledge of that vulnerability? This executive went through his day-to-day business life for years never knowing the answers to these questions.

If these disturbing possibilities aren't enough to set your teeth on edge, perhaps the following definition of leadership styles put forward by the Hay Group in corporate training centers throughout America will help to highlight the fundamental flaws in the "scientific" model's approach:

Leadership Styles
Behavior=f (Person, Situation)
   Behavior is a function of the Personnel and Situation we are dealing with, *i.e.,* your behavior as a Leader depends on the profile of the person you interact with.

Therefore, in different situations and dealing with different persons you can use/ need to use different Leadership Styles.[5]

This definition is not unlike the message put forward in the business books of Welch, Collins, and other management gurus on the subject of leadership. That is, much of what they teach isn't leadership at all, but rather a strategy for "situational" management.

The Hay Group encourages executives to adapt their message and leadership style to the *personality of the person being addressed within the specific situation they are addressing*. It therefore instructs them not to lead through vision or quality of message, but to manipulate based on the results of psychological profiling. It teaches managers the techniques necessary to control rather than lead, based on manipulation of message, style, and, ultimately, the individuals themselves (depending on the situation and the psychological profiles involved). This isn't leadership derived from the inside out (principles), but from the outside in (technique); and in the long run it seems, to me, doomed to fail.

SQUELCH WELCH

Similarly, business guru Jack Welch promotes an "ego-driven" model of leadership. In his Orwellian vision, salient leadership qualities one traditionally might begin with, such as personal values and belief, are almost nonexistent. Let's review this passage from his best seller *Jack: Straight from the Gut*:

> In GE every day, there's an informal, unspoken personnel review—in the lunchroom, the hallways, and in every business meeting. That intense people focus—testing everyone in a myriad of environments—defines managing at GE. In the end, that's what GE is. We build great people, who then build great products and services. Every year, we'd ask each of GE's businesses to rank all of their top executives. The concept was we forced our business leaders to differentiate their leadership. They had to identify the people in their organizations that they consider in the top 20 percent, the vital 70 percent, and the bottom 10 percent by name, position, and compensation. The bottom 10 percent had to go.
>
> The first time new managers name their weakest players, they do it readily. The second year, it's more difficult. By the third year, it's war. By then, the most obvious weak performers have left the team, and many managers can't bring themselves to put anyone in the C column. They've grown to love everyone on their team. . . .
>
> The problem with not dealing with the Cs in a straightforward manner really hits home when a new manager shows up. With no emotional attachment to the team, he or she has no difficulty identifying the weakest players.[6]

For me the problem with Jack Welch being seen as a truly "great" leader is evident in the titles of both his book and the chapter from which the above passage is excerpted, "The People Factory." The phrase implies that people can be manufactured, just like refrigerators or microwave ovens are produced at General Electric's plants. The more telling implication telegraphed in the book's title—*Jack: Straight from the Gut*—is that Welch seems to believe that he has somehow created the blueprint for the perfect employee that GE supposedly manufactures.

The flaw in the leadership style espoused by Jack Welch and other CEO authors, like Lee Iacocca in *Where Have All the Leaders Gone?*, is that it's ego-driven. For example, in one seven-line paragraph in his book, there are no fewer than eight references to "I": "I was an outrageous champion of everything we did . . . I had an idea . . . I wanted to drive . . . I could never say it enough . . . I repeated it over and over . . . until I could almost gag . . . I always felt . . . I had to be over the top.[7]" What a charmer Jack must have been to work with!

Additionally, Welch created a monstrous work environment, chock-full of continuous "personnel reviews," with "intense focus" in "lunchrooms, hallways, and in every business meeting." This atmosphere is only worsened by a human resources appraisal system that "forces" executives to rate their "team" in A, B, and C categories, knowing that anyone rated "C" (the bottom 10 percent) will be fired.[8]

Professor Rakesh Khurana of the Harvard Business School makes the point that highly directive leadership styles of CEOs like Welch and Iacocca ultimately lead to dysfunctional cultures which seemed obvious to me. Moreover, while the ego-driven leader is in power, a culture of distrust, based on wholesale firings and focus on short-term financial results, often takes precedence over the long-term interests of the corporation, its employees, and its shareholders. "You may get a burst of performance from a charismatic CEO," Khurana concludes, "but in the long run they tend to do more harm than good for a company.[9]"

Imagine, then, a situation where an executive, after two or three years of firing the bottom 10 percent, has no "C" players to list. At GE this can't be imagined, however, because Jack Welch, creator of "The GE Way," requires that every year 10 percent be identified for termination of employment regardless of whether they are "C" players! In Mr. Welch's world, even after continuous purging, "C" players must always exist.

Fortunately, critics like Khurana are now taking a closer look at GE's accounting systems under Welch and the company's reliance on acquisitions to spur growth. More to the point, they speculate that the spate of profit scandals at GE and its subsidiaries during Welch's reign may have been encouraged by his obsession with executive bonus programs and quick and dramatic bottom-line improvements. So far as I can tell—nearly the opposite of Welch—genuinely "great" leaders encourage teamwork and the basic concept of "doing things right," without shortcuts, and in a way that's sustainable.

IT'S MORE THAN NUMBERS

In his book *Leaders*, former president Richard Nixon argues that historical "impact" is what makes a leader great.[10] He fails, however, to make the more precise differentiation of *positive* historical impact. Certainly, Hitler, Stalin, or, more recently, Bin Laden have had tremendous historical impact. But they must justifiably be discarded from any list that defines great leadership as character-driven and built on principles.

So, too, business leaders like Welch, while successful and having "impact" on global business practices, must be scratched from a short list of great leaders because "greatness" in global business, as well as in global politics, must be *ennobling*. It must be grounded in inviolate principles that are universal—integrity, fairness, honesty, trustworthiness—and involve more than callously firing 10 percent of your staff every year and dropping those savings to the bottom line.

IT'S NOT ABOUT LUCK

The third traditional leadership model, called "Level 5" by Jim Collins (and the "leadership from forty-thousand feet" model by me), is put forward in his best seller *Good to Great*: "Level 5 leaders channel their ego needs away from themselves and into the larger goal of building a great company. It's not that Level 5 leaders have no ego or self-interest. Indeed, they are incredibly ambitious—but their ambition is first and foremost for the institution, not themselves.[11]" The "Level 5 Hierarchy" that Collins espouses is as follows:

Level 5—Level 5 Executive: builds enduring greatness through a paradoxical blend of personal humility and professional will.
Level 4—Effective Leader: catalyzes commitment to and vigorous pursuit of a clear and compelling vision, stimulating higher performance standards.
Level 3—Competent Manager: organizes people and resources toward the effective and efficient pursuit of predetermined objectives.
Level 2—Contributing Team Member: contributes individual capabilities to the achievement of group objectives and works effectively with others in a group setting.

Level 1—Highly Capable Individual: makes productive contributions through talent, knowledge, skills, and good work habits.[12]

While Collins's Zen-like perspective on leadership has its charm, the fundamental problem with his model comes to the fore when he gives examples of those whom he considers to be Level 5 leaders. One example is Alan Wurtzel, CEO of Circuit City: "You might expect that extraordinary results like these [Circuit City's] would lead Alan Wurtzel to discuss brilliant decisions he made. But when asked to list the top factor in his company's transformation, Wurtzel gave a surprising answer: The number one factor was luck. "We were in a great industry, with the wind at our backs."[13] Collins goes on to cite CEOs Darwin Smith of Kimberly-Clark and Joseph F. Cullman of Philip Morris as Level 5 leaders, each of whom, according to Collins, held to that same tagline—"I guess we were just lucky."

This is not helpful to any meaningful definition of leadership, nor is it instructional to anyone seeking to understand how to improve their own leadership skills. Men like Wurtzel, Smith, and Cullman simplistically, if not disingenuously, attribute their success to an external force (luck) instead of the considered actions they took, which, of necessity, derive from internal forces such as intelligence, experience, and critical thinking.

It is a fact that *great leaders must lead*. In order to lead well, they must *teach*, *influence*, and *inspire*. These are all characteristics that go far beyond the simple "good luck" or "bad luck" one experiences when playing roulette. Additionally, as an executive moves up Collins's Level 5 Hierarchy, he seems to progress further up and away from actually *doing things*. Level 1 refers to "good work habits"—that is, *you do it*; Level 2 refers to "group . . . work"—that is, *you do some of it*; Level 3 refers to "organizes people"—that is, *others do it*; and so on. By the time an executive reaches Level 5, he or she isn't leading but—as a CEO running a one-billion-dollar specialty chemical company recently described it—managing "from forty thousand feet,"[14] detached from both employees and customers.

The problem with this kind of top-down management is that from forty thousand feet away, an executive cannot discern constructive happenings (which should be supported) from destructive happenings (which should be discouraged or stopped). In short, Collins's hierarchical "pyramid," when used in this way, represents a total abrogation of leadership responsibility. It assumes that the leader is above all others and that his subordinates, like the pedestrians in Graham Greene's film *The Third Man*, are viewed from a kind of executive ski lift, mere dots to be added to or subtracted from the corporate landscape.

Clearly, the problem with Collins's Level 5 Hierarchy is that it's "situational" and based exclusively on external forces, whether they are metaphysical (luck) or organizational (Level 5 Hierarchy). Therefore Collins himself seems at a loss to explain how Level 5 leadership can be learned, taught, or otherwise acquired:

> For your own development, I would love to be able to give you a list of steps for becoming Level 5, but we have no solid research data that would support a credible list. Our research exposed Level 5 as a key component inside the black box of what it takes to shift a company from good to great. Yet inside that black box is yet another black box is yet another black box—namely, the inner development of a person to Level 5. We could speculate on what might be inside that inner black box, but it would mostly be just that—speculation. So, in short, Level 5 is a very satisfying idea, a powerful idea, and, to produce the best transitions from good to great, perhaps an essential idea. A "Ten-Step List to Level 5" would trivialize the concept.[15]

TRUE LEADERS "EARN THEIR STRIPES"

Contrary to Collins's model, "character-driven" leaders lead by example. A character-driven leader gives direction, influences, inspires, and, when the situation calls for it, decides boldly. Character-driven leadership is not ephemeral. Rather, it's substantive, based on the premise that the right to lead must be earned. It is founded on integrity, quality of vision, trustworthiness, perseverance, and the ability to inspire others to follow. In order to be a great leader, there must be something profound about the person and the leadership they offer. Great leaders, like great artists, must earn their stripes. They must take the talent that they possess and develop themselves so that they become worthy of attracting and keeping a following. They must be *real* in order for the leadership they exert to be credible.

Still, before we move on to examine closely the character-driven leadership exercised by six American presidents during periods of their greatest challenge, it's important to respond again to a pervasive and controversial question: can key elements of the leadership exercised by presidents in the administration of U.S. government be relevant to the leadership exercised by executives in the business world?

WHY EMULATE THE PRESIDENTS?

The key elements identified in *character-driven* leadership are relevant, and crucial, to the long-term success of executive leaders—and, in fact, almost every other kind of leader I can think of.

Situational leadership builds its foundation on the shifting sands of the personalities of the individuals involved and the situation that the "leader" finds him- or herself enveloped in. This prompts a shifting message to be delivered in a variety of ways. In short, the *situation* dictates who the leader will be at that moment, what the leader will say, and how the leader will say it. *Character-driven* leadership, founded on principles, derives its power from deep inside the leader and the culture. Thus it's stronger, more enduring, and, ultimately, more effective. This kind of leader also has more global appeal— as you shall soon see.

So what are *principles*, as used in the context of character-driven leadership? As the proud dad of two Eagle Scouts, I figured out the answer when I recognized the stark distinction between what celebrity authors and consultancy firms like the Hay Group teach future business leaders versus what tried-and-true programs like the Boy Scouts of America's Eagle Scout program instructs their future leaders to prize and adhere to. The principles admired by the Boy Scouts include virtues such as honesty, fairness, trustworthiness, vigilance (be prepared!), and courage, which are accepted and admired by nearly all cultures and individuals.[16] These principles represent concepts that encourage future leaders to eschew vice; develop their own character through self-discipline, practical knowledge, and purity of heart; and marshal the strength to lead others.

Character-driven leaders aren't shallow or arrogant; they are *ardent*. Their dreams, their actions, and their very presence ennoble the situation and the people they interact with each day because their overwhelming strength of character fosters words and actions that make people want to follow them to a forward-looking, more fulfilling future. Great leaders, whether in business or otherwise, are defined by their characters and their actions. In this way, America's greatest presidents can instruct us as we seek success as future leaders in our careers, our personal lives, and in the society in which we live.

NO MORE ENRONS!

A question you hear a lot these days, whether around the coffee machine at work or on television talk shows, is whether the misaligned values and amoral foundation prevalent in many of our leadership models helped to create corporate scandals like Enron and A.I.G., the banking crisis, and the cultural quagmire we find ourselves facing. Well, it seems to me that at the very least the type of instruction many of our current leaders adhere to contributes to these catastrophes because it creates an environment that places "winning" above all, views "profits" as the gauge of success, and overlooks character in favor of results.

In other words, *situational leadership* substitutes an executive's adherence to a specific business model for a character-driven leader's internal development and hard-won business savvy. In the latter, profits are the fruit derived from doing the right things consistently, leaving the executive capable of innovating based on a deep understanding of him- or herself and the surrounding business environment. In the former, profits are derived from doing what others say will work, devoid of core principles, leaving the executive foundationless, without any self-knowledge, deep understanding of the environment, or the necessary skills to innovate in times of hardship or change. Moreover, as this executive knows only the path of "winning" at any cost, he or she often feels trapped and desperate, compelled by a perverse character and lack of principles to resort to unethical or even criminal behavior.

Perhaps now, more than ever, it's easy to see why key elements of the leadership exercised by six character-driven presidents are applicable to business or any other kind of leadership role. The principles I'm writing about emanate, as Musashi in *The Book of Five Rings* tells us, from "the human conscience [and are] as universal and enduring as the earth that we stand upon."[17] Of course, by themselves, without the benefit of intelligence, experience, and viable instincts, no great leaders will emerge. But without the benefit of these universally accepted principles at his or her core, it can be guaranteed that no great leader will have even a chance of emerging.

Come with me now on the journey in which we explore and learn from key elements of the leadership as exercised by America's most formidable presidents during periods of their greatest challenge.

Chapter II

Abraham Lincoln
U.S. President, 1861–1865

In polls asking historians to rank the forty-four presidents—such as the one published by Zogby International in 2008—Lincoln invariably comes in, along with George Washington, as either the first or second "greatest."[1] Yet the greatness of Lincoln wasn't that he wanted to do great things, others wanted to accomplish those same goals. The greatness of Lincoln was his ability to navigate beyond obstacles and encumbrances, never losing sight of his objectives or his humanity, and through a sense of mission and steely determination to accomplish his goals.

In this chapter, we witness the leadership development of a simple, pragmatic man, an uneducated rail-splitter whose fundamental devotion to the principles he'd learned as a child both motivated and guided him to become a towering political genius—and perhaps the greatest of the American presidents we will study. If leadership is built from the inside out and brick by brick through self-development, discipline, and perseverance, then Lincoln is an astonishing example of that process.

Yet none of the leaders we will study was as innately complex and seemingly contradictory as Abraham Lincoln. How strange that a man who wrote and spoke in "plain diction and straightforward expression."[2] should be the subject of so many disparate interpretations of who he was, and what his motivations were in making the crucial decisions as commander in chief that preserved the Union and led the North to victory over the South.

Back in the 1950s, poet Carl Sandburg held a joint session of Congress spellbound with a speech on Lincoln that began, "Not often in the story of mankind does a man arrive on earth who is both steel and velvet, who is hard as a rock and soft as a drifting fog, who holds in his heart and mind the paradox of terrible storm and peace unspeakable and perfect."[3] Yet these beautiful phrases are contradicted by the strong and affecting words of Emory

University economics professor Thomas DiLorenzo, who sees Lincoln as a "water carrier for big business," instigating and presiding over an "unnecessary war"; as well as those of Josiah Holland, who saw Lincoln "as a religious doubter and perhaps even an atheist."

Who was Lincoln and what can he teach us?

Of all the presidents we will study, there is no better example of a man who led by unwavering principles than Abraham Lincoln. In his climb from poverty, his hunger for knowledge, and his burning desire to help others, we see not merely the character of an individual but a profound lesson in leadership.

To understand the qualities engendered within Lincoln as a youth, we must begin with the principles he espoused and lived by throughout his life and supplement them with the virtues that blossomed from that fertile ground. These traits included emotional intelligence, pragmatism, and an overarching ambition to set and accomplish long-term goals larger than himself or the times during which he lived. Lincoln, like all of the presidents we will consider, did not make little plans for his life. He did not have little dreams. He was a man of large ideas and great ambitions.

All too often, one sees the Mathew Brady photographs of Lincoln as president, bearded, somber, and dressed in a dark-vested suit with stovepipe hat atop his head. Nearly every day we Americans see Lincoln's image on the face of a penny or five-dollar bill; he's also been seen in venues as far afield from U.S. history as his "appearance" on the television series *Star Trek*, and, more recently, in the online cartoon *Hard Drinkin' Lincoln*, where the sixteenth president comes across as something of a hybrid between the animated television characters Homer Simpson on *The Simpsons* and Kenny on *South Park*.[4]

The truth is that Abraham Lincoln wasn't any of those caricatures—good, bad, serious, or comical. He was a man who, like each of us, evolved over time to become a doer of actions and the liver of a life, to be judged ultimately by the legacy he left behind and the future that was built on it.

Lincoln's early life was filled with tragedy. His mother, Nancy Hanks Lincoln, died when he was nine years old. His relationship with his father was such that when his father fell mortally ill, Lincoln told his brother it would be the "better for both" if he didn't see him again. His sister, Sarah, died when he was eighteen. His first love, Ann Rutledge, a woman whose hand in marriage he would surely have asked for, died at around that same time. After his marriage to another woman, Lincoln's son Eddie passed on at four years of age. This tragedy was followed by the death of his twelve-year-old son Willie, a loss so devastating that it forever changed the marriage and the lives of both Lincoln and his wife, Mary Todd Lincoln.

It's true that death—particularly involving young children due to illness; women during childbirth; and men and women, young and old, due to disease and war—was a constant companion to people in Lincoln's time. Yet in the case of Lincoln, the tragedies he experienced registered with seismic intensity, changing his mood and his life, because he was an abnormally sensitive man capable of an abiding empathy. If a president like Bill Clinton could say "I feel your pain," a man like Lincoln didn't have to say it: the carnage of five hundred thousand casualties in a fratricidal civil war, coupled with a life steeped in personal tragedy, was written in every line and furrow of his countenance.

The young Lincoln, without pen or paper, practiced his writing and arithmetic using black coal on the back of an iron shovel. His clothes were so tattered that even as an up-and-coming politician about to address hundreds of fledgling Republicans at Cooper Union in New York in February 1860, he had to be convinced by party loyalists to overcome his own sense of frugality and shyness to visit a Manhattan clothier and buy a new suit.[5] And because of his impoverished situation, as a young lad he had access to, and read again and again, only four books—and what a unique and serendipitous selection of literary works they were!

The books in which Abe Lincoln immersed himself during early childhood may have been meager in number because of his poverty, yet they were profound in both moral and political instruction. They taught Lincoln the principles and pragmatism that would become the bedrock of his character, informing his decisions, and his presidency, during the chaotic war years to follow.

Four—that's right, four—books were the only source of comfort Lincoln possessed as he tried to fill an emotional void created by the absence of material comforts, the lack of a father's love, and the absence of early friendships as he grew up in the back woods of Indiana. He himself tells us that he read and reread these four works, drawing from them intellectual, spiritual, and emotional nourishment. Whether by fate or happenstance, those earliest of psychical imprints could not have been more salient: morality (the Bible), fairness and justice (Aesop's Fables), human nature and the foibles of power (Shakespeare), and politics and communications (*The Columbian Orator,* a popular anthology of speeches).

The degree of impact that these books had on a boy of his temperament, reared by a stoical, hard-hearted father and an optimistic, encouraging stepmother (Sarah Bush Lincoln) was immense and helped develop the man and inform his presidency. Lincoln as a child may have been physically strong, but he was morbidly shy; he harbored in his mind a yearning for knowledge and in his heart a tenderness so overwhelming that he once stopped and tracked back half a mile to rescue a pig caught in a mire—not because he loved the pig, recollected a friend, but "just to take the pain out of his mind."[6]

His capacity for feeling would serve him well in his presidency. As business authors like Stephen Covey, author of *The Seven Habits of Highly Ef-*

fective People, observe, one of the cardinal rules of effective communication is to first "seek to understand before trying to be understood."[7] Called today *emotional intelligence*, it's the ability to not only understand the words, but to comprehend the emotions of another when they speak. It is communication on both a physical level—"I hear what you are *saying*"—as well as on a much deeper emotional level—"I understand what you are *feeling*." As such, Lincoln was a president whose listening skills operated at a heightened level, both verbally and emotionally. This left him not only with the desire, but also the psychological wherewithal both to understand his constituents' needs and fulfill them.

His ability to insightfully discern unspoken truths was not limited to others as was evident in Lincoln's prescient dream about his own assassination. Pulitzer Prize–winning historian Doris Kearns Goodwin recounts the president's April 1865 dream as follows:

> Curiously, Lincoln had recently experienced a dream that carried ominous intimations. "There seemed to be a death-like stillness about me," Lincoln purportedly told Ward Lamon. "Then I heard subdued sobs, as if a number of people were weeping . . . I went from room to room; no living person was in sight, but the same mournful sounds of distress met me as I passed along . . . Determined to find the cause of a state of things so mysterious and so shocking, I kept on until I arrived at the East Room [of the White House], which I entered. There I met with a sickening surprise. Before me was a catafalque, on which rested a corpse wrapped in funeral vestments. Around it were stationed soldiers who were acting as guards, and there was a throng of people, some gazing mournfully upon the corpse, whose face was covered, others weeping pitifully. "Who is dead in the White House?" I demanded of one of the soldiers. "The President," was his answer; "He was killed by an assassin!"[8]

The life of Lincoln abounds with such premonition-filled stories, and I believe that they have less to do with the supernatural than with his acute sensitivity to the people and environment that surrounded him. It would be a quality that would serve Lincoln well, time and again.

Perhaps the example that best demonstrates Lincoln's strong internal attributes during his presidency is his decision to write, then hold back, and then finally deliver the Emancipation Proclamation in January 1863, an order that declared the freedom of all slaves in the South. While on first consideration contradictions seem to abound, on reflection there is no question that through it all, Lincoln's basic morality, political genius, and effectiveness as a leader were never more shimmering.

It is necessary to first recognize the controversy, not only among historians and scholars, but also the contradictions in Lincoln's own words and writings, over his motives in declaring the Emancipation Proclamation. For example, in a public letter to Horace Greeley, founder and editor of the *New York Tribune*, the man dubbed the "Great Emancipator" wrote, "My paramount objective in this struggle is to save the Union and is not either to save or destroy slavery. If I could save the Union without freeing all the slaves I would do it; and if I could save it by freeing some and leaving others alone I would do that also."[9] In August 1862 Lincoln had met with a delegation of African Americans and urged them to emigrate to Central America, because "even when you cease to be slaves, you are yet far removed from being placed on an equality with the white race . . . It is better for us both, therefore, to be separated." This comment so infuriated Frederick Douglass, a fierce champion of the abolishment of slavery, that he called Lincoln "a genuine representative of American prejudice."[10]

It doesn't end there. In an article published in *Ebony* magazine in 1969, entitled "Was Abe Lincoln a White Supremacist?" Lerone Bennett Jr. makes the case that Lincoln was a crass man who told racist jokes, exploited the issue of slavery between the North and South for his own political gain, and, for the sole purpose of winning the war, manipulated the black population into soldiering on the side of the North.[11] Clearly, if any of these allegations are true, Lincoln by our own definition of character-driven leadership would fail miserably. Worse, he would have to be judged a monstrous man, no better or worse than Hitler, Stalin, or Bin Laden.

Which kind of man was he? If Lincoln was indeed a "great" leader demonstrating an adherence to principles and the other virtues put forward as essential to "greatness," how could his motives be so misunderstood? Why did he pen the Emancipation Proclamation to begin with? Why did he hold back its announcement, and then its effective date, for nearly six months? How can we be reasonably certain that his declaration of freedom for blacks in America was nothing but a Machiavellian ploy to undermine the Southern war effort by recruiting their work force and turning them against their former "owners" in order to tip the scale of the war in the North's favor?

Aside from the inevitable revisionism that surrounds Lincoln's motives in declaring the Emancipation Proclamation in a country struggling even today with race differences, there is a massive body of evidence that demonstrates that Lincoln's antislavery beliefs were well-formed early in his career, and that they are probably predicated on the reading he did as a boy in rural Indiana.

Despite his personal beliefs about the basic evil of slavery, however, Lincoln was deliberate in approaching the issue—he was anything but a backwoods yahoo. A shrewdly determined pragmatist, he understood that the fundamental principles that guided his life were not the only ones to be considered; moreover, if slavery was ever going to be abolished, it had to be done in a methodical, not an emotional, way. So strong and deceptive was this pragmatic and driven "other" side of Lincoln that the politically astute Edwin Stanton, Lincoln's secretary of war, was forced to concede that he had "never seen a man so open to the ideas of others . . . [yet] always get the better in things" over the strenuous arguments of far more experienced statesmen.[12]

But Lincoln, like FDR seventy-five years later, knew how to "juggle." He understood the dangers of a black and white approach to leadership and possessed the ability to preserve two parallel courses simultaneously knowing that the first (pro-slavery) would dissipate and the other (anti-slavery) would prevail. Lincoln's intellectual dexterity was matched only by the implacability of his moral diligence.

Lincoln had made his beliefs on slavery publicly known as early as 1837, when he protested against the institution in the state legislature. But as a president presiding over a fractured nation on the brink of war, he was in no position to deliver ultimatums. Worse for him, fewer than three years earlier the Supreme Court under Chief Justice Taney had ruled in the *Dred Scott* decision that slavery wasn't only *permissible* in those states designated "slave" states, but that the Missouri Compromise—which limited slavery's boundaries—was unconstitutional, making slavery, in effect, the law of the land.

Nevertheless, in his famous debates with Senator Stephen Douglas, held in August through October of 1858, Lincoln countered Douglas's clever rhetoric with a principle-based message that resonates with the language, imagery, and philosophy of the Bible, Aesop's Fables, Shakespeare, and *The Columbian Orator*. He cast the whole conflict with Douglas "as a battle between right and wrong."[13] In the doing, Lincoln was walking a political tightrope, and he had to fend off charges of promoting the "amalgamation of the races"—"Just because I am in favor of setting a black woman free doesn't mean I want to marry her!"[14]—which he did in his June 16 "House Divided" speech:

> Lincoln addressed the growing agitation over slavery and declared that the conflict would cease only when "a crisis shall have been reached, and passed." Taking a deeply familiar biblical text—"A house divided against itself cannot stand"—he set out the premise on which he constructed this and subsequent speeches. Slavery and freedom were incompatible. "I believe this government cannot endure, permanently half slave and half free." But the struggle had to be resolved within a continuing Union. "I do not expect the house to fall—but I do expect it will cease to be divided. It will become all one thing, or all the other." There could be no permanent middle ground between the two conditions.[15]

This excerpt, some of it in Lincoln's words, some of it in author Richard Carwardine's, tells us a lot about the predatory logic of Lincoln's principles, elocution, and political determinism. On one level, it is true that the Bible was a huge influence on Lincoln's life and thinking. On another, here was an individual who, while surrounded by the tsunami-like rising of the Second Religious Awakening in the United States, would not acknowledge that Jesus Christ was God's son, despite constant prodding by the Christian movement; in fact, he even wrote an article as he aspired toward political office on why he couldn't accept Christ as deity. His wiser—if not more honest—political handlers saw to it that the treatise never saw the light of day, but the well-documented fact remains that while Lincoln believed in God, he had little use for organized religion; in fact, he sometimes mimicked the hand-wrenching fervor of the itinerant preachers he'd witnessed while speaking as a young man in the West.[16]

While for more than a century the extent of Lincoln's religiosity has been debated, few have ever questioned Lincoln's deeply rooted connection to both the Bible and the soul of humankind. The lessons Lincoln did get from the Bible were more pragmatic than emotional, more spiritual than religious. Though the letter of the Word was unappealing to the iconoclastic Lincoln, its life lessons to him were sound, uplifting, and absolutely necessary for a society in search of a moral compass regarding the issue of slavery. As much as the moral principles that formed the lodestar for his message of freedom and American determinism, Lincoln took from the Bible a gift for language and an eye for parable that was startling in its accuracy when it came to striking at the heart of the American spirit during the 1850s and 60s.

Beyond any of this, there is a deeper lever of duality and logistical sophistication that permeates the House Divided passage. On the one hand, witness the moral certainty of his position: "I believe this government cannot endure half-slave and half-free." Further, he felt that the Republican (and his) position would lead to a public consensus "that it [slavery] is in the course of ultimate extinction."

Nevertheless, understanding that a unilateral outlawing of slavery where it already existed and was an economic necessity—eleven states, with a population of nine million inhabitants—would rupture the delicate balance that was the United States in 1858, Lincoln took a carefully reasoned, balanced position that would, in the end, achieve its goal of ending slavery without exacerbating the conflict between the Northern and Southern states. This "other" side of Lincoln's view is noted by Carwardine when he goes on to observe that "[Lincoln's] policy of arresting the spread of slavery while avoiding the direct assault on the institution as advocated by Northern abolitionists."

So artful is Lincoln in his layered House Divided statement that a Southerner might be persuaded to see him as simply against the *spread of slavery* into non-slave states. So tactical is Lincoln in what he's saying that a Northerner might rally around his words as a reasonable and sure path *to the abolition of the institution.* So strategic is Lincoln in what he's saying that non-radicals on both sides would find comfort in the familiar language of the Bible. Lincoln's was a remorseless, pragmatic, persevering logic at work, understanding the goal he wanted to achieve and never deviating from it, *while at the same time* carefully gauging his growing constituency.

Still, it's no wonder that Frederick Douglass—freed slave, gifted orator, and renowned author—cringed at Lincoln's emancipation strategy. Unlike Lincoln, who spoke of adherence to laws, both local and constitutional, Douglass was an advocate and planner of John Brown's failed and bloody attempt at creating a "slave insurrection" at Harper's Ferry in October 1859.[17] For Lincoln, however, unencumbered candor was a luxury he and the nation could ill afford.

In fact, his oft-stated position among members of the newly created Republican Party was to avoid the "passion and ill temper" that had secured him the presidential nomination over better-known and more experienced candidates like William Seward, destined to become his secretary of state, and Salmon Chase, who would be his secretary of the treasury. Even taking these two formidable names from the short list of prospective candidates, Lincoln arguably was fourth in line to be the presidential nominee after Edward Bates, who would become attorney general, and Simon Cameron, who would assume the position of secretary of war in his cabinet.

How did Lincoln overcome what seemed to be such overwhelming odds against him in gaining the Republican nomination, thereby gaining the distinction of running nationally against his longtime nemesis Stephen Douglas? To answer that it was by "being Lincoln" wouldn't be too facile a response because he took with him into the nomination process each of the leadership virtues he would later put to use as president.

Fundamentally, the three pillars of Republican ideology that became the party's platform going into the 1860 national election were: First, a denunciation of Stephen Douglas's popular sovereignty in favor of a plank that insisted on the federal government's constitutional responsibility to enforce a legal ban on slavery in the territories (a clear effort to secure the Northern states). Second, the promise to embargo slave labor outside its existing boundaries (a plank designed to crystallize the Republican's appeal as economic progressives, already established by their calls for a railroad link to the Pacific; this was a way to include the Western states beneath their political umbrella). Third was their belief in trade tariffs to safeguard domestic manufacturing (a plank that won the hearts of both Pennsylvania delegates concerned about iron interests and protectionists in the Northwestern states).

Given this agenda, no candidate appeared as fitting a choice as Abe Lincoln—owing to his already well-earned reputation for honesty, moderation, and inclusion. Wise enough to have always entertained the South's point of view concerning the economic necessity of slavery due to its plantation system, Lincoln never spoke about banning slavery overnight, as had Chase and Cameron, for example. Instead, he offered sensible plans involving a federal buyout of slaves from their owners in order to secure their freedom. His arguments, even after the onset of the Civil War, were based on logic rather than religious acrimony. He never called Southerners "evil," though he did call the institution of slavery "evil." More to the point, his chief arguments, beyond constitutional law, were economic and based chiefly on the classically American idea of a "meritocracy," "the labor theory of value," and the "relationship of labor and capital."[18]

Regarding meritocracy—a theme that resonated within his own personal climb and that of immigrants and other impoverished Americans—Lincoln was unabashed in his support of a shoemakers' strike in the East, never missing an opportunity to include his views on blacks and the institution of slavery along the way:

> I am glad to see that a system of labor prevails in New England under which laborers can strike when they want to . . . I like the system which lets a man quit when he wants to, and wish it might prevail everywhere, [purposefully adding to that,] I want every man to have the chance—and I believe a black man is entitled to it—in which he can better his condition—when he may look forward and hope to be a hired laborer this year and the next, work for himself afterward, and finally to hire men to work for him![19]

Using a more complex, and subtle, argument against the practicality of slavery, Lincoln meticulously explained his self-taught theories of economics during addresses given between 1858 and 1860 on the relationship of labor and value: "Labor was the prior engine of human activity. Through their industry, sobriety, and honesty men accumulated wealth. With that capital, laborers enjoyed the freedom to hire those who lacked land or their own workshops. Such hired hands were not consigned to permanent dependence . . . They understood the meaning of hope, opportunity, and self improvement . . . Slaves, however, knew only the lash and unremitting hopelessness. This was why 'the mass of white men are really injured by the effect of slave labor in the vicinity of the fields of their own labor.'"[20]

Strained though this logic may have been, it was Lincoln's way of keeping the dialogue both civil and intellectual as opposed to damning and emotional. The basis of his arguments demonstrated that he was not at heart an angry or vindictive man, but rather a man who could recognize the views of Southern whites even if he didn't agree with them. As important to would-be delegates, Lincoln was providing a window into himself and the leadership savvy he possessed even at this early stage of national prominence. It was a window that would serve him well, particularly when seen through the eyes of Wisconsin kingmaker Carl Schurz.

Carl Schurz was an admirer of Lincoln since the first of the Douglas debates. Of German descent, he noticed with interest not only Lincoln's message, but also his "purity" of character, "striking and original" appearance, "powerful" speaking voice, and personal history, which he believed would resonate with German immigrants flooding into the Midwest around that time. But for Schurz, there was more to this "strange, long-armed man" than even those unusual qualities.[21] Lincoln, who was born in the Southern state of Kentucky, had brought with him from that region more than mere pedigree. In many ways, he was the progeny of his political idol, nationally recognized orator and Great Compromiser Henry Clay, who had fashioned the Missouri Compromise when few saw a way out of a North-South conflict.

To Schurz, perhaps the rough equivalent of a modern-day political handler in the James Carvel mold, all of these assets must have tumbled around in his mind like alphabet soup. The words were there, the raw goods, the background, the unvarnished sentiment, and even the political pragmatism to become a major political player on the national scene—but how to put them together into a cogent image? At some point, it came to him: Abe Lincoln, the honest, workaday rail splitter. A man who didn't know how to lie—unlike Douglas, Seward, or Chase—he was "Honest Abe," a throwback to another time, perhaps even an idealized world, before the moral confusion of slavery and economic consideration that seemed to muddy the water between "right" and "wrong." Here was a Bible quoter, morally intransigent but not a religious fanatic; a self-educated Western woodsman who had himself earned a living with the sweat of his brow and the muscle in his arm. Abe Lincoln was to Schurz—and would soon be to others—the embodiment of the American dream: reasonable to Northerners, palatable to Southerners, and someone to whom the masses, especially immigrants, could relate.

Proof of this mass appeal was the fact that once the Lincoln-Douglas debates were published, no fewer than thirty thousand copies were gobbled up almost immediately by an engaged public, and two more editions had to be printed to meet the demand.[22] In 1859, after Lincoln's biography was published in the *Chester County Times*, the public had an opportunity to see, thanks to Schurz, exactly how impoverished Lincoln's early childhood had been. "Yes, it is true, I grew up in a log cabin," he told inquiring reporters. "Yes, I was a rail-splitter and can still cut with the best of them. . . . No, we did not have writing instruments and my arithmetic was practiced using coal on the back of a spade shovel."[23] By February 1860 the mythic Lincoln had emerged, a phenomenon documented for posterity in a well-distributed

Mathew Brady photograph that captures the image of a raw-boned giant, strikingly handsome with penetrating black eyes and high cheekbones, dressed in a brand-new three-piece suit. That same year a subsequent publication of Lincoln's biography sold over one million copies.[24]

All of this attention bemused Lincoln, who, despite trenchant bouts with depression throughout his life, possessed a fabled sense of humor and a disarming modesty. When a *Chicago Press and Tribune* interviewer commented that he found Lincoln "painfully impressed with the extreme poverty of his early surroundings—the utter absence of all romantic and heroic elements," Lincoln couldn't help but respond: "It is a great piece of folly to attempt to make anything out of my early life. It can all be condensed into a single sentence, and that sentence you will find in Gray's Elegy, 'the short and simple annals of the poor.' That's my life, and that's all you or anyone else can make of it."[25]

Nevertheless, with or without Lincoln's own help along these lines, but with a deceptively calculated hands-on approach to every aspect of garnering electoral votes from states essential for his victory, Lincoln triumphed both in his efforts to gain his party's nomination and to win the national election over Stephen Douglas.

After the election, when throngs of ordinary citizens flooded the White House and often gained an audience with the new president, Lincoln vowed to use "every indispensable means" to preserve the Union. He started by inventing what modern political advisers would call "focus groups" on the public's sentiments concerning abolition. In his time he was criticized for leading a "beggar's opera." According to Lincoln, "I feel—though the tax on my time is heavy—that no hours of my day are better employed than those which bring me again within the direct contact and atmosphere of the average of our own people . . . [These meetings] serve to renew in me a clearer and more vivid image of that great popular assemblage out of which I sprung . . . I call these receptions my 'public opinion baths.'"[26] In essence, then, Lincoln knew his own mind regarding the freeing of "all men, including slaves," but he still tried to gauge the mind of the *average* man in order to ascertain the right moment to issue a proclamation for national freedom. And when it came to the abolition of slavery, the fault line in public opinion fell squarely along the Northern and Southern border.

Later, in the summer of 1862, when a delegation of Quakers urged Lincoln to proclaim freedom for the slaves throughout America—something that Lincoln believed would provoke the conflicted border states—Lincoln's response was significant. It also offers a far deeper insight into the complex nature of this president's spiritual journey.

In response to the Quakers' call for freedom, Lincoln responded, "Perhaps God's way of accomplishing the end which the memorialists have in view may be different from theirs." Then, after the disaster at Second Bull Run, Lincoln wrote in a personal memorandum, "In great contests each party claims to act in accordance with the will of God. Both may be, and one must be wrong. God cannot be for, and against the same thing at the same time." Upon later reflection, Lincoln then seems to contemplate the possibility of yet another startling realm of logic: "In the present civil war it is quite possible that God's purpose is something different from the purpose of either party," he writes. "I am almost ready to say this is probably true—that God wills this contest, and wills that it shall not end yet . . . God chose to let the contest begin. And having begun He could give the final victory to either side any day. Yet," he wearily concludes, "the contest proceeds."[27]

Was ever a greater testimony of ultimate faith offered by any man? Here Lincoln acknowledges humankind's helplessness in the face of God, but he benignly accepts the blood, death, and carnage that God's will brings down on his country. Even more striking is the total lack of moral arrogance on Lincoln's part concerning the Union's versus the Confederacy's position on the subject of slavery. There is no rancor, there is no vengeful undercurrent—only the pure, unfettered heart of a man whose spirituality is evolving to a higher plane and who is trying to contend with the mundane yet nightmarish world into which he and his citizenry have plunged headlong.

No wonder Frederick Douglass and Lincoln were at once friends and enemies prior to Douglass's first visit to the White House. It's also no wonder that once Douglass understood the ethereal quality of Lincoln the man, he called him "the moral leader of his time" whose work on behalf of African Americans "made us [blacks and whites] kin uniting us forever."[28] Seward recalled that when discussions, often heated, took place among cabinet members on the subject of slavery, the president "listened intently" but "did not participate" for fear of influencing opinions before they were heard. Indeed, the makeup of Lincoln's own cabinet also revealed much about the man himself.

As Doris Kearns Goodwin points out in her book *Team of Rivals: The Political Genius of Abraham Lincoln*, Lincoln's cabinet was made up almost entirely of expert political rivals whom he'd vanquished but whose expertise and diverse opinions he'd learned to respect. Perhaps his deft combination of these talents into his cabinet was a stroke of political genius, but it was also a bold, courageous leadership decision that readied him for the conflict ahead.

Lincoln knew he had to keep an open mind to succeed at his long-term goal of a united nation. Unfortunately, for him, when he proposed his idea of compensated emancipation as a voluntary first step toward abolition, the border states flatly refused to endorse it.[29] The ideas of others—ordinary citizens, African American leaders, and cabinet members—percolated in his mind. On Sunday, July 13, 1862, while riding in a carriage with Secretary of State William Seward and Secretary of the Navy Gideon Welles on their way to the funeral of Stanton's infant son, the president proposed a new idea: emancipating slaves in the warring Southern states by overriding the constitutional protection the Supreme Court had given slavery with his own constitutionally sanctioned war powers. According to Welles, because the notion had never been discussed, both he and Seward hardly knew how to react. And because the occasion of the funeral wasn't the most propitious for political debate, the two men said little about the proposal, understanding that, at least to Lincoln, the subject of civil war and slavery was never very far from his mind.

But from this idea conceived by Lincoln, we see the inner workings of Lincoln's mind and decision-making process. Not only did he listen, but he listened to all sides, including those of Southern leaders and cabinet members with whom he fundamentally disagreed. Knowing what he wanted to do, however, and knowing when to do it in order to enhance the decision's chances for success, were two different issues—fortunately ones that he was more than capable of separating. Lincoln, like the other great leaders we will study—Reagan, Franklin D. Roosevelt, and Kennedy, all examples—had an unfailing sense of timing.

Only eight days after this historic carriage ride with Seward and Welles, the cabinet was convened and Lincoln shared with them the fact that he was "determined to take definitive steps in respect to military action and slavery." The research phase of his decision-making process had ended, the analysis phase was completed, the deliberation had occurred, and now it was time for action. The two decisions the president had come to were these: First, Union generals in Confederate territory would be authorized to appropriate property necessary to sustain their troops. Second, the Union government would sanction payment of wages to African Americans brought into the army's employ. The third issue, Lincoln confided, before asking that the cabinet convene the next morning in his office, was that he wasn't yet "prepared to decide" about the question of arming blacks accepted into the military.[30]

On July 22 Lincoln's cabinet must have felt shocked when, that morning, the president read them his first draft of the Emancipation Proclamation, a document that would free all slaves within states still in rebellion on January 1, 1863, "thenceforth and forever." Upon the reading, each man present understood that, in a single stroke, Lincoln had superseded legislation on slavery and property rights that had stood for nearly seventy-five years. The president was proposing to free, almost overnight, three and one-half million

African Americans who had been enslaved for generations. The prospect of such an act was, as Welles would later record, "fraught with consequences, immediate and remote, such as human foresight could not penetrate."[31]

Predictably, the reaction of the cabinet to Lincoln's startling proposal was mixed. Edwin Stanton, secretary of war, was for "its immediate promulgation." Edward Bates, attorney general, was for "its immediate promulgation." Gideon Welles, secretary of the navy, was against it because of its "unpredictable results," fearing that far from shortening the war, it would generate an "energy of desperation," thereby intensifying the South's conviction. Caleb Smith, secretary of the interior, was against it, confiding to John Usher, the assistant secretary, that if Lincoln issued the proclamation, he'd "resign and go home and attack the administration." Montgomery Blair, postmaster general, vigorously objected and asked to "formally file" his opposition, viewing Lincoln's proposed proclamation as "radical" and "dangerous." Though in favor of emancipation, Salmon Chase, secretary of the treasury, vehemently opposed Lincoln's proposal, calling it "beyond anything I have recommended . . . [its issuance] leading to depredation and massacre." William Seward, secretary of state, was against it because it "could provoke a racial war in the South . . . so disruptive to cotton [production] that the ruling classes in England and France would intervene [on behalf of the South] to protect their economic interests."[32]

Despite the fact that only two of seven cabinet members favored his Emancipation Proclamation and several questioned his constitutional right to do it, Lincoln remained steadfast about the proposal until Seward, whose expertise in foreign affairs was unquestioned, spoke up, adding to the discussion another dimension: "I approve of the proclamation, but question the expediency of its issue at this juncture . . . The depression of the public mind," he argued, "consequent upon our repeated reverses [battlefield catastrophes] is so great that I fear it may be viewed as the last measure of an exhausted government, a cry for help . . . our last shriek before retreat."[33]

No doubt contemplating the North's miserable performance against generals Lee and Jackson during the Peninsula Campaign, the Seven Days Battles, Bull Run, and others battles, the president listened closely and decided to reconsider—not the proclamation, but the timing of its announcement. His open-mindedness was again at work in changing the timing but he maintained his unwavering belief in the rightness of what he was doing. Lincoln later admitted to artist Francis Carpenter, "The wisdom of the view of the Secretary of State struck me with very great force . . . It was an aspect of the case that, in all my thought upon the subject, I had entirely overlooked. The result was that I put the draft of the proclamation aside, as you do your sketch for a picture, waiting for a [Northern] victory."[34]

Still, as the month of July concluded, Northern victories were nowhere in sight. August commenced with a string of unrelenting Union defeats at Manassas Junction and the Second Battle of Bull Run, leaving the president, as Seward reports, "ready to hang himself."[35] It was also in August that Lincoln met with a delegation of African American leaders to discuss solutions to the slavery issue, followed by his one-on-one meeting with Frederick Douglass. Lincoln listened patiently to the former slave—the first black man to have ever been a guest at the White House—as he vociferously attacked the president's "tardy, hesitating, vacillating policy."

Lincoln, for his part, agreed that "if slavery is not wrong, than nothing on this earth is wrong," but then defended himself on an extraordinary level, considering Douglass's passion on the subject: "While I may appear slow in acting . . . I do not waiver . . . when I have taken a position," Lincoln told him, "I have never retreated from it."[36] Lincoln again proved himself a man of principle. Douglass came away from the meeting deeply impressed with Lincoln's sincerity, honesty, and ability to feel the emotions that were coursing through him: "There was no pomp and ceremony about him . . . In his company I was never in any way reminded of my humble origin, or of my unpopular color . . . [Lincoln was] someone whom I could love, honor, and trust without reservation or doubt."[37]

Of course, what Frederick Douglass could not know when they first met on the afternoon of August 14, was that the president was holding in the top drawer of his desk a document that would free all slaves in the South. At the meeting, however, Lincoln assured Douglass that black soldiers would receive the same pay as white soldiers and promised to sign any promotion for blacks that the secretary of war recommended. In fact, prior to this meeting, Lincoln had already signed an order aimed at preventing Confederates from murdering blacks. It stipulated that "for every soldier killed in violation of the laws of war a rebel soldier shall be executed."[38]

Finally, on September 17 at Antietam, in a clash described by McClellan as the "most terrible battle of the age" and one that left six thousand soldiers dead and seventeen thousand wounded, Northern forces prevailed over Lee.[39] "At last our Generals have risen to the grandeur of the National crisis," the *New York Times* reported to the exhausted and demoralized Union citizenry. "September 17, 1862 will, we predict, hereafter be looked upon as an epoch in the history of this rebellion from which will date the inauguration of its downfall."[40]

Five days later, Lincoln convened his cabinet. The Emancipation Proclamation was published the next day, with an effective date of January 1, 1863, in order to give the rebellious states time to reconsider their war of secession. The next morning, the *Richmond Enquirer* was outraged as were scores of other newspapers in the South and surrounding border states: "[Lincoln] is guilty of inciting an insurrection that will inevitably lead to slaves being hunted down like wild beasts and killed . . . Cheerful and happy now, he plots their deaths."[41]

That evening, when throngs of well-wishers assembled outside of the White House to cheer the actions of the "Great Emancipator," Lincoln was as ardent as he had ever been when he told them from an upstairs window, "I can only trust in God that I have made no mistake. It is now for the country and the world to pass judgment on it . . . [Whatever difficulties I will face] are scarcely so great as the difficulties of those who, upon the battlefield, are endeavoring to purchase with their blood and lives the further happiness and prosperity of this country. Let us never forget them."[42]

Frederick Douglass and Lincoln would meet at the White House on two other occasions after that first August 1862 discussion: in August 1864 and March 1865, immediately after Lincoln's second inauguration and less than a month before the president was assassinated. The mood, according to Douglass, was celebratory. The war was nearly over, with 180,000 African Americans in uniform serving at full pay and with comparable status to white soldiers.[43] Two months earlier, the Thirteenth Amendment, abolishing slavery throughout the United States, had become the law of the land. Though not on Douglass's schedule, or with the timing that most of his own cabinet members agreed with, Lincoln—aware of his surroundings, informed about his options, and cognizant of the implications of his actions—had done exactly what he said he would do.

ABRAHAM LINCOLN'S LEADERSHIP LESSONS

The characteristic I find most impressive about Lincoln's life and presidency is his depth of judgment and consistency in applying it. In situations as gut-wrenching as the ones he faced—slavery, the breaking apart of the union, civil war—the temptation to be rash and judgmental must have been excruciating. So, as with our other great presidents, the presidential lessons Lincoln's leadership asks us to consider are based squarely on his strength of character.

Lesson #1
Don't Let Your Current Environment Dictate Your Future

Lincoln's early life wasn't only impoverished, it was filled with tragedy: the son of an itinerant dirt farmer, ill clothed, poorly nourished, uneducated, and living—literally—in a log cabin, his mother died when he was nine years old, his sister and first love, Ann Rutledge, when he was eighteen, and his two sons, Eddie and Willie, at the ages of four and twelve.

To understand the qualities engendered within Lincoln as a youth, we need to start with the principles he learned and lived by and the virtues he developed within himself. They include emotional intelligence, pragmatism, and an overarching ambition to set and accomplish long-term goals larger than him or the times during which he lived.

Lincoln didn't allow his environment to dictate his future.

Don't focus on where, or even what, you are today. Devote your energies instead to becoming the man or woman you want to be, and the destiny that awaits you.

Lesson #2
Surround Yourself with Positive Influences

Lincoln's early influences provided valuable rhetorical lessons (The Columbian Orator), insights into human nature (Shakespeare), storytelling (Aesop's Fables), and a gift for language (Bible), that he used to maximum effect during his "House Divided" speech, and debates with Stephen Douglas.

It was these positive influences—morally sound and spiritually uplifting— that informed his moral compass on the issue of slavery and formed the lodestar for his message of freedom, democracy, and American determinism.

The effect of "positive influences" extends to the people you choose to have around you. In the case of Lincoln, the Cabinet members he selected— Stanton, Bates, Seward, Chase—were drawn from the ranks of political rivals but, more important, they were the best minds available.

The point is, the books you read, the music you listen to, the people you spend time with, all determine the individual you will become, early in life, and throughout your career.

Spend time with people who share your passion for a "larger" purpose. Immerse yourself in a world of activities that will help you to build a "better self" by surrounding yourself with positive influences, not negative ones.

Lesson #3
Avoid the Pitfalls of a "Black and White" Approach

Sometimes a leader is better off moving a situation closer to his or her ultimate objective rather than trying to achieve it, if the timing is dead wrong. As President Ronald Reagan once said, "I've never understood people that would rather have 100% of nothing than 70% or 80% of what they're after. Wait, and go back later for the other 20% or 30%."[44]

Lincoln knew that the institution of slavery was unsustainable. He also understood that a "black and white" approach to the issue of slavery would shut down communication, exacerbate conflict, and negate the possibility of lasting resolution, so he held his Emancipation Proclamation in his desk drawer for six months waiting for the right moment.

Develop your emotional intelligence. Work hard at listening to the perspectives of others. Accommodate other ideas whenever possible and the positions you take will have more standing with others. Don't be petty. Discussions, negotiations, and the decision-making process should never be encumbered by likes or dislikes, personal prejudices, or supposed moral superiority.

As Lincoln's handling of the problem of slavery demonstrates, enduring leaders are open-minded, mindful of differences of opinion, and stay true to their ideals but avoid the pitfalls of a "black and white" approach.

Lesson #4
Great Leaders Know What They Don't Know

Lincoln's decision-making process was pragmatic: listen, deliberate, analyze, and act never losing sight of your ultimate goal. Yet, when confronted with a point of view more considered than his own, or an external environment that altered, Lincoln changed his mind or—as in the case of the Emancipation Proclamation—the timing of his actions.

Lincoln was not blinded by the shimmer of his own logic and the pride that often goes along with it. Great leaders are also great listeners capable of changing their thinking on a subject, but never their principles, as circumstances change or the external world evolves around them.

The leadership lesson Lincoln demonstrates in his handling of the Emancipation Proclamation is clear: surround yourself with the best people and listen to them. Changing your mind in the face of a dynamic situation, or in light of new information, is not a sign of weakness. It is a sign of intelligence.

Great leaders "know what they don't know" and act accordingly.

Lesson #5
Character-driven Leadership Never Goes Out of Fashion

The wondrous element about character-based leadership is that it never goes out of fashion. There is no new theory, model, or book to replace it. The reason historians like Lerone Bennett Jr. and Josiah Holland struggle to find the true Lincoln is that, despite his straightforward speeches and humble trappings, he was a complex man.

Lincoln did what he believed in regardless of the consequences, even as his decisions were constantly informed by alternate views and the overriding empathy he felt for others. As a result, his opinions were constantly evolving because he was consistently remaking himself to fit into his own, and his nation's larger dreams. It was this relentless pursuit of ideals, running parallel with his own simple hands-on pragmatism, that made him perhaps the most visionary and yet the most effective leader in our nation's history.

Remember, that great leaders run their own race.

As Lincoln demonstrated in his handling of the Emancipation Proclamation, and throughout his presidency, listen to others, compromise when appropriate, but never lose sight of your principles or your humanity

Chapter III

John F. Kennedy
U.S. President, 1961–1963

John F. Kennedy, our nation's thirty-fifth president, served only about one thousand days in office. Yet in poll after poll the American public and many historians place him among the greatest presidents both of the twentieth century and all of American history. In this chapter, we'll examine the hard-won development of JFK's leadership, up to and including the Cuban Missile Crisis. In doing so, we will witness the evolution of our nation's youngest elected president, his bitter failures and his stunning successes, in order to understand how a man whose presidency was so brief could be elevated to the stature of Washington, Lincoln, Teddy Roosevelt, Franklin D. Roosevelt, and Ronald Reagan.

Some see his assassination as the sole reason for JFK's historical impact. One would do well to consider William McKinley, however, another important president also struck down by an assassin's bullet, but one who enjoys no such distinction in the hearts of Americans. The secret of JFK's searing impact on the American public is the courageous leadership of a master critical thinker, something that he demonstrated in his life and the political career leading up to his death.

In a post–World War II America energized by victory and restless for a new direction, Kennedy epitomized a new generation ready to engage the future head-on. The U.S. Food and Drug Administration approved the world's first oral contraceptive in 1960, a tiny white tablet that hit the nation with the social ferocity of the atom bomb. In Greensboro, four African American freshmen from North Carolina Agricultural and Technical State University sat down in protest at an all-white lunch counter in Woolworth's department store. They were joined by eighty-five additional activists, the sit-in sparking similar nonviolent demonstrations across the country and opening a new phase of the civil rights movement. In music, it was Chubby Checker and the twist, an apt metaphor for the coming sexual revolution. In world affairs, it was the catastrophic U-2 incident in which CIA pilot Francis Gary Powers's spy plane was shot down above the USSR. The Eisenhower administration claimed it was a civilian craft that had somehow drifted into Soviet airspace. Unfortunately, Khrushchev held the trump card, because Powers, who had survived the crash only to be captured by the Russians, had already confessed to high-altitude spying.[1]

With all that was going on, American politics needed a bridge, someone to fill the gap between Eisenhower—rooted deep in the tradition of the World War II power structure—and the new generation: someone younger, more vigorous, and even sexy, who would lead America into the modern space age where competition was keen and minds sharp. The landscape was, indeed, that of a new frontier. Kennedy quintessentially captured this vision for a strong and daring America in his 1961 inaugural address:

> Let the word go forth from this time and place, to friend and foe alike, that the torch has been passed to a new generation of Americans—born in this century, tempered by war, disciplined by a hard and bitter peace, proud of our ancient heritage, and unwilling to witness or permit the slow undoing of those human rights to which this nation has always been committed, and to which we are committed today at home and around the world . . . Let every nation know, whether it wishes us well or ill, that we shall pay any price, bear any burden, meet any hardship, support any friend, oppose any foe, to assure the survival and the success of liberty . . . I call on the country and the world to begin anew—remembering on both sides that civility is not a sign of weakness, and sincerity is always subject to proof . . . Let both sides explore what problems unite us instead of belaboring those problems that divide us . . . Let both sides seek to invoke the wonders of science instead of its terrors. Together let us explore the stars, conquer the deserts, eradicate disease, tap the ocean depths, and encourage the arts and commerce. Let both sides unite to heed in all corners of the earth the command of Isaiah—to "undo the heavy burdens and let the oppressed go free."[2]

JFK's inaugural address was a clarion call, not just to citizens of the United States, but to citizens of the world. Like Teddy Roosevelt, who initiated America's rise to the status of world power, Kennedy asserted his leadership and that of the United States as a defender of the free world and humankind's best hope for the future. Given the ferocity of the times, what better example could there be of the integral binding of conviction and courage within a great leader?

When the forty-three-year-old Kennedy declared, "We shall pay any price, bear any burden, meet any hardship . . . to assure the survival and success of liberty," it wasn't a threat, but a declaration of commitment to confront communism throughout the world. Openly displaying both carrot and stick to the Soviets, he took care to deepen his message by adding a second dimension that welcomed dialogue and acknowledged the desirability of peaceful coexistence between competing political systems.

While the first half of his address was a declaration of resolve followed by an appeal for open communications, the second was a challenge to Americans to apply themselves to the higher purpose of national service: "And so, my fellow Americans: Ask not what your country can do for you—ask what you can do for your country," he declared, but he didn't leave it at that. Then he presented a bold, universal vision for a radically different world based on mutual interests and shared humanitarian goals. "Let both sides seek to invoke the wonders of science instead of its terrors," he offered his cold war adversaries. What he offered was more than mere words. Over the next thousand days, JFK proposed and delivered specific and concrete actions to back those words up, including the moon project to explore space; a Peace Corps to aid struggling countries; a civil rights bill to guarantee the freedoms of minorities; a nuclear test ban treaty to stem the rising tide of weapons proliferation; and a strategic alternative to nuclear war with the Soviets over Cuba.

Still, beyond these extraordinary initiatives, there was something much deeper to John F. Kennedy, his leadership, and the love affair Americans had with him than the tragedy of his assassination, his rhetorical eloquence, or even his accomplishments as president. Unlike the scientific detachment of the Hay Group's leadership model, Jack Welch's ego-driven CEO, or Collins's Level 5 guru-leader, John F. Kennedy—perhaps through his own frequent brushes with death—had learned to make a genuine connection with the humanity in each of us. More than words, programs, or legislation, this soul-to-soul engagement shone through in everything he did and everything he projected.

More, like Washington and Lincoln before him, he had the insight to realize that the American people had outgrown the society in which they lived. Their dreams were bigger than the environment they occupied. It was necessary to move on: without fear, and understanding that sacrifice is necessary to achieve meaningful change, whether personally or in the systemic change he challenged the nation to achieve.

As former White House physicians and intimates of JFK now reveal, JFK was a man who knew that he would "die young," even in the absence of an assassin's bullet. Perhaps—as with Lincoln—it was this sense of predestination, mortality, and imminent personal collapse that freed him to be himself without veneer, an individual thoughtful, and even gentle, who possessed the uncanny ability to check those instincts when necessary, gather himself up, and be tough. The Kennedy whom people saw during his inaugural address and at weekly press conferences—bold, confident, and assertive—was only a portion of the full man. Clearly, as those close to him witnessed, there were virtues and flaws that were not evident—his sensitivity, kindness, and abiding empathy—elements that the American public may have intuited but could not fully comprehend.

In fact, few saw the underbelly of Kennedy's day-to-day existence outside of his immediate family and personal physicians. At forty-three years of age, despite his tanned, movie star countenance, continuous references to aggressiveness and vigor, and athletic prowess (as seen through televised footage of touch football games at his family's Hyannis Port retreat), John F. Kennedy was a chronically ill man whose physical condition (according to sealed medical records released in 2003) may not have allowed him to survive a second term as president: "By the time he was in his mid-thirties, Kennedy can't go up a staircase the way a person with normal flexibility can . . . He can't turn over in bed at night, can't take the shoe or sock off his left foot because of his back . . . His Addison's disease was life threatening. It shuts down the body's ability to produce certain hormones that control vital organs."[3] At the time of his death, the president was being treated with no fewer than seven different medications to combat conditions ranging from colitis to Addison's disease, and undergoing a regimen of six injections directly into his back weekly (and sometimes daily) to control pain.

The portrait that emerges after these revelations doesn't minimize Kennedy's stature as a leader but, upon reflection, serves to enhance it. Here was a man leading the most powerful nation on earth through one of the most perilous times in history, and yet he'd grown from a sheltered childhood dominated by unremitting illness to an adult life in which nearly every day lived was one wracked by physical pain. Yet JFK rose to the occasion—as witnessed during the Cuban Missile Crisis—with a sense of mission, coolness, and intellectual probity rivaled in the twentieth century only by the likes of Churchill, FDR, and Charles de Gaulle.

During Kennedy's 1960 campaign for president, Lyndon Johnson wasn't kind or accurate in summing up his opponent for the Democratic nomination as "all style and no substance, too rich."[4] Afterward, when a reporter told Kennedy what Johnson had said, JFK told the newspaperman to take a trip to the modest home in blue-collar Brookline, Massachusetts, where he was born on May 29, 1917. John's father, Joseph Patrick Kennedy, was the son of an Irish-born Boston saloon keeper. His mother, Rose Elizabeth Fitzgerald, was daughter of John "Honey" Fitzgerald, mayor of Boston. "Johnnie," as his father called him, a sickly infant diagnosed with an adrenalin deficiency called Addison's disease, was given the last rites of the Catholic Church at birth.[5]

The second of nine children, little "Jack," as everyone else called him, survived in the rather imposing shadow of firstborn son Joseph Patrick Jr. So enamored were both father and father-in-law with the contrasting good health and robust athleticism of JFK's older brother that they nicknamed Joseph Jr. "Future President" when he was a child. Still, there was no sibling rivalry between the two brothers; there was little reason for it. Joseph was the stronger, the smarter, the better looking—but not the funnier.

Even as a child, Jack Kennedy was known as a quick-witted jokester and a boy happy to be alive. In the winter of 1920, when he was three years old, little Jack contracted scarlet fever, was administered last rites by the local priest (for the second time), and nearly died. Like Theodore Roosevelt, Kennedy used his frequent prolonged hospital stays to sharpen his reading skills and develop his lifelong interest in history. Not nearly the romantic that TR was, Kennedy nevertheless devoured books like *King Arthur and His Knights of the Round Table*—appropriate reading for the man credited by some with creating his own Camelot—and volumes on American history, an interest cultivated by his mother, who took him often to historical sites like Plymouth Rock and the Old North Church.

Several early episodes undoubtedly helped to create the man John F. Kennedy became. Viewed fondly as the "runt of the litter," young Jack, who was bedridden for a large portion of his childhood, had to invent ways of attracting people to spend time with him. Surrounded by nurses while recovering, and sent along with Joe Jr. to Dexter, a private school with only female teachers, Kennedy's appeal to women may well have been shaped by his need to charm and entertain females from a very early age.

Just prior to the stock market crash of 1929, Joseph Kennedy Sr. sold his holdings "short" and invested his substantial gains in a Hollywood movie studio. Embarking on a highly publicized affair with starlet Gloria Swanson, he started introducing his frail, freckled-faced eleven-year-old son to the company of movie stars. This influence can be seen later in JFK's life as president, when his penchant for "action" would lead him to his own not-so-publicized romances, as well as his highly visible friendships with Hollywood stars like Frank Sinatra, Dean Martin, and Sammy Davis Jr.

Yet beyond this, there were at least two other imprints that Joseph Sr. left on Jack and other members of the Kennedy family. The first was an appreciation of the importance of leadership in public service. "To [John F. Kennedy], the highest service people had was in government," recalls Harvard University's John Kenneth Galbraith, chief economist during the Kennedy administration. "You reached the top of human activity not in business, not in the arts, not in writing, but in Washington, D.C. in the government."[6] Much of this probably had to do with Joe Sr.'s own obsession with social acceptance.

Despite his wealth, his movie studio, and his homes in Palm Beach and Hyannis Port, as the son of an immigrant saloon keeper he would never be part of the Brahmin elite dominated by old-money families like the Peabodys, Cabots, and Lodges. To shrewd patriarch Joseph, leadership in government meant legitimization; consciously or unconsciously, each of his offspring would carry this attitude along with them into adulthood.

In the meantime, however, Joe's gritty mental toughness was a second characteristic passed along to Jack and the others. In school at Dexter, Joe Jr. and Jack remained great friends, calling themselves the Catholic "Mucks" and singling themselves out from the silver spoon–fed Protestant boys, with whom they often picked fights. Joe Jr. seemed to take this all in stride. He rarely got angry, had exceptional grades, and dominated the school in football, track, and tennis. For Jack, often too sick to attend classes, life was not nearly so exceptional, although he made the most of it, capitalizing on his good looks, charm, and ability to make people want to be around him. Despite the fact that he was a C student, young Kennedy campaigned to be voted "Most Likely to Succeed" on a lark and won, infuriating schoolmasters who saw it for what it was and tried to have him expelled on the eve of graduation. To Jack and his coconspirators, this was funny and not very intimidating, especially to one who just a year later would again be hospitalized, this time with what doctors diagnosed as leukemia.

Prevented from joining his brother Joe at the London School of Economics after his graduation due to another serious but undiagnosed illness, Jack eventually joined his older brother, but then fell ill, and had to be hospitalized in London before being sent home to recover. Later, at the age of eighteen, he attended Princeton University for a short period; at six feet one and weighing just 135 pounds, however, when he began rapidly losing weight he was again sent home and hospitalized to undergo a series of harrowing medical tests, which would lead doctors to decide that he had cancer of the blood.[7]

Perhaps the true grit of John F. Kennedy can be seen in these early days, because even with his prognosis now as dire as anyone's could be, those attending to him reported that he was "lighthearted, pleasant, and totally at ease." A note written to a friend from Kennedy's hospital bed reflects a strange Lincoln-esque quality to his writing. It was as if he was free of time, disembodied, and watching himself and world around him from a unique, almost otherworldly vantage point: "Took a peek at my chart yesterday and could see they were mentally measuring me for a coffin . . . Tomorrow or next week I suppose we will attend my funeral."[8]

With his health improved but uncured of the mysterious illness that would plague him for the rest of his life, Kennedy began his first semester at Harvard University in the fall of 1936. He campaigned to gain entrance into one of the university's exclusive social clubs that his father and even his brother Joe, being Irish, would never have aspired to joining. It was a testimony to Kennedy's mental toughness, tenacity, and social adaptability that he was able to navigate his way into acceptance. Later that year he injured his back in a freak accident while playing touch football on campus. Problems related to that incident, exacerbated four years later during the sinking of PT Boat 109, would loom large in his life and presidency years later.

One of the seminal moments in Kennedy's evolution as a leader, and which initiated a philosophy he would espouse during the most challenging moments of the cold war, came about as the result of a car tour he took through Europe with a fellow student during the summer of 1937. Driving an old convertible jalopy, Kennedy witnessed firsthand the military buildup that foreshadowed Germany's inexorable march through the Continent. The influence of Hitler and Mussolini was ubiquitous around him and his companion during their entire tour, Kennedy noted, and he no doubt questioned his own father's passivity toward the dictators in his position as U.S. ambassador to the United Kingdom.

Upon his return to Harvard, Jack was ardent in his belief that the United Kingdom, and Neville Chamberlain specifically, were making a catastrophic mistake in their policy of appeasement. The issue became such a bone in his throat that his final thesis, "Why England Slept," examined how a nation as historically savvy as Britain could be lured into such complacency. Ambassador Kennedy certainly could not have enjoyed the later discussions inevitably initiated by his son while meeting British royalty or socializing with members of their diplomatic corp. It was Joe Sr.'s belief that "dictatorships and democracies need to learn to live together," which is where he and Jack, who viewed such statements as a tacit endorsement of Hitler, parted company.

Upon returning to Europe in August 1939, the U.S. ambassador sent Jack back with a message for his father. "War within two weeks," it read; one month later, Germany invaded Poland. At that time, even Joe Sr. had to concede that the primary focus of Jack's argument—"The German people are being whipped into fierce hatred of British, but England remains unprepared, why?"[9]—no longer seemed the empty warnings of an overexcited youth.

In the days that followed, young Kennedy would meet and watch the bigger-than-life historical giants of World War II: Churchill, de Gaulle, and Roosevelt. He even would engage them in discussions. History was alive before him—he'd found his true love and calling. In August 1940, with many of his thesis arguments vindicated, he was offered a book deal for "Why England Slept" and expanded it for publication. Its two major themes were ones that Kennedy was destined to remember in later dealings with Khrushchev and the Soviet Union. First, democracies cannot survive without the vigilance and sacrifice of their citizens. Second, appeasement of tyrants and tyrannical governments is a sure path to war. Based on the relevance of the topic, *Why England Slept* became a best seller and launched Kennedy into a career as an author/journalist.

In 1940, after a brief stint at Stanford School of Business, Jack wrote articles siding with Churchill about the inevitability of U.S. involvement in what he saw as an epic battle to defend democracy and stop the forced spread of totalitarian regimes. Realizing that his father was still against U.S. engagement and had dodged the draft himself in 1917, Jack and his brother Joe sought to enlist in October of that year—Jack in the army and Joe in the navy. For Joe, as always, the path was paved. He wasn't only accepted but was enrolled in the elite Navy Aviators School. For Jack, as always, the path was less than smooth, and he was rejected outright due to his erratic health, driven primarily by Addison's disease and Crohn's disease, an intestinal disorder that had crept into his life.

Such was the patriotic fervor of Kennedy, however, that he would not accept the decision. He'd been vocal in his beliefs concerning the dangers of Hitler, and he wanted to fight for his country! Taking his rejection as a challenge, Jack began a regimen of marathon swimming, weightlifting, and running to improve his fragile health; he then asked Joe Sr. to pull whatever strings he could from his position as U.S. ambassador to the United Kingdom to help get him into the navy. Whether his father, who was opposed to either of his sons enlisting, ever did anything to clear Jack's path is unknown, but in August 1942 Kennedy was commissioned ensign in the navy and assigned to the Office of Naval Intelligence in Washington DC.

From the beginning, unsatisfied with his desk job, Jack repeatedly petitioned his superiors for a post fighting on the frontlines. After a brief stint in PT Boat Officer's Training, he got his wish. He became one of the thousands of graduates dubbed "90 Day Wonders," a jab at the fact that the men's training was for a maximum of three months. By the beginning of 1943, at the age of twenty-six, Lt. John F. Kennedy was commanding his own PT boat in the Solomon Islands. The vessels were equipped with light armament but seemed more engine than boat: while carrying a crew of thirteen, they could blast through the open seas at speeds of better than seventy miles per hour. Their mission was to patrol Japanese-infested waters and to spot, report, and sink enemy ships.

It was on one of these late-night missions in August of that year, with the ocean cloaked in a heavy blanket of fog, that PT Boat 109 was rammed and sliced literally in half by an oncoming Japanese destroyer. It immediately caught fire and sank, killing two men on impact and leaving eleven others floating amid burning fuel. Assuming responsibility for saving those who would otherwise drown, Kennedy, whose own back had been severely injured, took one man in tow as he led his crew through four miles of open sea before arriving safely on an uncharted cay. For seven days the men survived on coconuts, bugs, and rainwater. Each night Kennedy would swim far out into the channel hoping to hail a passing ship; finally an SOS written on a coconut shell was passed from a native to an Australian coast watcher, and the men were rescued.

Noteworthy is the fact that JFK never ducked the responsibility of service to his country despite his own father's encouragement to do so. Indeed, like Teddy Roosevelt, Kennedy went out of his way to face personal challenge, engaged it, learned from it, and eagerly absorbed lessons about life, death, and his own internal fortitude.

Proclaimed a hero for his acts of bravery, Kennedy, with his back in a cast and overall health plummeting, was sent home. That same month, he and his family learned that Joe Jr., after volunteering for a dangerous B-24 mission over Europe, had disappeared in an explosion. He was never to be seen again.

After the war, Kennedy returned to Germany—specifically Berlin—as a journalist working for the *Chicago Herald-American*. While there he gained a deep insight into the perils of world war: "Not a single building not gutted . . . On the streets, the stench, sweet and sickish, from dead bodies is overwhelming."[10]

Kennedy was seeing the effects of war on a massive scale. Even more, he'd felt its awful sting with the death of two crew members and his brother Joe, who was as near to him as a twin. While history and journalism remained passions for him, a complex of influences must have come upon him at this point in his life. Certainly, his father, the ultimate pragmatist, knew how to leap from one horse to the next. With Joe Jr. gone and the senior Kennedy obsessing for most of his adult life about having a son become president, it's fair to assume that Joe Sr.'s hopes were transferred almost automatically to his bright, personable, but sickly second son. But there was more than his father's aspirations at work in the shaping of the adult Jack. The war had matured Jack from a young man with dreams of existing in the lofty cocoon of university life to a man ambitious in his desires to profoundly influence the world and assume a leadership role, as he had in the navy, and as his hero, Sir Winston Churchill, had in Europe.

The coupling of these forces didn't take long to mesh. In 1946 Kennedy became a candidate for the Eleventh Congressional District in Boston. He fiercely campaigned for the position, but a discerning voter could see that he appeared uncomfortable when he spoke before crowds. Moreover, Jack was frighteningly underweight, his ringed eyes giving the appearance not of a robust leader, but rather of a gaunt tubercular.

Despite these obvious drawbacks, there were at least as many positives. In open dialogue with groups of voters, particularly women, Jack was at ease, witty and totally charming. Regarding the issue of the day—communism—he was quick with the facts and clear in his opinions. Finally, he was a Kennedy; as such, he enjoyed the unbridled support of every family member: Former Boston mayor "Honey Fitz"—Jack's maternal grandfather—was there for him with political advice and contacts. His mother, Rose, and his sisters were said to have practically "drowned" women voters with "political tea parties" held on his behalf. But of all his supporters, the most powerful was the willful patriarch Joseph, who funded and directed strategy from behind the scenes.

Kennedy easily won the Eleventh Congressional District seat in 1946, but in September 1947 he was again stricken by a serious illness and hospitalized. This time it seemed there would be no recovery. His father, mother, brothers, and sisters held vigil at his bedside. The doctors concluded that he wouldn't live another year. In desperation, they finally prescribed a new "miracle" drug called cortisone, a first-generation steroid, which they hoped would stem Jack's rapid physical decline. Joseph Kennedy spent the thousands of dollars necessary to buy the drug and stockpile it once doctors determined that it was helping to stabilize his son. By early 1948 Jack was back to politics but still suffering from chronic fatigue.

Encouraged by his family, Jack doggedly continued to represent his constituency when yet another blow struck the Kennedy family. In May of that year Jack's younger sister Kathleen died in a plane crash over Europe. It was a tragedy that his family took in stride with the kind of Irish pluck that seemed to strengthen the bond among them. Shortly after this death of a second family member in their prime, Jack set his sights on the Senate seat occupied by Henry Cabot Lodge Jr., the son of his father's nemesis.

One may wonder if, at this point in his life, John F. Kennedy wanted to be president of the United States, or if it was his father's own raging ambition that was the heartbeat beneath his 1952 Senate run. By most accounts, his congressional career was less than stellar; moreover, based on recent medical revelations, Jack must have been fighting mightily just to live something that approached a normal life. But there was always more to Kennedy than met the eye.

As with all great leaders, beneath the exterior—his good looks and boyish charm—there was a reach-down-into-your-guts grit, a capacity for self-sacrifice, courage, and heroic action that he drew from during moments of challenge and crisis. And thanks to his family's support, his father's political contacts, and the steely resolve that had rescued him so many times before, Kennedy came out the winner over Lodge by more than seventy thousand votes.

For Jack, the weary, battle-tested candidate, the political win must have been gratifying. For Bobby, his younger brother and campaign manager, it must have been exhilarating. For Joseph Kennedy, the son of an Irish Catholic immigrant, who felt perpetually denigrated by Boston high society, it must have been a kind of sweet revenge that he would savor until his son's next step: the presidency of the United States.

Kennedy's health held out for the next two years and during that time, far from the scrawny jokester of his early youth, he developed his own brand of leadership—confident, self-assured, witty, and intellectually curious. Cortisone helped to control his Addison's disease, and with a side effect that was a pleasant surprise to everyone involved. Daily injections of the drug had the effect of building and defining his musculature, as well as filling out his six-feet-one frame from what had been a weight of about 140 pounds to a healthy-looking 170. His face, once accentuated by sallow cheeks and sunken eyes, was now full and virile in appearance, especially since his movie star friends had taught him the value of a Palm Beach tan and a dash of henna to lighten his naturally brown hair. The Kennedy "persona" was beginning to emerge. Women had always liked him, but now they were attracted to him. As Evelyn Lincoln, his White House secretary, later observed in regard to rumors that Kennedy chased women, "Jack Kennedy never chased women. *They chased him!*"[11]

During his first term in the Senate, Kennedy began dating Jacqueline Bouvier, a young and beautiful reporter working for the *Washington Times-Herald*. An experienced traveler twelve years his junior, Jackie had studied at Vassar and the Sorbonne, and graduated with honors from George Washington University. Kennedy was immediately attracted to Jackie Bouvier not just for her stunning appearance, but for her social grace, ability to speak foreign languages, knowledge of ancient history, and love of fine arts. A writer like him, she'd won several awards for essays she had written, and this too made them simpatico.

Yet beyond these obvious attractions, there was certainly another draw for a thirty-six-year-old politician ambitious to become president: Kennedy needed to be married. It may have been charming when a newspaper gossip columnist wrote about one of his flings (with actress Gene Tierney) when he was in his twenties, but by the time he was a politician beyond his mid-thirties, Kennedy knew the voting public preferred to see him anchored, serious, and *monogamous*. For Kennedy there could be no better choice of a mate than the beautiful, elegant, and classy Jacqueline Bouvier. In September 1953, after a four-month engagement, the couple had a storybook wedding that marked the beginning of the most glamorous political marriage in the history of American politics. What began as a romance between Jack and Jackie would lead to a deeply rooted emotional relationship among the American public, its president, and its First Lady.

What Massachusetts voters, and most Americans, didn't know back then was that between October 1954 and February 1955 their senator's life was in danger. With his Addison's disease flaring, his intestinal condition worsening, and his back ruined, the pain that Kennedy lived with became unbearable, forcing him to use crutches during most of that period. The operation proposed by doctors to correct his chronic back pain called for the insertion of a stainless steel plate, which, when coupled with the complications of his adrenalin deficiency, would leave him with only a 50 percent chance of surviving. Yet Kennedy told his new wife, "I'd rather be dead than spend the rest of my life on these goddamned crutches."[12] And so he underwent not one, but two major surgeries. The first was to insert the steel plate. The second was to remove it once a deadly infection had set in. After the surgeries, with doctors predicting the worst and after having again been given last rites, JFK beat the odds to survive. "I know nothing can happen to him now," confided his father to their local priest. "I've sat at his deathbed three times now, and he's always pulled through stronger than before."[13]

During his recovery, much like TR, Kennedy refused to remain idle, and instead began writing a book entitled *Profiles in Courage*, which would become a *New York Times* best seller and win him the Pulitzer Prize. A compilation of biographies of American leaders who put public welfare before personal gain, the book was as much a statement about Kennedy's view of himself and his place in the world as it was about the men he exalted. Chapters describing heroic deeds by John Quincy Adams, Daniel Webster, Thomas Hart Benton, Sam Houston, Edward G. Ross, Lucius Q. C. Lamar, George Norris, and Robert Taft became a personal testimony about John F. Kennedy's own faith in democracy, undaunted courage, and "unyielding devotion to absolute principle."

Profiles in Courage was to boost Kennedy's visibility in early 1956. In February he made headlines and attracted the ire of party stalwarts like Lyndon Johnson by calling on the Democratic Party to unequivocally support the Supreme Court decision ending segregation in public schools, even if it meant alienating Southern Democrats. When presidential nominee Adlai Stevenson backed his stand, Kennedy endorsed Stevenson's candidacy without reservation. In August, during the Democratic National Convention, Kennedy nearly garnered the second spot on the ticket because of his public persona, waxing national on the basis of his Pulitzer Prize, appearances on the television program *Face the Nation*, and a *Look* magazine cover story entitled "Can a Catholic Become Vice-President?"

After the closely contested floor battle with Tennessee's Senator Estes Kefauver, an articulate and charming Kennedy strode to the podium and onto the nation's television screens, graciously asking the delegates to make Kefauver's nomination unanimous. The gesture, and the impression he gave of a "clean-cut boy who'd done his best and who was accepting defeat with a smile," struck at people's hearts across America. With his proposal accepted, Kennedy left to a thunderous ovation, making him, as Arthur Schlesinger Jr. writes, the "only real winner coming out of the convention."[14]

As early as December 1958, Kennedy, his eye set squarely on the White House, had gathered a brain trust second to none, consisting of intellectuals from Harvard and MIT, like Archibald Cox, Arthur Schlesinger Jr., and John Kenneth Galbraith. It would take more than an advisory committee and hard campaigning, however, for Kennedy to win his party's nomination for the presidency.

Overall, Kennedy's stints in the House and Senate had been unimpressive. To many, he was immature, more of father Joe's creation than an authentic leader, and best remembered for his absences, rather than attendance, in Congress. More to the point, Kennedy, despite his youth, carried as much baggage into his campaign as strength. When he visited Eleanor Roosevelt to win her support, she refused, berating him for his and Bobby's failure to disavow Joe McCarthy during his Senate term and for absenting himself from the vote on McCarthy's censure. Lyndon Johnson—running number two in the presidential polls at the time—was savage in his loathing of the young senator and attempted whenever possible to tie the elder Kennedy's past to the candidate before him. Former party standard-bearer Harry Truman, when speaking of "John," pretended a slip, calling him "Joe"; when questioned about Kennedy's Roman Catholicism, Truman scratched his head and wondered out loud whether he should be more concerned about the "pop" or the "pope."[15]

On January 1, 1960, during a strategy session held at the Carlyle Hotel in New York City, Kennedy and aides Kenneth O'Donnell and Larry O'Brien caucused with Jersey City Mayor John Kenny, and Congressman Neil Gallagher concerning these "hurdles":

"Hurdles? Oh, yes, we've got hurdles," Kennedy joked. "Youth, inexperience, soft on Communism, and Catholic to boot, but since you bring it up, what are your thoughts?"

"Hit them head on. It's the only way," Gallagher insisted. "Youth? Turn it into an advantage. With Sputnik up there circling the globe, does anyone believe that Eisenhower or Nixon kept pace? Soft on Communism? You're a war hero, Jack. You fought while Nixon could only talk with Hiss and all the rest about it. Catholic? Concede publicly that it's a problem for some and appeal to

Americans' basic sense of fairness. No one wants to be a bigot. Explain how you would separate affairs of state from religion in a speech. Most people see themselves as fair. Position this Catholic thing as an opportunity for them to prove it."

Kennedy nodded. "Those are some goddamned good ideas, Neil," he said walking toward him and extending his hand, "but the Kennedy administration is going to be talking about the future, not the past, a New Frontier: Space, civil rights, economic expansion and an end to this arms race with the Soviets that threatens to destroy our very existence. Peace, Prosperity, Progress. In the end, that's what it's all about, isn't it?"[16]

Aggressively taking all negatives without rancor and without looking back, Kennedy used his private plane, *Caroline*, to zigzag across the country more than a dozen times; attend meetings held in schools and churches; out-work his opponents in primaries held in Oregon, Wisconsin, and Nebraska; and appear regularly on television shows such as *Meet the Press* and *Face the Nation*.

While campaigning in the West Virginia primary and sensing that his Catholicism was obscuring his proposals for federal aid for education, highway expansion, and safer working conditions for miners, he took his message directly to the coal miners in an extemporaneous speech that made the television news that night: "Nobody asked me if I was Catholic when I joined the United States Navy," he said, confronting the gathering of miners. "And nobody asked my brother if he was a Catholic or a Protestant before he climbed into an American bomber to fly his last mission!" So strong was the stand he took, and so powerful was the image of him standing gaunt and resolute before the rugged West Virginia miners, that it changed the course of the campaign.[17]

Kennedy swept West Virginia, collecting 219,246 votes to Hubert Humphrey's 141,941. In fact, he carried forty-eight of the state's fifty-five counties. The *New York Times*, embracing Kennedy's underdog status, called the victory a "smashing upset" and carried numerous stories pointing to an "emerging Kennedy bandwagon."[18]

The 1960 Democratic National Convention opened on July 11 in the new Los Angeles Memorial Sports Arena. Just days before, a congressional quarterly poll of senators and representatives showed that 54 percent of the members responding thought Lyndon Johnson was the party's strongest candidate, with only 20 percent naming Kennedy. But these were the opinions of insiders and party bosses, not the delegates or masses who voted. And the people loved JFK. More than a man, he was a leader creating a new vision for America, and party insiders had never before seen anything quite like it.

That night, by the time roll call for balloting among the states' delegations started, the momentum among Kennedy supporters was unstoppable. To them, *this was the next president of the United States*; and the man bold in his ideas, strong in his commitments, and courageous in the stands he took, both at home and abroad, won on the first ballot. The convention went wild, and a motion to nominate by acclamation was passed unanimously. In a whirlwind of exuberance, John F. Kennedy, with his New Frontier, was ready to reshape America.

The first televised debate between the two presidential candidates, Nixon and Kennedy, was held in Chicago on September 26, 1960. Eighty million American citizens watched a forty-two-year-old stand toe-to-toe with a political veteran and foreign statesman of note—not only did he hold his own in the debate, but he also presented a stark contrast in style, personality, and vision.

Despite the fact that popular opinion today ballyhoos the appearance of Kennedy—tanned, trim, self-assured—versus that of Nixon—sweaty, grim, with eyes darting and a five o'clock shadow—the true distinction was Kennedy's personal judgment and powers of discernment. The first correct decision Kennedy made was to focus on the first debate over all others, not only because of its lasting first impression that voters would carry into the voting booth, but also because it would be the most watched. The Nixon camp took a diametrically opposed position, and they were wrong, for twenty million more viewers watched the first debate than any of the others.

The second, and more telling, decision made by Kennedy was to stop campaigning one week before the debate. This way he could relax at his family's Palm Beach home, ensure he looked as good as possible by debate time, and cram with experts peppering him with likely debate questions. Unwisely, Nixon campaigned full throttle right up until the afternoon of the debate, then did it sick with a 103-degree temperature while stubbornly refusing to wear makeup in the first-ever televised presidential debate. One might attach little significance to these choices, but truly, as Kennedy's hero Sir Winston Churchill observed, "small decisions affect great outcomes,"[19] and one of the qualities of a great leader lies in his or her ability to identify which "small decisions" matter.

In Kennedy's case, he correctly judged where best to focus his energies for maximum impact (the televised debate) and how best to do it (intense preparation). The net result of these two small decisions, based on correctly prioritizing the tasks ahead, led to the greatest of outcomes: winning the debate and presenting himself favorably to the American people. As important, that night Kennedy, fortified by solid preparation and his presidential appearance, had the prescience to grasp the historical imperative the 1960 election carried, something he crystallized in his overriding challenge to every American watching the debate with the mantra "We can do better . . ." JFK had listened. He heard the unspoken aspirations of an emerging superpower and responded to it:

> In the election of 1960 . . . the question is whether the world will exist half slave or half free, whether it will move in the direction of freedom, in the direction of the road that we are taking, or whether in the direction of slavery . . . Therefore, I think the question before the American people is: Are we doing as much as we can do? Are we as strong as we should be? I saw in West Virginia, here in the United States, where children took home part of their school lunch in order to feed their families . . . I'm not satisfied when many of our teachers are inadequately paid . . . I'm not satisfied when I see men like Jimmy Hoffa, in charge of the largest union in the United States, still free . . . I'm not satisfied until every American enjoys his full constitutional rights . . . I think we can do better.[20]

Easily as important to the outcome of the debate, and the election, is the vision that John Kennedy put forward. With a broad stroke, he laid out the broth and marrow of the challenges confronting the United States, leader of the free world, in 1960: the spread of communism and its implications to the world, the issue of national strength to combat the communist threat and support our allies in democracy, poverty, education, the influence of organized crime in America, and finally the conundrum of civil rights for African Americans. Faced with the fact that the Eisenhower-Nixon record was sound in terms of unemployment, the economy, and world peace, Kennedy—as any good salesman—needed to "create a need," and the need was a call to the nation to not just "do good" but to truly and deeply "excel."

This was the battle cry of the new generation moving forward into a new decade. Kennedy's strategy was to identify, demand, and expect "continuous improvement" of our elected officials, our government, and ourselves. Herein was Kennedy's leadership genius. He appealed to the citizenry's patriotism to galvanize the dormant power of the United States collectively, as a nation. The lesson we see exemplified here is simple yet profound: exceptional leaders rarely discuss the current wants of their following, but rather anticipate their needs, and offer them a roadmap to a better, more meaningful, future. They master the art of communicating to them that every person, every human soul, possesses the seeds of greatness.

Further, he rose above the entrenched cold war mentality of his times and, through sheer force of will and a dazzling agenda of "large ideas," changed America and enlightened the world, setting both on a course to achieve the vision articulated in his 1961 inaugural address. This was not leadership from "forty thousand feet," the pedantic maxims of an egomaniac, or the scientific manipulations of an elite coterie of behavioral psychologists. Rather, it was visionary leadership at its best, backed by superior listening skills, exceptional advisors, and moment-to-moment participation in situations that required direct attention.

Kennedy's unique ability to see the big picture, while understanding the history and detail that it comprised, was his real edge over Richard Nixon, who was never able to capture the public's imagination of what could be. Instead, Nixon drowned them in facts without telling them *why* those facts should matter to them, their country, and future generations. This "gap" between the two candidates was evident in the second debate, which focused on civil rights; the third debate, which focused on China; and again during the fourth debate, when the candidates clashed over Cuba and the harsh cold war realities that neither could ignore. There is no better example of Kennedy's determination on the issue of communist expansion than this excerpt from a speech he gave just two days before the general election:

> Four years ago the Cold War was being carried on thousands of miles away. This year it spread to within 90 miles of Florida, to Cuba. Next week when Mr. Khrushchev and Mr. Castro arrive in New York, they will bring the Cold War within twelve miles of Journal Square. And yet the administration has told us that all is well. In the 1930s while England slept, Hitler armed. Today, while we stand still Khrushchev moves, and, I tell you, we must rebuild our nation's defenses because it is not a question of quarreling with Mr. Khrushchev, as Mr. Nixon has done. It is a question of making ourselves stronger than Russia.

On November 8, 1960, when it was all said and done, Kennedy squeaked by Nixon with 49.7 percent of the popular vote versus 49.5 percent, a difference nationally of just 118,574 votes.[21]

How strange to consider the fact that this "happy-go-lucky" journalist, historian, and war hero had gravitated, despite all odds, to become chief executive and commander in chief of the U.S. armed forces during the most perilous time in our nation's history. On the day that he took office, JFK was greeted with the stone-cold fact that 40 percent of the American public believed that an all-out nuclear war with the Soviet Union was inevitable.[22]

Within days of Kennedy's inaugural address, which promised that America would "bear any burden . . . face any hardship," Khrushchev answered the president's perceived challenge by announcing his intention to support the expansion of Soviet communism throughout the Third World. In response to this test of America's resolve, Kennedy called for a 30 percent increase in defense spending just two weeks into his term. Seven weeks later, the new president would face his first cold war crisis in Cuba with a CIA-hatched plan for the Bay of Pigs invasion.

As early as November 18, 1960, the CIA had briefed Kennedy at his Palm Beach retreat on its plans for an invasion of Cuba. The CIA's attempts at assassinating Fidel Castro had failed, and Soviet weapons had been pouring into Cuba on a daily basis. Mindful of the fact that Cuba had already established ties to the Soviet Union, JFK reluctantly agreed to go along with the scheme, based on the endorsement of CIA Director Allen Dulles and former president Eisenhower. Kennedy undoubtedly depended on the advice of others: some from the intelligence community, like Richard Bissell; and others from the State Department, like Chester Bowles and Dean Rusk. His approval of the plan was predicated on the fact that the U.S. military would have no direct involvement, for Kennedy believed that such an action could trigger a nuclear war with the Soviets.

It was here that Kennedy's inexperience surfaced in ways both subtle and obvious, for the mission's odds of success were never very high. By the afternoon of April 18, 1961, thirty-six hours after the invasion of Cuba had begun, not a single element of the Bay of Pigs had succeeded. Castro was still alive. One CIA-sponsored air attack emanating from Nicaragua had minimal results, with a second having been canceled. Castro's army, fully prepared for the assault, had killed 114 men and captured another 1,189. Castro's spies among the Cuban exiles had given him the entire plan, thus bringing about the most significant international embarrassment of the Kennedy administration.[23]

In a televised address to the American public, the president denied that the United States was directly involved in the attack, but in an oblique reference to the nation's indirect involvement, he noted, "There is an old saying that 'victory has one hundred fathers and defeat is an orphan.'"[24] The subtlety of the comment was not lost on political analysts or Republican adversaries, who viewed the entire affair as a major embarrassment to the United States before the world community.

Kennedy immediately demanded a thorough analysis of the debacle. As a first move, he recalled General Maxwell Taylor from civilian life to recast the country's paramilitary planning, including "intelligence, guerrilla activity and any other pursuit to gain politico-military objectives." The changes were sweeping, including the firing of longtime intelligence icon Allen Dulles, director of the CIA, and the creation of smaller, more elite combat specialists, beginning with the U.S. Army's Green Berets and, after that, the top-secret Delta Force.

According to Kennedy confidant and speechwriter Theodore Sorenson, "In the aftermath of the Bay of Pigs, Kennedy . . . mostly . . . blamed himself for relying on experts. He said, 'I got where I am by not relying on experts. Why did I do this, Ted?' The experts had misled him and now he wanted generalists to sit in from then on. He wanted Robert Kennedy and me, and others who knew him, knew his mind, who knew and shared his goals, his objectives and wanted to protect his interests."[25] Yet, there was more to the Bay of Pigs episode than the American public, and even Kennedy's closest advisers, had any way of knowing at the time. The first concerned John F. Kennedy's chronically poor health. The second regarded his unflagging resolve to study the Bay of Pigs fiasco.

Regarding the president's health at the time, Dr. Jeffrey Kellerman observes, "There are episodes during that period when sitting at a table he had to have aides stationed at both shoulders because he couldn't lean forward to get papers. So to make certain that it didn't look like he couldn't lean forward, the aide would lift the paper and put it in front of him. There were periods where he had to use a standup desk because he couldn't sit down, and there were periods when before he could go into conferences, he'd have to get painkillers injected into his back."[26]

All of this is not to offer an excuse for the outcome of the Bay of Pigs fiasco, and Kennedy certainly didn't excuse himself: "*The 'best and the brightest'!*" Secretary of Defense Robert McNamara remembers him fuming. "*Jesus, Bob, how could I have been so stupid!*" But the failed invasion never escaped John F. Kennedy's purview. Obsessive in his resolve to never repeat a mistake like it, he exhaustively researched how the plan came into existence, who was responsible for its creation, the skewed cold war logic from which it derived, and—most importantly—his own weaknesses in terms of analytical ability, personal judgment, and self-confidence in his role as commander in chief.

A testimony to the bond that Americans shared not only with the president, but with Jackie, then pregnant with John Jr., was the fact that immediately after the Bay of Pigs and Kennedy's national address where he deftly took responsibility for the disaster, a Gallup poll measured his approval rating at an all-time high of 81 percent.

Nevertheless, the trials of John Kennedy were far from over.

On May 16, 1961, following an address to the Canadian Parliament, Kennedy dug a shallow hole in the ground outside the Canadian Government House for a tree-planting ceremony that didn't even make the evening news. What for most men his age would have been a routine gesture was, for him, anything but routine in its effect on him and his presidency. When he left Canada that afternoon, his back was so severely aggravated that the president had to board Air Force One on crutches and deplane at Andrews Air Force base standing on a forklift. He was unable to walk down the ramp stairs under his own power.

The severe health problems that Kennedy had kept to himself during his campaign ranging from chronic back pain to life-threatening Addison's disease would now consume a significant portion of his daily life and presidency. Confined to bed for most of the days leading up to the most important overseas trip of his administration so far—a meeting with French President Charles de Gaulle in Paris and participation in a summit with Soviet Premier Nikita Khrushchev in Vienna—Kennedy had precious little time to recover.

On May 25 he went before Congress to warn of the dangerous escalation of the cold war in other countries and in space; he urged Americans to be prepared for the unthinkable: a nuclear war. "The possibilities for an irrational attack," Kennedy stated, "a miscalculation, an accidental war, or a war of escalation, in which the stakes by each side gradually increase to the point of maximum danger, cannot be either foreseen or deterred. It is on this basis that civil defense can be readily justifiable."[27]

Kennedy then went on to announce an even more startling initiative. With Soviet cosmonaut Yuri Gagarin already the first man in space—the achievement being hailed by Khrushchev as "a triumph that proves communism, not capitalism, would lead exploration into the new frontier"—the president went before Congress to request a nine-billion-dollar appropriation for space exploration, boldly declaring, "I believe that this nation should commit itself to achieving the goal, before this decade is out, of landing a man on the moon and returning him safely to the earth. No single space project in this period will be more impressive to mankind or more important to the long-range exploration of space and none will be so difficult, or expensive to accomplish."[28]

Kennedy's astounding ambition was, in 1961, literally fantastic—a fantasy that was in defiant ignorance of the Soviet Union's huge head start in the space race and America's apparent inability to keep pace. The president had identified a goal that was neither Republican nor Democratic, and one that few in the House of Representatives would oppose. Here was the great national challenge—in addition to the Peace Corps, civil rights bill, civil defense programs, and modernization of U.S. intelligence—that so many found lacking during the Eisenhower years. It was the embodiment of the New Frontier.

Having thrown down the gauntlet to American scientists with his moon project, Kennedy felt that he'd gained the initiative over the Soviets and thus was ready to head for his European meetings. In Paris he and Jackie were greeted by thousands of enthusiastic well-wishers. Addressing the crowd, who loved the First Lady and her ability to charm them in fluent French, he jokingly referred to himself as "Jackie's husband."

Yet, behind closed doors, away from the cheering citizenry, the mood was somber. President Charles de Gaulle was deadly serious in cautioning the president about Khrushchev and the upcoming summit in Vienna. Terrified by the mass of Russian tanks and troops gathered at the German border, he asked Kennedy's reassurance that if Berlin was attacked, the United States would come to its defense. "You won't use nukes?" De Gaulle tested. "Yes, we will," the president promised, guaranteeing a first-strike nuclear assault if Western Europe came under siege. De Gaulle seemed heartened by this response. "Don't show weakness," the president of France soberly advised, "especially on Berlin . . . This will be a psychological testing ground to see if you are tough . . . Do not budge."[29]

Since the end of World War II, Berlin had been divided into East and West. On June 3, 1961, when the two leaders of the most powerful nations on earth met, Khrushchev was robust and surly, Kennedy physically spent and in agonizing pain. To Khrushchev, who'd witnessed and personally ordered any number of executions under Stalin, this was a test of wills, his versus that of what he considered to be a spoiled preppy whose father had pampered him for most of his life. To Kennedy, a student of history and a pragmatic idealist, this was an opportunity to develop a relationship with the Soviet leader in the hopes of setting a new course, one away from cold war and toward a mutual understanding and cooperation.

Over the two days of intensive meetings, two morning and two afternoon sessions, Kennedy's personal physician administered injections of painkillers to the president before the start of each. Somewhere along the way, the wily Khrushchev, sensing that Kennedy was distracted as the sessions lengthened and the painkillers wore off, pressed on, insisting that he had the right to support "wars of liberation" in the Third World, and especially Vietnam. Finally, understanding that thousands of East Berliners were fleeing to the West, Khrushchev moved his queen in this chess match of wills: within six months he intended to sign a "peace treaty" with the East Germans that would end the Allies' right to occupy West Berlin!

Kennedy understood the threat immediately and drew a line in the sand. If the Soviets did that, and acted on it accordingly, the president informed Khrushchev, it would mean war. At this statement, the cold-blooded Khrushchev did not blink. Kennedy pressed on. If there was a war over Berlin, Kennedy expanded, it would involve a nuclear exchange that would kill seventy million people in the first ten minutes. Was Khrushchev aware of that? Khrushchev seemed unmoved. He'd seen war before, Khrushchev informed the American, and death on a massive scale was nothing new to him. "If that's the case, it's going to be a long cold winter," Kennedy solemnly swore, and, with those words, the meeting ended.[30]

On the return flight from Vienna, author Richard Reeves reports, JFK looked totally fatigued, gray, and was hardly able to stand. "He came in and he had a hat with him which was rare for him . . . He put the hat over his eyes lying down on a sofa. 'How did it go?' an aide asked. 'Worst day of my life,' the president said grimly. 'He walked all over me.'"[31] Afterward Kennedy—bedridden with back pain and exhaustion for two weeks following the summit—was concerned and frustrated by his apparent inability to convince Khrushchev that he would not yield to bullying: "We have wholly different views of right and wrong, of what is an internal affair, and what is aggression. And above all, we have wholly different concepts of where the world is and where it is going," he explained during a televised speech.[32]

Within weeks of the meeting, to stem the growing tide of East Berliners defecting to the West, Khrushchev, in a direct affront to American power in the region, ordered the construction of a twelve-foot-high concrete-and-barbed-wire wall to divide the city. The approach to the wall was laced with landmines and guarded by tanks and infantry soldiers. From prison-like towers equipped with prowling searchlights, marksmen watched for potential defectors. Their orders were to shoot to kill. Kennedy's response was to amass U.S. troops at the border, but he eschewed the advice of military advisors to use the occasion to confront the Soviets militarily. Instead, he transformed the building of the wall into a propaganda triumph that demonstrated to the world the repressive nature of Soviet communism. Then, taking a page from Churchill's initial warnings to Hitler, JFK stated his position, and that of the United States: "We do not want to fight, but we have fought before, and others in earlier times have made the same dangerous mistake of assuming that the West was too selfish, and too soft, and too divided to resist invasions of freedom in other lands. To sum it all up, we seek peace but we shall never surrender."[33]

Beyond the temperance Kennedy exercised in his initial response to the Berlin standoff, it was easy to see that he'd learned from his mistakes and taken them to heart. Unfortunately, being immured in their own cold war isolation, the Soviets could not see what the rest of the world was learning about the president and his ability to get tough while keeping options for political maneuvering wide open. Evan Thomas, ambassador to the Soviet Union at the time, remembers Kennedy's cool and reasoned approach to crisis resolution:

> JFK learned from his father, a smart Irish politician, you have to do things in many different ways. You go through the front door, but you also have to go through the side door and back door. You need several channels, one is not enough. And he brought that instinct, that practice, to foreign policy . . . that while, of course, we dealt with the Soviets through the U.N. and State Department, Bobby [Kennedy] ran his own back channel with George Bolshikov, a Soviet spy based in D.C. who was to deliver messages to the Kremlin.[34]

It was through his brother Bobby and Bolshikov that private assurances were delivered as the world awaited either nation's next move until, finally, like a tide receding, both sides simultaneously withdrew forces at Checkpoint Charlie, the guarded passageway to East and West Berlin. The wall stood.

Kennedy had made his point to the world—but not to Khrushchev, who, trampling on a nuclear test ban commitment made at Vienna, ordered the test detonation of a fifty-megaton atomic bomb, one ten times more powerful than all of the weapons used during the Second World War, including Nagasaki and Hiroshima. Forced into action by the Soviet leader's audacity, JFK called for an immediate and unprecedented defense spending increase to demonstrate resolve. He again took the contest beyond brute force, however, using the U.S. space program to demonstrate to the world the difference between "free" and "communist" systems, as well as the difference between a tyrant and a great president.

After ten aborted attempts, on February 12, 1962, at Cape Canaveral, Florida, astronaut John Glenn was put in a space capsule mounted atop an Atlas intercontinental ballistic missile (where a nuclear warhead would normally have been placed) and successfully launched into outer space. Unlike Soviet missions, which were cloaked in secrecy and not publicly aired, the space program's successful and unsuccessful launches, including that of *Friendship 7*, were covered "live" on national television.

In a speech at Rice University, Kennedy defined the very essence of the New Frontier and his world leadership in his answer to the question, "Why go to the moon?"

There is no strife, no prejudice, no national conflict in outer space as yet. Its hazards are hostile to us all. Its conquest deserves the best of all mankind and its opportunity for peaceful co-existence may never come again. "But why," some say, "the moon?" Why choose this as our goal? And they may well ask, "Why climb the highest mountain? Why, thirty-five years ago, fly the Atlantic?" We choose to go to the moon in this decade, and do the other things, not because they are easy, but because they are hard. Because that goal will serve to organize and measure the best of our energies and skills . . . Because that challenge is one we're willing to accept, one we are unwilling to postpone, and one we intend to win, and all the others, too![35]

As important as the accomplishments themselves was the perspective that JFK's optimism offered both Americans and modern civilization. He was telling all that the world didn't have to be mired in the politics of global confrontation. There were alternatives to strife and war if only world leaders could disengage themselves from the mentality and the mistakes of the past.

In this sense, Kennedy tapped into Americans' sense of unlimited possibility, inspiring their imagination to take on modern fears and transform them into hope. This was not wasted on the rest of the world, who saw not only what American ingenuity could achieve, but also the positive motives behind the accomplishments. Eighteen months into his presidency, JFK was defining a new kind of America and a new kind of life for it citizens. The New Frontier would extend far into space but also deep into the American psyche.

Two months after *Friendship* 7's successful mission, Kennedy showed a side of himself that, if the Soviets had studied and understood it, would have told them volumes about the character-driven nature of his leadership. In April 1962, at the behest of steel executives, the Kennedy administration, citing national interests, had helped mediate a union contract with steel workers that held wages flat but offered a ten-cent-an-hour raise in pension contributions. Expecting "big steel" to take a similar approach concerning the price of steel after Kennedy's plea for asceticism in the dead of the cold war, the president was shocked when U.S. Steel Chairman Roger Blough raised steel prices a hefty 3.5 percent, an increase repeated within the week by each of the remaining suppliers!

To Kennedy the increase was no small matter. At that time, steel was the largest single factor in the U.S. economy. It accounted for a half million jobs, and the industry's power was such that 40 percent of the increase in overall prices from 1948 to 1958 could be traced to above-average increases in the price of steel. Soon after, when Blough came to the White House to meet the President personally, a seething JFK informed the chairman, "Mr. Blough, you have made a terrible mistake. You have double-crossed me!"[36]

John F. Kennedy didn't like to lose. Worse, he didn't like to be either cheated or intimidated. During a press conference held on April 11, the president publicly lambasted Blough and the other steel executives: "In this serious hour in our nation's history, when we are confronted with grave crises in Berlin and Southeast Asia, when we are devoting our energies to economic recovery and stability, when we are asking reservists to leave their homes . . . and servicemen to risk their lives . . . and asking union members to hold down their wage requests . . . the American people will find it hard, as I do, to accept a situation in which a tiny handful of steel executives can show such utter contempt for the interests of 185 million Americans."[37]

The public attack was notably strong in its tone and language. Kennedy's private attacks were even more withering, as the attorney general began to investigate potential violations of monopoly laws in the steel industry, FBI agents visited the offices of steel executives inquiring about expense accounts and personal records, and IRS agents called them in for tax audits. Faced with this onslaught, big steel backed down within days, returning prices to their original level.

If Kennedy's decisiveness in handling U.S. Steel didn't give the Soviets pause, then surely his display of moral courage during the integration of the

University of Mississippi should have had them reassessing his capacity for strong stands and bold action in crisis situations.

The conflict began when an African American named James Meredith applied for admission into "Ole Miss," a state-funded public institution that admitted only white students. When his application was denied, he filed a lawsuit against the university in September 1962. Ultimately the Supreme Court ordered that Meredith be admitted.

Given the fact that federal troops were required to enforce a court order during a similar desegregation incident in Little Rock, Arkansas, five years earlier, Kennedy worried that an escalation would lead the world to witness to an ugly display of racism at its worst. As the United States and the Soviets edged toward the precipice of what would become known as the Cuban Missile Crisis, Kennedy understood that America's image abroad and the support of its allies would be a vital factor in winning the propaganda contest between the two systems. The last thing he wanted was a federal versus state battle over the fate and civil rights of one man. But that was exactly the situation that confronted him.

While Mississippi Governor Ross Barnett ranted publicly, swearing to his constituents that he wouldn't allow Meredith admission into the university, Kennedy had his brother, the attorney general, engage Barnett in a series of telephone calls, trying to work out a way for the governor to save face. During those discussions, Bobby made it clear to Barnett that Justice Hugo Black's order would be followed, but that the president also understood his political predicament and wanted to find a nonconfrontational path for Meredith, the governor, and the administration. Matters worsened when local law enforcement, heeding Barnett's refusal to comply, followed suit, and angry mobs turned back federal marshals attempting to escort Meredith to his dormitory. Barnett, for his part, publicly argued that his state's rights were being violated and that Meredith was being supported by a "communist front"—the NAACP—accusations that further solidified the divide.

Faced with the option of either backing down or enforcing the law, Kennedy responded by federalizing the Mississippi National Guard, taking control from the governor, and making himself their commander. On September 30 he addressed the country, and the citizens of Mississippi specifically: "You have a new opportunity to show that you are men of patriotism and integrity," he argued. "For the most effective means of upholding the law is not the state policemen or the marshals or the National Guard. It is you. It lies in your courage to accept those laws with which you disagree as well as those with which you agree. The eyes of the nation and the world are upon you and upon all of us, and the honor of your university and state are in the balance."[38]

Just prior to Kennedy's words, federal agents had successfully escorted James Meredith to his residence on campus, but immediately afterward the two hundred state troopers assigned to protect them walked off, leaving them to fend for themselves. The agents were forced to fire tear gas grenades into the roiling mob in order to protect themselves and Meredith, and the situation further degenerated when gunshots were fired, killing a journalist and a nearby construction worker. It was at that moment in real time while monitoring the situation that the president ordered the National Guard, supplemented with regular army troops, to move in. The following morning, on October 1, James Meredith attended his first class. Two men had died and more than two hundred federal agents and troops had been wounded, with about the same number of civilians jailed and later prosecuted.

Kennedy had risked his political career by potentially alienating the Southern vote while jeopardizing the propaganda battle with the Soviets at a time when it counted most by taking an unwavering stand on what he correctly defined as a "moral" issue that the U.S. government could no longer ignore. In the end, the purity of his motive, and the courage that he demonstrated by protecting the rights of a single individual against the masses, was the greatest display of American righteousness that anyone could have wished for. Kennedy proved to the nation and the world that the Constitution mattered and that, like all of our great presidents, he knew where and when to draw a clear and unmistakable line in the sand. His idealism and moral courage won him the respect and support of voters, as evidenced in the Gallup polls that followed. More importantly, Kennedy's stand at Ole Miss was further evidence that he had grown in his leadership and was now ready to face the greatest challenge of his presidency—the most perilous thirteen days the world had ever seen.

It's been said of Kennedy's hero Winston Churchill that everything he did and all that he learned before World War II prepared him to face the crisis of 1940 when Britain stood alone against Nazi Germany. The same held true for Kennedy. The lessons he learned during the Bay of Pigs, at the Vienna Summit, the Berlin Crisis, and Ole Miss had seasoned him for his role as president. Still, not even these experiences could totally prepare any leader for what historian Arthur Schlesinger calls the "the most dangerous moment in all of human history," with its potential to incinerate millions of people and level entire cities in an instant.[39]

In spring 1962, while domestic issues took center stage for the president, Khrushchev was meeting with the Soviet's high military command at a Black Sea resort. Informed that the Soviet military wouldn't be able to respond to an American first strike, Khrushchev proposed a "different way" to keep the United States in check. The plan called for the installation of medium-range ballistic missiles on the island of Cuba. With Khrushchev still stubbornly seeing Kennedy as a man who would cave in to threats of a nuclear war, and understanding that these offensive weapons were virtually indistinguishable from defensive surface-to-air missiles, it was decided that Soviet Foreign Minister Andrei Gromyko would make private assurances to Bobby Kennedy that the missiles posed no threat while piece by piece the offensive missiles and payloads were delivered and assembled. Interestingly, Khrushchev's ploy was based on the premise that Kennedy led from "forty thousand feet," was unengaged in the management of his cabinet, and lacked the historical perspective to see the comparisons between Hitler's pre–World War II gambit and the Soviet's capacity for aggressive deception.

Khrushchev was wrong on both counts.

His miscalculations became obvious from the onset when, on Tuesday, October 16, 1962, Kennedy's assistant for national security affairs, McGeorge Bundy, brought the president photographs taken from a high-altitude U-2 reconnaissance plane over Cuba showing what appeared to be nuclear-armed IL-28 medium-range missiles targeted on U.S. cities. These were *supposed to be* surface-to-air missiles and radar, but the problem, as Director of Intelligence John McCone told Kennedy, was that there was no foolproof way of verifying Khrushchev's claim of defensive weaponry. Worse, the CIA estimated that the missiles would become operational within two weeks.

The president ordered an emergency meeting of ExCom—a committee of national security advisers that included Lyndon Johnson, Secretary of Defense Robert McNamara, Rusk, Undersecretary of State George Ball, and Bobby Kennedy—that same morning. As ExCom members report, and recently released tapes of the meetings confirm, Kennedy remained in control of himself and events as they unfolded despite intense pressure from the military establishment, the CIA, and vocal political opponents to bomb the missile sites and invade the island.

Kennedy's resistance resulted from his desire to gain a full perspective of the situation before committing to irrevocable actions. The president's sentiments and the power of his resolve to stay objective are palpable in an anecdote conveyed to aide Kenny O'Donnell when, based on an ExCom leak, New York Senator Kenneth Keating took to the Senate floor denouncing Kennedy's deliberation as a signal that he was "soft on nukes." Kennedy said:

In 1914, with World War I underway, Prince von Bulow, the former German chancellor, said to the current chancellor, Bethmann-Hollweg, "How did it all happen?" to which Bethmann-Hollweg replied, "Ah, if only one knew." If this planet is ever ravaged by nuclear war, if the survivors can endure the fire, radiation, and catastrophe, I don't ever want one of those survivors to ask another,

"How did it happen?" and receive the reply, "Ah, if only one knew." But I'm
going to tell you something, that's what Keating and LeMay and the others are
pushing us toward and I won't do it!

From the beginning, Kennedy was convinced that Khrushchev had misled
him about the nature of the weaponry. Moreover, he saw its implications in
the context of the Cold War. The Soviets, through their Cuban clients, had
embarked on a breathtaking provocation. Military leaders like General Curtis
LeMay were adamant in their calls to bomb and invade, and even ExCom
moderates, understanding that an invasion would require between 100,000
and 150,000 troops and lead to a massive Soviet military response in Cuba
and elsewhere, were of the mind that it might be a price worth paying. For
Kennedy, however, the question that loomed wasn't whether to act, but how
to show unshakable resolve without instigating World War III.

McNamara, who eventually came to understand and agree with Kennedy's more strategic approach, comments: "Kennedy was first to see the
big picture. This was more than a Soviet attempt to protect an ally. This was
about strategic balance. This was about Berlin . . . with a potential nuclear
war over Cuba on one hand and what he [Kennedy] perceived to be a potential nuclear war over Berlin with even greater stakes and an even worse
position a month later."[40]

The first ExCom meeting began in the Cabinet Room of the White House
on the morning of Tuesday, October 16, 1962 just three hours after Bundy
had shown Kennedy the most revealing of the nearly one thousand U-2 photos taken over Cuba. Unclear as to whether the missiles shown could be used
to carry nuclear warheads, the president ordered a doubling of U-2 missions
to clarify the situation.

On Thursday morning, October 18, with the options before him ranging
from bombing and invasion to strategic air attacks on the missile sites still
under discussion, Kennedy emphasized that the Cuban crisis did not exist in a vacuum and that another Cold War flashpoint—Berlin—was very
much in play. He feared that a U.S. attack on Cuba would be answered by
a Soviet assault on West Berlin, a move that the United States could only
stop with the use of first-strike nuclear weapons. Given the world situation,
Kennedy favored a strong but less provocative response than bombing and
all-out invasion.

Partway through the meeting, the president excused himself to meet with
Soviet Foreign Minister Andrei Gromyko. With the presence of intercontinental offensive missiles with a range of 2,200 nautical miles confirmed
by subsequent U-2 missions, Kennedy was withering in his scorn for Gromyko, who held to the Soviet deception. Stating that he had "never heard so

many barefaced lies," Kennedy ended the encounter with a blunt message for Khrushchev, instructing his foreign minister to "tell his boss" that if the missiles were not dismantled and removed, "the United States would remove them at the risk of nuclear war."[41]

When Kennedy returned to ExCom, an uneasy consensus had developed, away from the advantages of a first strike and around his initial idea of a naval "quarantine" that would put the nation "one step short of an invasion." The word "blockade" was one that Kennedy refused to use, because it was associated with the Soviet attempt to starve out West Berlin in 1948. The quarantine would not be enacted to stop the supply of food and medical supplies to the Cuban people, Kennedy noted, but to prevent delivery of military hardware requisite to making the missile sites.

On Monday afternoon, October 22, when the president met with congressional leaders to brief them on his decision of a naval quarantine, he expected their support but was startled to encounter vehement resistance and even more pressure to invade. Like General LeMay, some went so far as to compare Kennedy with Neville Chamberlain in his dealings with Hitler, a bit of nastiness that would have provoked even a less-confident president, especially one who'd written a book like *Why England Slept*.

Six days into the ExCom meetings, Kennedy states in a tape-recorded diary that "nuclear war might be unpreventable," a fear that has him working 24/7 despite a host of medical complications that would certainly have been crippling to a less committed individual.[42] But Kennedy was used to pain and had mastered the art of rising to the occasion. In addition to diphenoxylate, atropine, and paragoric used for Crohn's-related intestinal inflammation; trasentine and phenobarbital, used as an antispasmodic and muscle relaxant; and corticosteroids used to control his Addison's disease, JFK was given "trigger point" injections of procaine and lidocaine directly into the muscles of his back to relieve debilitating pain. According to his medical records, Kennedy needed six injections into his back just to relieve the pain "on a momentary basis" throughout the crisis.

Fortunately, because Kennedy's tapes, medical records, and recorded diary have now been released, there are available today several barometers with which to gauge Kennedy's leadership during one of the world's most sobering moments. The portrait that emerges is that of a lucid leader engaged by Cuba but intensely aware of the "big picture"—a man doggedly in search of clarifying information and alternative opinions that would lead him to a clear and informed resolution of the crisis.

During the Cuban Missile Crisis, Kennedy brought to the table much more than a sense of duty. He acted with a sense of history in real time, understanding what was at stake, the implications of his actions, and the unimaginable consequences of getting it wrong. For him it was an amazing display of critical thinking and "grace under pressure," as Ernest Hemingway has defined it, at the most critical moment and under the most precarious personal circumstances.

On the night of October 22, 1962, nearly two-thirds of the nation's total population—one hundred million Americans—watched spellbound as JFK addressed the world on national television explaining his decision to enforce a naval quarantine, his rationale for doing so, and the firm stand that the United States had taken regarding the dismantling of the missiles: "Within the past week, unmistakable evidence has established the fact that a series of offensive missile sites is now in preparation on that imprisoned island . . . Each of these missiles, in short, is capable of striking Washington, D.C., the Panama Canal, Cape Canaveral, Mexico City, or any other city in the southeastern part of the United States, in Central America, or in the Caribbean . . . Other sites, presently under construction, will house missiles with even longer ranges from as far north as Hudson Bay, Canada, and as far south as Lima, Peru."[43]

His words showed his grasp of the big picture: by listing potential targets in countries outside the United States, he'd skillfully made the case that the missiles in Cuba were *hemispheric* threats, not limited to sections of the United States. At a time when the administration worried about communist insurgencies in Central and South America, the president was tacitly warning neighbors to the south that they, too, were vulnerable, not only to the missiles, but to internal communist aggression, thus broadening the crisis beyond U.S.-Soviet relations.

Then, seizing the moral high ground, Kennedy went on to deliver a larger message to American citizens, and the world, about the Soviet's trustworthiness as a foe or an ally. He quoted public statements made by the Soviets to the United States and the United Nations concerning their military buildup in Cuba as "designed exclusively for defensive purposes," then added pointedly, "*That statement was false.*" He then moved on to his private discussions with Gromyko to demonstrate the Soviet's calculated pattern of deceit. "The Soviet Foreign Minister told me in my office and I quote him, 'training by Soviet specialists of Cuban nationals in handling defensive armaments was by no means offensive, and if it were otherwise,' Mr. Gromyko went on, 'the Soviet government would never become involved in rendering such assistance." Kennedy then added pointedly, "*That statement also was false.*"[44]

Afterward, as if in answer to General LeMay, Senator Keating, Senator Russell, and others who criticized his naval quarantine as a weak response to Soviet aggression, Kennedy made it clear to the world that he as president, and the United States as a sovereign nation, had taken to heart the lessons taught by Neville Chamberlain in his dealing with Hitler in Munich:

> The 1930s taught us a clear lesson: aggressive conduct, if allowed to go unchecked and unchallenged, ultimately leads to war . . . This nation is opposed to war. We are also true to our word. Our unswerving objective, therefore, must be to prevent the use of these missiles against this or any other country, and to secure their withdrawal from the Western Hemisphere . . . To halt this offensive buildup, a strict quarantine on all offensive military equipment under shipment to Cuba is being initiated. Further, it shall be the policy of this nation to regard any nuclear missile launched from Cuba against any nation in the western hemisphere as an attack against the United States requiring a full retaliatory response upon the Soviet Union.[45]

Finally, after making the important distinction that unlike the Soviet's "blockade" of Berlin in 1949, ships carrying food and medical supplies would not be turned back from Cuba, the president concluded his address with a startling personal plea to the Cuban people that, in one brief paragraph, sums up the sophistication of his strategy and, in many ways, his own multifaceted approach to leadership:

> I speak to you as a friend, as one who knows of your deep attachment to your fatherland, as one who shares your aspirations for liberty and justice . . . These new weapons are not in your interest. They contribute nothing to your peace and well-being. They can only undermine it. The United States has no wish to cause you to suffer or to impose any system upon you. We know that your lives and land are being used as pawns by those who deny your freedom . . . Our goal is not the victory of might, but the vindication of right—not peace at the expense of freedom, but both peace and freedom, here in this hemisphere, and, we hope, around the world.[46]

Sixty-three ships were put in place to enforce the quarantine of the island, and on Wednesday, October 24, two Russian ships approached the quarantine barrier, five hundred miles from Cuba. Word then arrived that the Russian ships had stopped dead in the water at the edge of the quarantine line—but Khrushchev was clever, and what seemed like a stalemate was not. U-2 photos taken that day showed that the material in transit may not have been needed to make the missiles operational after all. Meanwhile, missiles were still being assembled in Cuba, and sites were still being constructed. Understanding that soon all the missile sites would be ready for activation, if they weren't already operational, Kennedy perceived that the only viable alternative left to removing them was to invade Cuba, an act that would almost certainly escalate the standoff into nuclear war.

Unable to accept nuclear weapons ninety miles from the coast of Florida, Kennedy put U.S. troops on high alert in Berlin and around the world, ordered his Joint Chiefs of Staff to begin plans for invasion, and readied America's nuclear arsenal for war. That night, the president's patience was rewarded when John Scali, an ABC television State Department correspondent, stepped forward, claiming that Aleksandr Fomin, a high-ranking Soviet diplomat, had told him that Khrushchev was desperately looking for a way out of the crisis but needed to find a way for him and the Soviet government to save face. A similar message had been communicated to veteran diplomat Averill Harriman, who sensed the same willingness but added that Khrushchev was under tremendous pressure from the right wing in his country to "teach the Americans a lesson."

The next morning, news arrived at the White House that an American U-2 plane was shot down over Cuba, killing the pilot, Major Rudolf Anderson. "This means war!" McNamara charged, but Kennedy would hear nothing of it, moving ExCom away from the U-2 incident and getting them to focus instead on the unique possibilities presented by Harriman's communication. If Khrushchev was looking for a mouse hole to escape the crisis, why not help him stand down right-wing generals by offering something in return for dismantling the missiles?

For the rest of the day, a debate within ExCom raged until a proposal arose that perhaps offered the Soviet premier a way to save face while getting the president what he demanded: in exchange for the Soviets taking the missiles off the island, the United States would issue a nonaggression pledge to Cuba and withdraw obsolete short-range nuclear missiles from Turkey six months afterward. "Now that's what we ought to think about," Kennedy advised, again seizing control of the meeting. "Number one, we just last year tried to get the missiles out of there [Turkey] because they're not militarily useful. Number two, it's going to—to any man at the United Nations or any other rational man—look like a fair trade."

The very next day, Friday, October 27, a top-secret communiqué was carried to Soviet Premier Nikita Khrushchev outlining the plan. Seeing the president's proposal as the only way to avoid what he believed would be nuclear annihilation, Khrushchev agreed to Kennedy's terms in an open letter read by him in a televised broadcast that night and printed the following morning in newspapers around the world. Construction of the missile sites would stop, and within days the missiles themselves would at last be dismantled and removed from the island of Cuba.[47]

The crisis was over, yet it was only recently, with the perspective offered through documents made available after the collapse of the Soviet Union, that the most shocking aspect of the Cuban Missile Crisis came to light: at the time of Kennedy's decision to opt for a quarantine rather than invasion, 170 nuclear-tipped Luna missiles were in place, *armed and ready to fire*, with ninety to be used against military targets and the remaining eighty against civilian targets up and down America's Eastern seaboard. Additionally, General Anatoly Gribkov, the Soviet chief of general staff, who was charged with the defense of Cuba at that time, later confirmed that he was under orders to "use every weapon available versus an invasion" by the United States.[48] Were it not for Kennedy's cool head and ability to think critically, an estimated one hundred million American citizens and countless others would have lost their lives in the nuclear cataclysm that would have followed.

Regarding the leadership that Kennedy exerted during this, the world's most dangerous hour, author Robert Dallek observes: "If you listen to the tapes in the missile crisis it's obvious that Kennedy is the best and the brightest in the room. That he's often one or two steps ahead of all of his advisors in thinking through the implications. He's asking the best questions. . . . Because his capabilities can be so impressive, he regularly rescues the system from disaster."[49] Of the one thousand days during which JFK occupied the White House, the thirteen days running from the middle to the end of October 1962 were the most difficult and the ones most historians use as a gauge to measure Kennedy's leadership and presidency. Still, there was something remarkable about the man who emerged from the precipice over which he stood to look down into the nuclear abyss. This was a different John F. Kennedy, one who through study and personally developing his own internal fortitude, the art of staying "calm at the center" during what many historians describe as the world's most dangerous hour. In truth, after what he had gone through, how could anyone be unchanged?

There is a story that tells us much about what John F. Kennedy was thinking during this period of his life and presidency. After the missile crisis, with both the Americans and Soviets still testing dangerous nuclear devices in the earth's atmosphere, toxic residues of the tests began showing up in the world's food supply. One rainy morning the president stared from a window in the Oval Office. "After a nuclear blast," he asked, "how does radioactive material return to earth?" "In the rain," he was told. "You mean," he said, "it's in the rain out there?" It was, the aide told him, at which point Kennedy nodded and then fell silent, horrified at the prospect of poisoning the planet for future generations.[50]

In fact, the president was haunted not only by the threat of nuclear contamination, but also of proliferation and the possibility that ten nations would possess nuclear weapons by 1970, and as many as twenty by 1975, all testing and all capable of launching first-strike attacks that could lead to a shooting war. "I see the possibility in the 1970s of the president of the United States having to face a world in which fifteen to twenty or even twenty-five nations may have nuclear weapons," he stated at a 1963 news conference, even as China, with its more aggressive brand of communism than the Soviets, was in the process of testing hydrogen-bombs in the atmosphere.[51]

For Kennedy, the post–Cuban Missile Crisis period was a time to rethink cold war attitudes. Conventional thinking had brought both sides to the point of annihilation, he understood, and with both the American and Soviet populations chastened, he was prepared to bring about the far-reaching paradigm shifts he'd promised during his inaugural address. He was an idealist who no longer feared the political swipes of the right wing, that had taunted him through both the Cuban Missile Crisis and the Bay of Pigs.

In a speech given at American University on June 10, 1963, John Kennedy started to become a man who existed outside of his time. Shocked by the crises in Berlin and Cuba, numbed by the billions of dollars spent on weapons of mass destruction each year, and sobered by experiences in Vienna, where two world leaders had casually talked about the death of millions, Kennedy challenged American citizens, and their government, to start thinking about peace instead of war:

> Total war makes no sense in an age when great powers can maintain large and relatively invulnerable nuclear forces and to surrender without resort to those forces . . . It makes no sense in an age when a single nuclear weapon contains almost ten times the explosive force delivered by all the Allied air forces in the Second World War. It makes no sense in an age when the deadly poisons produced by a nuclear exchange would be carried by wind and water and soil and seed to the far corners of the globe and to generations yet unborn. Today the expenditure of billions of dollars every year on weapons acquired for the purpose of making sure we never need to use them is essential to keeping the peace. But surely, the acquisition of such idle stockpiles—which can only destroy and never create—is not the only, much less the most efficient, means of assuring peace.[52]

Understanding the radical nature of his words, the president purposely kept the text of the speech away from Secretary of Defense McNamara and Secretary of State Rusk prior to its delivery. He also announced that he wished to take "first-step measures of arms control designed to limit the intensity of the arms race and reduce the risk of accidental war . . . [and] to draft a treaty that would ban nuclear testing."[53] Khrushchev praised the speech as "the best statement made by any president since Roosevelt."[54] Less than two weeks later, the United States and the Soviet Union agreed to establish a direct line of communication, and by fall 1963 a limited test ban treaty was signed, lead-

ing to a comprehensive ban treaty that was a landmark in easing the dangerously escalating arms race.

That same month, after Governor George Wallace refused admittance into
the University of Alabama to two black men, President Kennedy signed an
executive order federalizing the Alabama National Guard and deploying four
hundred additional army troops. There was a tense standoff with students,
the governor, and gangs organized from the ranks of the Ku Klux Klan, until
Wallace finally left the campus, clearing the way for the students to register.
With that, racial segregation came to an end at the university. Still, urged by
his brother Bobby and Vice President Lyndon Johnson, Kennedy drew a line
in the sand that would forever define civil rights in the United States as a
"moral" as well as a "legal" issue.

In his "Report to the American People on Civil Rights," televised on June
11, 1963, Kennedy's principle-based position transcended rhetoric to become
a shining moment in American history:

> The Negro baby born in America today, regardless of the section of the nation
> in which he is born, has about one-half as much chance of completing . . . high
> school as a white baby born in the same place on the same day, one-third as
> much chance of completing college, one-third as much chance of becoming a
> professional man, twice as much chance of becoming unemployed, about one-
> seventh as much chance of earning $10,000 a year, a life expectancy which is
> seven years shorter, and the prospects of earning only half as much. This is not
> a sectional issue . . . Nor is it a partisan issue . . . This is not even a legal or
> legislative issue alone. It is better to settle these matters in the courts than on
> the streets, and new laws are needed at every level, but law alone cannot make
> men see right. We are confronted primarily with a moral issue. It is as old as
> the scriptures and it is as clear as the American Constitution . . . The heart of
> the question is whether all Americans are to be afforded equal rights and op-
> portunities, whether we are going to treat our fellow Americans as we wanted
> to be treated.[55]

During the summer of 1963, Kennedy continued to try to close the dangerous chasms that had developed among races, political systems, and countries. Addressing a joint session of the Irish Parliament, he declared, "There
are no permanent enemies," thereby seeking to reframe the relationship
between the United States and the Soviet Union. Never did that statement
seem truer than on June 26, 1963, when Kennedy stood facing the Berlin
wall before more than one million admiring West Germans. In a strong voice
carried through the wind over the wall that separated the city and to all of
the world, Kennedy's words became as much an invitation as a challenge to
the people of East Berlin, and to Soviet Premier Nikita Khrushchev, to join

with the president in the creation of a bold new world where walls, real and
metaphorical, no longer separated people, cities, or nations:

> Freedom has many difficulties and democracy is not perfect, but we have never
> had to put a wall up to keep our people in, to prevent them from leaving us
> . . . While the wall is the most obvious and vivid demonstration of the failures
> of the Communist system for all the world to see, we take no satisfaction in it
> for it is . . . an offense not only against history, but an offense against humanity,
> separating families, dividing husbands and wives and brothers and sisters, and
> dividing a people who wish to be joined together.[56]

Kennedy had hit his stride in terms of what he felt was important, not just
to the United States, but for the world. In fact, during the last six months of
his presidency, no less than one-half of the speeches he delivered involved
either support for civil rights or the quest for world peace.

He continued to battle valiantly on behalf of African Americans in the
South, and in September he put forward to Congress the Civil Rights Act
of 1963, which strengthened guarantees of constitutional protection for all
American citizens. Overseas, with the success of the Peace Corps, young
Americans learned about other languages and cultures while helping to lift
the burden of abject poverty from millions around the world in dozens of foreign countries. And on September 24, 1963, the president's Atmospheric Test
Ban Treaty passed the Senate by a vote of eighty to nineteen, marking the
beginning of what would later become known as détente. Four days earlier,
while addressing the UN General Assembly, Kennedy had called the test ban
treaty "a vision not of what we are but of what we might become." He now
added to the news of his triumph an astonishing offer that would take him
full circle, back to his inaugural address and the signature issue of the New
Frontier as a prospective avenue for U.S.-Soviet cooperation.

With whatever gap that had existed between the two space programs
closing rapidly since astronaut John Glenn's successful orbit of the earth,
Kennedy, who had suggested technological cooperation between the two
superpowers at an earlier speech at Rice University, now boldly called for
a joint U.S.-Soviet expedition to the moon. "Space offers no problems of
sovereignty . . . Why, therefore, should man's first flight to the moon be a
matter of national competition?" he asked. "Why should the United States
and the Soviet Union, in preparing for such expeditions, become involved in
immense duplication of research, construction, and expenditure?"[57] Jaws at
the Pentagon must have dropped to the desktops. John McCone, CIA director
at the time, must have reached for a nitroglycerin capsule. Lyndon Johnson
must have thought he was hearing things. This stunning gesture on Kennedy's

part, coupled with his speech to Ireland's Parliament declaring, "There are no permanent enemies," represented a radical cold war thawing that the United States and the Soviet Union would have to wait two decades to see again.

Yet this was the kind of courageous gambit that Kennedy believed was necessary after the two superpowers had brought the world to the brink of disaster during the Cuban Missile Crisis. Just one year earlier an intensely competitive Kennedy had insisted that the race to the moon was worth the effort only if the United States was committed to being first. Now he was offering his adversaries a shared vision, one that Soviet strongman Nikita Khrushchev, also chastened by the Cuban crisis, found equally alluring: the prospect of a profoundly different relationship where the United States and Soviet Union directed their vast resources toward solving the challenges of poverty, famine, and disease, confronting an ever-shrinking world, and not toward proliferating weapons to destroy that same world.

Kennedy understood that the contest between "those who see a monolithic world and those who believe in diversity" was destined to continue. Still, joint cooperation such as the one he proposed could act as a lever for peace. From out of the profound experience Kennedy had endured came an abiding moral conviction that the survival of civilization depended upon nations' working together toward the shared vision of a safer, more harmonious, world. But in the early afternoon of November 22, 1963, all of these plans and hopes and dreams ended with the assassination of John F. Kennedy.

There is an anecdote told by Viktor Sukhodrev, Khrushchev's official translator, that tells us much about John F. Kennedy and the evolution of leadership that he passed through on his way to greatness and immortality. Nikita Khrushchev went to the American embassy to sign the book of condolences; he then sent Anastas Mikoyan, his closest adviser, to represent the Soviet people at the funeral. According to Sukhodrev, who had accompanied him, Jacqueline Kennedy was standing near the casket dressed in a black dress with veil, in mourning, when Mikoyan came abreast of her in the funeral line to pay his condolences. As he outstretched his hand toward her, she took his hand into both of her hands and said, "Mr. Mikoyan, thank you for coming. I have a message for Mr. Khrushchev that I'd like you to deliver. Tell Mr. Khrushchev for me that he and my husband could have brought peace to this world by working together. And that now he will have to do it alone." It was a moment the weight of which, Mikoyan tells us, neither man will ever forget.[58]

Of the thirty-three presidents who preceded Kennedy and the nine who have followed, how many have accomplished more than JFK? In his short time in office, Kennedy accomplished: historical advances in civil rights; the strongest ties with our allies in post–World War II history; diplomatic expansion with programs like the Peace Corps; a modernization of U.S. intelligence and the military to deal with the cold war nuclear threat as well as local insurgencies; a nuclear test ban treaty that was the forerunner of détente; and a deftly handled escape with honor from the Cuban Missile Crisis that could have triggered World War III.

For those who would question the practical idealism that JFK brought to the office of president, I can think of no better example than Kennedy's landmark decision to "send a man to the moon and bring him safely back to earth" by the end of the decade. Out of that project came the following practical benefits, along with commercialized technologies that we are still using today:

- Creation of a wartime economy without firing a single shot
- Computerization of project management
- Advances in satellite communications
- Government loans for higher education, particularly in the sciences
- A military edge in surveillance and rocketry that has sustained itself for more than forty years

When a European colleague and I discussed this aspect of Kennedy administration, he asked, "Could Kennedy really have known all that?"

"No," I answered, "but he listened to himself and others and created an innovative environment that allowed it to happen."

President John F. Kennedy was an unabashed idealist. But he was also a pragmatic visionary whose powers of critical thinking during the dark days of the Cuban Missile Crisis may have saved the planet from destruction. Additionally, his character-driven leadership left Americans with a blueprint for success based on an unfailing belief in democratic principles, the courage to defend them, and the open-mindedness to understand the enormous potential that the future affords those strong enough to believe in it.

JOHN F. KENNEDY'S LEADERSHIP LESSONS

To me, the most outstanding characteristics of Kennedy's life and presidency were his courage and powers of critical thinking. Unlike Franklin Roosevelt, who preceded him, or Ronald Reagan, who followed, he may have lacked the grace to make his time in office "look easy." But if, like me, you're someone who has to work hard for everything they achieve, JFK's presidential leadership lessons couldn't be more relevant.

Lesson #1
Meaningful Change Requires Sacrifice

JFK's 1961 inaugural address challenged Americans to apply themselves to the higher purpose of national service: "And so, my fellow Americans: ask not what your country can do for you—ask what you can do for your country."

Over the next thousand days, he proposed and delivered concrete actions to back those words up, including the moon project to explore space; a Peace Corps to aid struggling countries; a civil rights bill to guarantee the freedoms of minorities; a nuclear test ban treaty to stem the rising tide of weapons proliferation; and a strategic alternative to nuclear war with the Soviets over Cuba.

Despite his tanned movie star countenance and continuous references to aggressiveness and vigor, Jack Kennedy was a chronically ill man. Yet, for the three years he held office, and for the thirteen days of the Cuban Missile Crisis, he rose to the occasion with an unrivaled sense of mission, coolness, and intellectual probity.

The real John Kennedy was not a rich, spoiled playboy who happened to become president, but rather a courageous man who understood the meaning of self-sacrifice as well as national sacrifice in an effort to shift the United States beyond its own societal limitations and Cold War paradigm.

Like Kennedy, in his 1961 inaugural speech, enduring leaders challenge those that depend upon them to sacrifice now, never accept the status quo, and continuously improve in order to better construct a future business, organization, or society.

Great leaders and great athletes share this in common: they train early, long, and hard, doing the right things with mind-wrenching discipline, to become the man or woman they want to become.

Lesson #2
Understand the Value of Your Time

Like TR, as a boy Kennedy used his frequent hospital stays to sharpen his reading skills and develop his lifelong interest in history. JFK devoured books like *King Arthur and His Knights of the Round Table*—appropriate reading for a man credited with creating his own Camelot—biographies, and volumes on American history.

Between October 1954 and February 1955, Kennedy's life was in danger. With his Addison's disease flaring, his intestinal condition worsening, and back ruined, doctors proposed surgery that required the insertion of a stainless steel plate into his back that would leave him with only a 50 percent chance of surviving.

Even during his excruciating recovery, Kennedy refused to remain idle, and instead began writing a book entitled *Profiles in Courage*, which won him the Pulitzer Prize. "For Kennedy every day was a gift," biographer Richard Reeves explains, "and he didn't want to waste a moment. And that was the attitude he brought to the Presidency. Every minute that you're president is a gift and no single moment can be wasted."

To future leaders, this is a lesson that cannot be emphasized enough: live your life like "your hair was on fire," legendary Samurai Musashi writes, sucking the marrow of knowledge from every minute of every day.

Think about where you are now and where you want to be. Make a careful assessment of the actions you perform each day, the way you spend your time, and who you spend your time with, then ask the question: how did these actions move me closer to my goal?

Like an arrow shot with a steady hand from a sturdy bow, you should be moving consistently each day toward your target of becoming the man or woman you want to be, headed for the leadership position you understand is your destiny.

Lesson #3
You are the Hero of Your Own Epic Journey

Kennedy, in his life, faced more trials than most, but got through it with a hero's courage and conviction, battling the status quo, critics, fault-finders, and cynics to claim the kind of future the American people demanded.

One of the most stirring images I have of John F. Kennedy is of him campaigning during the do-or-die West Virginia primary surrounded by hundreds of grizzled coal miners skeptical of his programs and blinded by the fact that he was Catholic.

Sensing that his planned speech was not connecting with them, he dealt with their personal prejudices head-on, never flinching, "Nobody asked me if I was Catholic when I joined the United States Navy," he said, confronting the crowd of miners. "And nobody asked my brother if he was a Catholic or a Protestant before he climbed into an American bomber to fly his last mission!"

So strong was the stand he took, and so powerful was that image of him, standing gaunt and resolute before the rugged West Virginia miners, that he swept the state 219,246 votes to Hubert Humphrey's 141,941 and changed the course of the campaign. Like John Kennedy, know that your life matters.

In his epic tale *The Odyssey* Homer's hero, Odysseus, faces mortal enemies and colossal trials on his sea voyage, a metaphor for every hero's journey through life. Great leaders see themselves exactly that way.

Once you understand that you're the hero of your own epic journey, nothing—not the flailing claws of Scylla, nor the spiraling whirlpools of Charybdis—can stand in your way.

Like John Kennedy, know that your life matters, and the way that you live it can change the world.

Lesson #4
Admit Mistakes and Learn from Them

JFK knew where he was in his life. He had the ability to stand outside his own circumstance to see his strengths, weaknesses, vulnerabilities, and opportunities in a given situation. He was objective, not subjective, in the assessment of his own leadership performance.

Credibility is a leader's most cherished possession. When JFK exercised poor judgment in his decision to invade Cuba during the Bay of Pigs fiasco, he admitted it forthrightly and soon, knowing that time only exacerbates the problem. Once a mistake is admitted, those following your leadership will want to move toward remedies, not recriminations. Admitting mistakes forthrightly and soon as Kennedy did enables a leader to maintain his or her credibility based on strength of character, self-knowledge, and an accurate assessment of the situation.

Once JFK admitted his mistake, he analyzed the cause—whether systems, strategy, communication, or people—considered corrective actions, determined appropriate and effective solutions, and acted in a way that guaranteed the same mistake could never happen again.

Most important, John Kennedy learned from his mistakes. He understood his own personal foibles and shortcomings and learned to correct or operate around them.

Treat failures as a learning experience as Kennedy did after the Bay of Pigs disaster. After all, it may well have been the lessons he learned from that mistake that enabled him to navigate the nation, and the world, through "the most perilous thirteen days in all of human history" during the Cuban Missile Crisis just eighteen months later.

Lesson #5
Know Where to Draw the Line

When, in September 1962, James Meredith, an African American, was denied admission into "Ole Miss" on the basis of race, the Supreme Court ordered that he be admitted. JFK understood that an ugly display of racism would severely damage the image of the United States abroad, and likely cost him the support of southern Democrats in his upcoming re-election bid. Faced with the option of either backing down or enforcing the law, Kennedy responded decisively, federalizing the Mississippi National Guard, taking control from the governor, and making himself their commander.

The confrontation that followed was violent and bloody. Two hundred state troopers assigned to protect Meredith walked off the job. Agents were forced to fire tear gas into the incendiary mob. Gunshots were fired killing a journalist and a nearby construction worker, and Kennedy was forced to call in the National Guard, supplemented by regular army troops, and two hundred were wounded in the melee that followed.

The next morning, James Meredith attended his first class. JFK had risked his political career and jeopardized the propaganda battle with the Soviets at a time when it counted most in order to draw a line in the sand on what he correctly identified as a moral issue that the U.S. government could no longer ignore.

Character-driven leaders who draw a line in the sand—like Kennedy in his confrontation with Governor Barnett—can never be defeated because even in losing a battle they maintain the respect of their followers who know that, in the long run, stands based on moral principle rather than expediency always win-out.

Learn where and when "to draw a line in the sand."

Lesson #6
Stay "Calm at the Center" of the Storm

During the Cuban Missile Crisis, Kennedy brought to the table more than a sense of duty. He acted with a sense of history in real time, understanding the implications of his actions, and the unimaginable consequences of getting it wrong.

Unwilling to accept nuclear weapons ninety miles from the coast of Florida—and resistant to withering pressure from military zealots to blindly attack Cuba—on October 24, 1962, he ordered sixty-three ships to enforce a quarantine of the island, ordered his Joint Chiefs of Staff to begin plans for invasion, and readied America's nuclear arsenal for war.

That evening the President's patience was rewarded when a State Department news correspondent, stepped forward claiming that Khrushchev was desperately seeking a way out of the crisis but needed a way for his government to save face. From that point on debate raged within ExCom until it was proposed that in exchange for the Soviets taking the missiles off the island, the U.S. would issue a non-aggression pledge to Cuba and withdraw its short-range nuclear missiles from Turkey six months later.

The next day, on Friday, October 27th, a top-secret communiqué was carried to Khrushchev outlining the proposal. Seeing it as the only way to avoid what he believed would be nuclear annihilation, the Soviet Premier agreed to Kennedy's terms in an open letter read in a televised broadcast that night.

The crisis was over, yet the most shocking aspect of the Cuban Missile Crisis was still to come: at the time of JFK's decision to opt for a quarantine rather than invasion, 170 nuclear-tipped Luna missiles were in place, *armed and ready to fire* at military and civilian targets up and down America's Eastern seaboard.

Were it not for Kennedy's ability to "stay calm at the center of the storm," an estimated one hundred million Americans and countless others would have lost their lives in the nuclear cataclysm that would have followed.

Great leaders stay composed. They ratchet-up their listening skills, not down, and direct others to do the same. Their thinking is unemotional. They become more analytical than ever. They evaluate. Ask questions. Consider options and deliberate with their team. Once a decision is made, they act boldly and with the courage of their convictions.

Never manage a crisis from "40,000 feet." Understand that your behavior, as a leader, sets the tone for those around you. Like Kennedy in the Cuban Missile Crisis, you may be in the center of the storm but never let the storm inside you.

Chapter IV

George Washington
U.S President, 1789–1797

While psychologists tell us that the character of most individuals is molded by early experiences, in the case of George Washington a confluence of his own boundless ambition and external fate seem to have coalesced to create a life unparalleled in American history. Many of the opinions, talents, and propensities that the future leader of the American Revolution would later exhibit can be traced directly back to seminal experiences that occurred prior to his twenty-sixth birthday. This formative period, leading up to the stunning victory of the colonists over the British, will demonstrate the key leadership qualities of America's first president.

If unique aspects of Washington's character did meld with specific early life experiences to form what was to become his destiny as a great leader, what were those traits? What were those experiences? In *His Excellency*, Joseph Ellis writes: "If we are looking for emergent patterns of behavior, then it is the combination of bottomless ambition and near obsession with self-control . . . He combined personal probity with a demonstrable flair for dramatic action wherever the opportunity . . . presented itself. He took what history offered and was always poised to ride the available wave in destiny's direction."[1] At the core, Washington's personal ambition made him something of an opportunist. If there's a set of early characteristics that leaps off the pages of account after account, it most certainly begins with a penchant for upward mobility, no doubt catalyzed by his own modest beginnings in a tiered societal structure that saw him as little more than a physically impressive, undereducated upstart.

It's interesting that he is popularly regarded as the "father of our country," because George Washington was an underdog with a questionable background, driven by a searing passion to be accepted by his presumed betters—in this case, the British. Indeed, the first twenty-six years of his life were dominated by his ardent, nearly heartbreaking attempts to simply become a "Regular" in the British Army.

As a boy, Washington idolized his older half brother Lawrence, an officer in an American regiment enrolled in the British Regular Army for an expedition in Cartagena, now Colombia. Despite Lawrence's complaints concerning British officers' scorn for the American troops, he remained enamored with the notion of becoming an officer in the British Army, consumed by an overwhelming need to overcome the odds and achieve "success" through initiative, hard work, and ingenuity. Years later, when Lord Loudoun rejected his pleas to fulfill what he saw as the destiny he was born to achieve, it's not difficult to discern Washington's disappointment and horror when he wrote, "We cannot conceive that being Americans should deprive us of the benefits of being British subjects."[2]

This emotional rawness, however, could never have occurred without there first being an emotional need, which we will witness time and again in the internal composition of the six greatest presidents. In Washington's case this came very early, and perhaps was even influenced by events that had occurred before his birth—specifically those involving his grandfather, John Washington, an impoverished adventurer, who first reached Virginia in 1675.

Pegged an "unscrupulous" businessman soon after his arrival, John Washington was implicated in the murder of five Indian ambassadors. He also married three times, twice to women of questionable moral scruples who had been brought before him when he served as justice of the peace. One had been running a "bawdy house," and the other had been the "governor's whore."[3] Later in life, when George, as a young colonial, first met Half King, the diplomatic representative of the Iroquois Confederacy, the tribal leader called him "Conotocarius," which meant "devourer of villages," based on the Indians' experience with his conniving grandfather.[4]

Not only did Washington's grandfather have an unsavory reputation, but young George was no doubt uneasy with the reputation of his father, Augustine, who'd died when George was just eleven. Restless, unsure, and bumbling, Washington's father was only a modest business success, depicted in court records as making deals and then reneging on them nearly instantaneously. Augustine was twice married, with two sons from his first marriage and five children from his second marriage. Upon his father's death, George eventually inherited Ferry Farm, the modest house where the family lived, while the majority of his estate, including what was to become Mount Vernon, went to his older half brothers.

Additionally, Mary Ball Washington, George's mother, was a tough, demanding woman who "was given neither to acquiescence nor compromise."[5] She herself was orphaned early in life and had grown up to be self-reliant.

Married at a late age for those times—at twenty-five—she gave young George meager quarter from her overbearing nature after the death of Augustine. She didn't approve of George inheriting Ferry Farm upon his father's passing; even later in life, with her son's ascension to the pinnacle of success and honor, she showed him little in the way of approval. No wonder that it was his half brother Lawrence to whom George fled emotionally, attaching himself to the upwardly mobile adjutant general of the Virginia militia like a love-starved son to a surrogate father.

If Washington's historical persona is one of an elusive stoic who kept his own counsel and rarely displayed emotions other than anger, surely it can be traced to an emotional vacuum filled not nearly so much by sentiment as by aspiration, nurtured by the politically astute, ever-supportive Lawrence. In truth, Washington was already on his way to becoming an amalgam of three men, with the influence of each showing itself during his later life as commander of America's army and our nation's first president. The first was John, his tough and ruthless grandfather, who was obsessed with material wealth and rent-generating land. The second was Augustine, a quietly diffident and self-effacing individual uncertain of the true worth of his abilities. The third was Lawrence, a man of modest background who married into the wealthy Fairfax family, parlaying his newfound marital status and modest military credentials into social credibility.

It was Lawrence who fired the flames of young George's military fantasies with stories of foreign adventure, enflaming an ardor that peaked with the renaming of their father's estate to Mount Vernon after Admiral Edward Vernon, commander of the Cartagena expedition. So close did the two become that the only foreign travel George Washington embarked on in his life was with Lawrence to Barbados.

As in all colonies, Virginia supported a volunteer militia, that operated as much like a social club as an army. Interestingly, while Lawrence held the rank of general, George's grandfather John had held the rank of colonel when leading the militia in a punitive campaign against the Indians which gained him his fearsome reputation. Still, while Grandfather John bared teeth and murdered, Lawrence taught George the art of conviviality and the power of a smile.

Working as a surveyor and stopping overnight for stays at inns and taverns, Washington cultivated a set of social skills that would serve him well later in life: a spirited sense of humor, a fondness for ale, and a talent for billiards, cards, and engaging pretty girls in conversation. Standing a strapping six feet three and weighing 180 pounds, the strong and agile George Washington was a superior horseman, a graceful dancer, and a "man's man": physically imposing, mentally enigmatic, and emotionally restrained.

But Washington's capabilities didn't end with anything as superficial as appearance or even charisma. Smoldering deep inside of this not-yet-twenty-year-old was an ambition that yearned to bridge financial and social gaps—bridges that were needed to meld the money-grubbing avarice of cold-blooded John with the smooth opportunism of the social-climbing Lawrence. Controversy exists among historians as to why young George so painstakingly hand copied each of the 110 precepts from the Jesuit book on etiquette *Rules of Civility and Decent Behavior in Company and Conversation* over and over again. While some maintain that he did it to burn into his brain those cardinal rules that promised to prime him for a life's mission, others suggest that he did it for a simpler reason: the improvement of his penmanship. Both postulations make little difference: Washington did it because he was obsessed with improving himself.

After his father's death it is no coincidence that young George spent much of his time at Mount Vernon with Lawrence and his wife, Anne Fairfax of the Fairfax dynasty. The Fairfax land claim was immense, covering more than five million acres, most of it west in the unexplored Northern Neck region. Washington must have watched raptly as his half brother spent his time engaged in the "assiduous courting of the great."[6] In fact, it was William Fairfax, cousin of Lord Thomas Fairfax and manager of the estate, who gave sixteen-year-old George the job of surveying the rugged Indian-plagued perimeters of his massive landholdings. For three years, Washington bore firsthand witness to Indian massacres and the mind-wrenching physical hardships known to only a handful of white men. During that same period, he handily purchased nearly 1,500 acres of property for himself.

Afterward, in June 1752, when an militarily inexperienced Washington petitioned Virginia's Governor Dinwiddie for Lawrence's adjutant general post, he did so not by learning more about the military, but by asking William Fairfax to use his influence to help get him the job. So we see the beginnings of a formidable force in American politics, at once driven, mentally tough, and perhaps even ruthless when it came to vanquishing his enemies, but also one that was savvy politically, knowing whom to go to for advancement, as well as how to impress his social betters into helping him move ever closer to what he saw as a preordained position of leadership.

Early signs of just how burning was Washington's ambition and how resourceful his nature surfaced publicly in 1753 when, at twenty-one, he boldly volunteered for a mission to deliver a letter from Governor Dinwiddie to the commander of the French troops, Jacques Legardeur de Saint-Pierre. Legardeur had marched into the vast region west of the Blue Ridge Mountains. With Britain and France engaged in a cold war and the Ohio Valley claimed by both rivals, Dinwiddie and other prominent men invested in the Ohio Company saw this not only as a military threat, but a financial one as well.

On October 23, 1753, after Lord Holderness, the secretary of state for the colonies, received confirmation that the French had "invaded our province of Virginia," he ordered Dinwiddie to evict them "by force of arms" if necessary.[7] Supported by both Dinwiddie and the Fairfax family, and already known to be an expert on wilderness survival owing to his surveying experience, Washington set out on his dangerous journey braving wild animals, hostile French troops, and unfriendly Indians.

Two months later, after a grueling winter trek, Washington and his small expedition eventually met with Commanding Officer Legardeur at French Creek. "France owns this country," he was stunned to hear, "and we have the right to take prisoner any Englishman attempting to trade here or on its waters!"[8] Convinced that a confrontation between France and Britain was in the works, Washington embarked on a brutal winter journey, over ice and water, for Venango County, Pennsylvania, where he'd be able to resupply and rush back to Dinwiddie. When Washington discovered, on the second leg of his journey, that his horses were too sick to continue, he left them behind and moved ahead on foot through heavy snow. Frostbitten men were quartered in shacks along the way, and soon it was just Washington and fellow traveler Christopher Gist who forged ahead in what had become a race against time.

It was emblematic of the incredible will, physical stamina, and sheer luck of Washington that he survived untouched when a seemingly friendly Indian they encountered along the way shot a musket at him point-blank. Then, demonstrating the sense of self-discipline that was later to become his hallmark, Washington insisted that the traitorous Indian be freed, understanding the possibility of reprisal from hostiles in a nearby village ominously named "Murderingtown."[9] Finally, after enduring five weeks of fierce winter conditions and a spill into icy river waters during a crossing that surely would have drowned a weaker man, Washington delivered the crucial information to the governor. Dinwiddie then urged Washington to write an account of his adventures in order to convey France's military ambitions, as well as to firm up British involvement in protecting the Ohio Company's land interests. In response, he committed to paper a spine-tingling account entitled *The Journal of Major Washington*. The work basically mapped out a justification for what would later become the French and Indian War. After its first appearance in several colonial newspapers, Washington's journal was reprinted by magazines in England and Scotland, elevating its twenty-one-year-old author from a wannabe military officer to a celebrity-like status among Virginians and a stalwart example to the British of that curious breed known as "American frontiersman."

Regardless of what the future held, that moment of recognition must have seemed nearly miraculous to Washington. They were the first early steps toward the fulfillment of his dreams: George Washington was now distinguished from others—physically, experientially, and militarily—a reputation marked by his willingness to courageously pursue endeavors involving extraordinary challenge against all odds. He was, in the eyes of his fellow colonials, a "hero."

If there were lessons to be learned by the young colonial officer over the next three years, however, one of the most poignant must have been that fame is fleeting. The reasons for this revelation-to-come began in February 1754, when Dinwiddie sent a party—made up of three hundred Virginia militia and British Regulars—to garrison a newly constructed fort at Ohio Forks, in an effort to stem the tide of French advancement. It was Washington, now a lieutenant colonel, who led the westbound force, but before he and his troops arrived, the French seized the British fort by summons, demolished it, and replaced it with a better-fortified compound of their own called Fort Duquesne.

Washington was little more than one hundred miles from Fort Duquesne when intelligence concerning the French seizure of the British fort reached him. The nature of his mission obviously had changed—but how? The answer came in the form of a French advance party that he and his troops would encounter—and devastate—on May 28, 1754. Washington's volley came as a total surprise to the French troops. Nearly a dozen French soldiers were killed or wounded, including the commander, Joseph Coulon de Jumonville. Led by Washington, the colonials were ferocious in battle, but not nearly as savage as their Indian guides, spurred-on by the vengeful Half King, who claimed that the French had boiled his father and eaten him in a previous encounter. Washington and his men watched in horror as Half King and his warriors scalped dead and living men, then "brained" them by washing their hands in the now-gaping skulls.

In the end, the stunning victory for the twenty-two-year-old lieutenant colonel was one that would be remembered not nearly so much for its tactical brilliance as for its brutality and intemperance. Still, convinced that he and his troops had destroyed a French enemy before they could destroy his own forces, Washington withdrew to a place called Great Meadows, where his men constructed an ill-conceived stockade that they named Fort Necessity. During the withdrawal, Washington heard and dismissed ill-translated information from Jacob Van Braam, a fellow colonial who claimed that the slain French commander was on a diplomatic mission when attacked.

Whether true or not, Canada and France seethed over the massacre, and nine hundred soldiers were dispatched under the command of Jumonville's brother Louis Coulon de Villiers to take vengeance against Washington and a force one-third as strong. On July 3 the French attacked Fort Necessity. It was here, if not in the initial encounter, that Washington's inexperience surfaced. Under-fortified and positioned indefensibly, Fort Necessity was relentlessly lambasted by cannon and musket fire. Attacking from behind trees and makeshift redoubts, the French were virtually invulnerable. In contrast, Washington and his troops were under-protected and therefore forced to remain stationary.

With no hope of anything but a bloody rout to look forward to, Washington dispatched an emissary to "seek terms" from the French. Again having to depend on translator Jacob Van Braam's questionable grasp of the French language, Washington signed what seemed to be a remarkably generous surrender, considering the circumstances. It allowed him and his men to vacate the fort, British flag held aloft as they marched back to civilization. What Washington did not know was that the terms, written in French, contained a damning admission that Jumonville had been "assassinated."[10] Washington returned to Wills Creek, West Virginia, and then on to Virginia, where this time something less than a hero's welcome awaited him. The prevailing view was that he'd been rash in his attack on the French advance troops and unable to control his Indian forces; his choice of location for Fort Necessity amateurish; and his subsequent admission to murder ("assassination") perceived as an act of cowardice in order to save his own life.

The French commander in North America, General Duquesne, wrote of Washington: "He lies to justify the assassination of sieur de Jumonville, which has turned on him, and which he had the stupidity to confess in his capitulation [journal] . . . There is nothing lower and even blacker than the sentiments and way of thinking of this Washington. It would have been a pleasure to read these charges under his very nose."[11] Given what we already understand about Washington's character, what opinions or rumors could possibly be more devastating? Hadn't his courage been proven just one year earlier while carrying Dinwiddie's message? Hadn't both the colonialist and British publics embraced him as a hero? Washington vociferously protested: First, he'd attacked the French advance troops *after* it was known that they had forcibly taken a British fortification just one hundred miles from his troops. Wasn't a "war" already started? Second, he had no way of knowing that the French terms—written in a language unknown to him and signed in the midst of catastrophe—contained an admission of murder or assassination, because his "translator" himself didn't realize it.

With these circumstances understood, the colonials leapt to his defense. Unfortunately, the British were unforgiving and attributed his ineptitude not to inexperience so much as to being an unsophisticated—and quite typical— American. Proof of the stigma left on Washington was that when Governor

Horatio Sharpe of Maryland—a former British officer—took command of one thousand Regulars to take back Fort Duquesne in fall 1754, Dinwiddie dissolved the Virginia militia entirely and offered Washington a mere captaincy in the new army.

At various points during these accounts, one can discern the beginnings of what the world would come to know as George Washington the Revolutionary leader: a man who *lived* his life, learning from early failures, humiliations, heartbreak, and the experience of others. As his brother Lawrence might have done, he used politics in order to get his military post. As his intemperate grandfather, John, might have been inclined, he attacked his enemies with reckless abandon. Yet it wasn't until the year 1754 that the self-doubt and private recriminations that plagued his father, Augustine, surfaced in the iron-willed Washington.

Convinced that the British would never have undercut a British officer as they had him, and that taking Dinwiddie's offer of a captain's post would leave him subject to the orders of British Regulars of the same rank, Washington refused the commission and resigned, marking yet another escalation in what would become a virulent anti-British sentiment. In December 1754, during a time when Governor Sharpe's Fort Duquesne campaign was falling apart before it started, Washington returned to Mount Vernon to start a new life outside the military while simultaneously admitting that "my inclinations are strongly bent to arms."[12] Later, when Governor Sharpe offered him an honorary title of "colonel" in order to entice him into serving as an adviser to the Regulars, Washington found the very request insulting: "You must entertain a very contemptible opinion of my weakness," the former lieutenant colonel begrudgingly responded.[13] This last insult, whether real or perceived, may have marked the low point of George Washington's young life.

Even at this early stage of his leadership development, it was clear to anyone who knew Washington that the "life of a planter" could not offer a man of his vaulting ambitions and need for action the kind of stimulation that he craved. In fact, it may have been something even more personal in his nature that spurred him back into military action.

Soon after Washington's return to Mount Vernon, George William Fairfax, his close friend and benefactor, married Sally Cary—a woman whom many historians considered the love of Washington's life. Without protest or contest, Washington watched the union happening before him, understanding that his family was not the social equal of the Fairfaxes, inexorably torn between his dependency on the Fairfax family's influence for his career advancement and his desire to marry Sally himself.

The hand of destiny again played its role, however, for even as France and Britain prepared for war, the British armada sailed on the Potomac past the very lawn of George Washington's home. Thus, in March 1755, when Major General Braddock came to Alexandria, Virginia, with two regiments, he was met by Washington, who'd invited his neighbors along to wish the troops well in an effort to ingratiate himself with the major general. Informed by others—most probably Fairfax—that Washington was an extraordinary frontiersman with an unparalleled knowledge of the wilderness, Braddock supported an arrangement that gave Washington no rank but allowed him to lead the colonials. Braddock also vowed that once the campaign was successfully completed, he would secure for George his dream of preferment in the Regular Army.

Soon after, Braddock undertook his mission to capture Fort Duquesne. But even before they'd engaged the enemy, conflicts emerged between Washington's advice and Braddock's preset strategy. Understanding the influence that the Indians had on the Canadian French regarding wilderness fighting, Washington warned the bullheaded British general that the battles to come wouldn't resemble engagements with the French in Europe, but Braddock rejected his advice. Worse, despite the fact that Braddock respected Washington, he demonstrated nothing but disdain for his "irregular" forces, subjecting them to callous disinterest publicly while berating them privately in front of their leader.

Another factor that Washington understood but Braddock didn't was that given the slow advance of the British troops, it would be impossible to arrive at Fort Duquesne before winter, leaving them ripe (uniformed in bright red as they were) for guerrilla attacks carried out by Indians warriors along the way. To make matters even more untenable, around this time Washington had became mortally ill with malaria and had to be left behind in a wagon. Separated from his troops but desperate not to miss the upcoming battle, a still-weak Washington managed to catch up with Braddock's forces just twelve miles from the French fortification.

The next day, July 9, 1755, as the forces marched through a twelve-foot-wide clearing cut by British engineers, a solitary shot rang out from the woods. It was followed by the blood-curdling cries of warring Indians, a barrage of musket fire, and troops dropping to the ground, dead. Mounted on his horse, Washington stood shoulder-to-shoulder with Braddock, who led the main column forward. But—as Washington had predicted—there were no similarly formed columns before them filled with Indian warriors. In fact, their enemy was invisible. Eerily, only the result of their enemy's attacks could be witnessed, with body after bloody body falling to the soil.

Washington understood the hopelessness of the situation and requested that Braddock allow him to lead the provincial troops into the woods and "engage the enemy in their own way."[14] The general would hear nothing of it, insisting that the columns re-form. Washington's horse was shot out from under him, but he leapt on another as he watched Braddock topple from his mount, wounded. Amid the hellish smoke of musket fire, war whoops, and the screams of Indian-ravished soldiers, no fewer than four bullets tore Washington's coat as he moved Braddock's body out of harm's way. Taking command of the troops, Washington had a second horse killed beneath him and his hat shot off as he led into retreat those soldiers who could stand. He also managed to load the mortally wounded Braddock into a cart, carrying him to safety.

In the final throes of death, the British general ordered Washington to ride forty miles to Philadelphia in order to summon reinforcements while still cursing his men for a lack of bravery and military prowess in fighting the enemy. Following his commands, Washington rode alone to Philadelphia, only to find the remaining British troops unwilling to go along with him. When he returned to the army's makeshift encampment, Braddock had died. Taking care to bury him in the center of the road, where wagons and boots would compound his grave's soil so that the Indians couldn't uncover it, Washington led what remained of Braddock's forces back to Philadelphia.

Once the facts surrounding Braddock's catastrophic defeat had settled, Washington, who held nothing as sacred as his reputation, was astonished to find even his most heroic efforts twisted into negatives by the British military establishment. A subsequent inquiry into the causes of Braddock's defeat attributed the army's panic not to faulty strategy, but to the colonials, and to Washington specifically. Washington's admirers, now spread across the colonies, would not countenance such revisionist explanations; they steadfastly regarded him as the hero of Braddock's defeat. The colonialists argued that not even the British questioned the fact that Washington had warned Braddock about the potential for a surprise. Nor did anyone dispute that Braddock had disregarded his advice. Beyond that, it was Washington, the natural leader, who took command, leading the surviving troops out of the ambush, dodging bullets himself, and taking care to remove his mortally wounded superior to safety. The split between viewpoints on the "Battle of the Wilderness" was symptomatic of a much deeper chasm that existed between the British and their colonial subjects. The fact was that their hero had again been made into a scapegoat in order to cover British incompetence. For Washington it was another bitter experience, yet he possessed an abiding sense of mission that made even the most onerous situations survivable: he learned from everything he did.

In the social realm, he'd seen the near impossibility of upward mobility among the British. To him, they viewed Americans as subjects of the Crown when convenient but as second-class citizens when it was to their liking. The prospect of a military man, even one as extraordinary as himself, ever rising to an officer's rank in the British Regulars was also not realistic, he realized, because such positions weren't earned on the battlefield but bestowed by birthright and financial arrangement—neither of which he possessed. Still, perhaps most importantly, through each of these experiences Washington discerned other truths about the British and their much-vaunted military superiority. Like a young boxing contender observing the style, stamina, and habits of a champion he might someday challenge, he'd seen vulnerabilities in the British command that he would someday be called on to remember and exploit. Given the forward-looking mind of Washington, would it be too far a stretch to wonder if, like that young contender in boxing, he wasn't even then calculating how he would go about defeating the British Army as commander in chief of American forces?

First, Washington may have reasoned, the British system was based on bloodlines and societal position, not merit; therefore it was intrinsically discriminatory toward its American subjects. Second, this system impinged on the military in that British officers were selected on the basis of social standing, not military acumen. The net effect was that many of the officers—for all of their social superiority—were in fact inferior military men. Third, as they were used to confronting the enemy in stand-up columns, British forces were defenseless against the guerilla combat tactics employed by the Indians. Fourth, convinced of their superiority in birth, culture, and battle, they were stubborn in their refusal to adjust to wilderness fighting. Fifth, unfamiliar with the Western frontier that Washington had so vigorously studied as a surveyor and soldier, British troops were easily ambushed and subject to the deleterious effects of an unfamiliar climate, rugged terrain, and disease.

The sum of these and other factors, Washington may well have surmised, could coalesce into a David-versus-Goliath military scenario whereby a smaller, less organized force would be able to defeat the larger, better-trained, British Army by virtue of the underdog's courage, will, and adaptability. In other words, time would be on the side of the indigenous troops—no small revelation to a man of Washington's iron will and boundless personal ambition.

During the following year, George Washington, still only twenty-two years old, was elected colonel of the Virginia regiment and commander in chief of all Virginia forces. Given the miserable outcome of their first wilderness battles, the British command abandoned completely the Shenandoah Valley between the Alleghenies and the Blue Ridge Mountains, where Washington and his army of 1,200 men were left to defend homesteaders against hit-and-run Indian attacks. As historian James Flexner notes, "George Washington and his regiment . . . had been assigned an impossible task. A force many times larger could not have defended so wide a frontier from the endlessly mobile Indians."[15]

To make matters worse, the politics of the British military system again began to encroach on Washington's efforts. Rivalries developed between British officers like Captain John Dagworthy, in Maryland, who not only insisted that as a Regular he had the right to order Washington about, but also proved it by commandeering what few supplies the colonial troops could muster whenever he wanted. Despite these significant obstacles, Washington earned the respect of the settlers and the undying support of his men. Passionate in his command and immensely loyal to his officers, he repudiated the British system of family influence in basing his army's reward and promotion system entirely on merit.

Washington did not give up. With a level of bulldog perseverance not to be seen again among presidents until the dawn of Theodore Roosevelt's rise to power, he continued to try to seize his destiny. After two years of enduring Indian fighting and political subjugation by mere lieutenants in the British Regulars, he pounced on the opportunity to get his career back on track when Lord Loudoun was given the American command. Believing even at this time that his efforts could not go unrewarded, Washington wrote a long letter criticizing, among others, his old ally Dinwiddie for not supporting his ardent belief that an army of Americans under his command could be entrusted to accomplish what Braddock could not: drive the French from Fort Duquesne. Later, after receiving no response to his pleas, he traveled to Philadelphia to meet Loudoun in person, only to find himself shunned for four days and then accorded only a brief, cold reception during which he was given a tongue-lashing by the indignant British commander. It was after this disillusioning episode with disappointment after disappointment no doubt resounding in his mind, that the young Washington wrote into his diary the infamous complaint, "We cannot conceive that being Americans should deprive us of the benefits of being British subjects."[16]

The following year, Brigadier General John Forbes recruited Washington to aide him in the capture of Fort Duquesne, employing forces three times the size of those used in Braddock's failed campaign. Ironically, the fort— and Washington's obsession—would be taken without a shot being fired, but again the wounds of vanquished pride would be opened by Forbes's unwillingness to listen to him. One year after that, in January 1759, another landmark event in Washington's life would occur with his marriage to Martha Dandridge Custis, a wealthy widow considered by many to be the "prize catch of Chesapeake society."[17]

Both the Custis marriage and an altercation with Forbes revealed Washington's typical penchant for financial sobriety and social advancement. In 1758, the campaign Washington waged against Forbes was almost as total as the one he wanted to wage against the French at Fort Duquesne.

Washington was vehement not only for military reasons, but for economic ones as well. He presumed that Forbes's forces would follow Braddock's former trek through Maryland. It was a route vastly preferable to him because it linked the prospective bounty of the Ohio Country to Virginia—and Washington's property holdings. Forbes decided instead to take his troops, based in Carlisle, Pennsylvania, straight across that colony, thereby cutting about thirty miles from the march. To Washington this was heresy and a slap in the face. While Washington argued the strategic benefits of the Maryland route because it followed an old Indian trail familiar to them, few historians would deny that the financial well-being of Virginians, and Washington himself, was also a factor.

During the course of Forbes's march on Fort Duquesne, however, Washington again would prove the duality of his nature, at once a man of block-upon-block pragmatism but also an action-oriented leader of thrilling military bravado: "But on the next day, November 12, the Virginia Regiment encountered a reconnaissance patrol out from the fort. In the skirmish that ensued, Washington stepped between two groups of his own troops that were mistakenly firing at each other, using his sword to knock up their muskets . . . The regiment suffered heavy casualties, most the result of 'friendly fire,' but captured three prisoners who reported that Fort Duquesne was undermanned and vulnerable."[18]

Washington's marriage to Martha Dandridge Custis can also be seen as in keeping with his devotion to courting continuous upward mobility. Historians like Ellis noted that all the women whom Washington courted had been wealthier than he was, with Martha perhaps the wealthiest widow in Virginia. Her estate of eighteen thousand acres—valued at thirty thousand British pounds—afforded her new husband two of the prizes he had strove most of his young life to attain: money and social status.

If within that equation it appears difficult to uncover virtue, one would do well to consider the fact that throughout Washington's life he remained an exemplary husband and father to both Martha and her children. What's more, if he had indeed fallen deeply in love with Sally Fairfax, the wife of his good friend William, he once again exhibited his legendary self-control in tempering the fires of passion to friendship and maintaining a sense of honor throughout what was to become a lifelong relationship: "Washington possessed a deep-seated capacity to feel powerful emotions. Some models of self-control are able to achieve their serenity easily, because the soul-fires never burned brightly to begin with. Washington became the most notorious model of self-control in all of American history . . . but he achieved this posture . . . the same hard-earned way he learned his soldiering, by direct experience with difficulty."[19]

This man weighed his every action against every consequence and had, very early in his life, honed every fiber of his being into an iron-cast stanchion of self-will.

Washington's first call to national duty came in 1774 when he was selected as Virginia's delegate to the first Continental Congress. Already seething at Britain's draconian economic policies, delegates became incensed when in May 1775 British troops massacred eight colonial minutemen in Lexington, Massachusetts leading to calls for revolution and the formation of a Continental army led by him.

The first challenge that General Washington faced after assembling his army—along with chronic shortages of food, training, and munitions—was maintaining morale given the daunting prospect of warring against vastly superior British forces. Early losses due to his troops' lack of experience and his own tactical errors didn't inspire much hope for victory. After just six months even loyal officers questioned the revolution's chance for success as Congress became vocal in its disapproval of Washington's "hit and run" military strategy. But Washington forged ahead, his belief in himself and his cause perhaps the only constant that kept the army from dissolving entirely due to illness and desertion.

Then, on Christmas night 1776, Washington accomplished what many believed to be impossible by crossing the frozen Delaware River undetected and launching a successful surprise attack on a British stronghold. The guerilla tactics he'd perfected as a wilderness fighter proved too quick and too powerful for the British. The Continental army's resounding victory not only vindicated Washington and the effectiveness of his methods but buoyed the flagging spirits of Americans throughout the colonies.

While the timing of his win was essential to morale, the victories to come would be as brutal as the hardships he and his troops endured. The key to success, he knew from his battles alongside the British, was holding the Continental army together and wearing down British resolve over time. For six bleak years Washington demonstrated a revolutionary ardor that would sustain his under-supplied soldiers through conditions as grueling as any army had ever endured until, in 1781, he delivered a death blow to British hegemony with a stunning victory at Yorktown, Virginia over General Charles Cornwallis. Two years later, the Treaty of Paris was signed by England and the United States, effectively ending the Revolutionary War.

Never were the bedrock principles that guided Washington more apparent than on the evening of December 23, 1783, when after defeating the British Army—the greatest fighting force in the world at that time—he ceremoniously stepped down from power by turning over his sword to the people's representatives, the Congress of Confederation. "Having now finished the work assigned me," he pledged, "I retire from the great theatre of Action . . . I here offer my Commission, and take my leave of all the enjoyments of public life."[20]

Of course, this wasn't the end of his leadership. A little more than four years later, Washington would be elected the first president of the United States, having proved that his heroism was not driven by self-interest, but rather by the principles he was willing to die for.

GEORGE WASHINGTON'S LEADERSHIP LESSONS

So often in business and in life we see so-called leaders who ask the impossible of their subordinates—longer hours, the achievement of unrealistic goals, even benefit and pay cuts—but make few, if any, of those sacrifices themselves. The most important presidential lesson I've learned from Washington is to lead by example, but the leadership lessons of George Washington go far beyond that.

Lesson #1
Work to "Build a Better Self"

Washington possessed a combination of bottomless ambition and obsession with self-control. Viewed as an under-educated, upstart by the British, Washington was—like each of us—a "work in progress." Standing 6'1" and 180 pounds, an expert horseman-frontiersman graceful enough to dance with the best of his social "betters," his capabilities didn't end with anything as superficial as appearance or even charisma.

Washington learned to be tough, even ruthless, when necessary from his grandfather, John; recognized the value of self-worth from his father Augustine's diffidence; and charm and the art of upward mobility from his half-brother, Lawrence. As a youth, he painstakingly copied each of the 110 precepts from *Rules of Civility and Decent Behavior* over and over again because he yearned to improve himself and his lot in life.

No one is born great. Each of us is a work-in-progress. In the end, as with great presidents from Washington to Reagan, becoming the character-driven leader we strive to become has much to do with having goals, learning from experiences, setting a true course toward achieving our dreams, and continuously improving to "build a better self."

Lesson #2
See Opportunity and Seize It!

Washington had what many saw as an opportunistic nature. His was a steady march from oblivion to the greatness accomplished step-by-step from the time he ingratiated himself with William Fairfax to get the job of surveying his land holdings, to using that contact to procure a military commission from Governor Dinwiddie, to volunteering for the harrowing mission of confronting Commanding Officer Legardeur at French Creek, to becoming Commander of Colonial forces, to the presidency of the United States.

Washington's ability to recognize opportunity, his willingness to take risks to pursue them, his talent for making the most out of each and, finally, his fluidity in moving from one opportunity to the next milestone on the path to accomplishing their ultimate goal, is what made him "great."

Opportunities are what you make of them. When you see one, take the risk, and seize it. It won't be there forever.

Lesson #3
Failure Is Part of the Journey

We learn more from our failures than our successes *provided we learn from them.*

Each great president suffered monumental setbacks. Washington's repeated rejection by the British to become a "Regular," presumed incompetence during the Jumonville fiasco, the Battle of the Wilderness, and Brigadier General Forbes' march on Fort Duquesne are all examples of early failures. Lincoln, too, lost two national elections before his rise to the presidency while few presidents endured the public humiliation of Kennedy after the Bay of Pigs fiasco.

Aside from the fact that each experienced these dramatic failures, the more important point is the attitude with which they accepted it. Each admitted their failure, analyzed what had gone wrong, recalibrated their approach to prevent repeating the same mistakes, and moved into the future tougher, wiser, and better prepared for the challenges ahead.

The word "failure" doesn't exist for those who, like Washington, turn personal and professional setbacks into opportunities for continuous improvement.

Lesson #4
Great Leaders Are "Heroic"

If ever there was a president whose leadership flies in the face of Collin's leadership from "40,000 feet," Welch's "ego-driven" model, and Hay's use of "scientific" manipulation, it is George Washington.

Like Teddy Roosevelt traveling to Panama to run a bulldozer in the middle of a malaria epidemic to inspire workers to complete the project, Washington's leadership was totally engaged and always "hands-on." Whether taking command of troops after Braddock was mortally wounded at the Battle of Wilderness, being shot point blank by a traitorous Indian on his mission to warn Governor Dinwiddie about France's incursion into the state, or charging through friendly fire to prevent disaster during Forbes' march on Fort Duquesne, Washington was heroic.

But even for Washington, being "heroic" didn't always mean performing swashbuckling acts or saving the day with sensational exploits. In fact, his most "heroic" act, and most remarkable, had nothing to do with combat. Rather, it came when after having defeated the most powerful military force on earth he quietly and magnanimously surrendered his sword and his commission as Commander of American troops to the Continental Congress in the name of democracy.

Great leaders like Washington are by definition "heroic" because they are character-driven. Their dreams, their actions, their very presence ennobles the situation and the people they interact with because their overwhelming strength of character fosters words and actions that make people want to follow them to a forward-looking, more fulfilling future.

In all that you do each day, strive to be "heroic."

Lesson #5
Suck the Marrow from Experiences, Good and Bad

Ironically, the rejection Washington faced attempting to advance within the British military turned out to be the very experience that gave him the insights he'd need to defeat them two decades later. More, it was the realization that the lives of all Americans would forever be subjugated unless another path was taken.

One of the great lessons of Washington's life is that often from out of our greatest rejection comes our greatest re-direction. Washington didn't get bogged down in self-pity or what the naysayers told him about his dream of becoming a great military leader. Rather, from out of that rejection sprung the revelation that his dreams were bigger than his environment and so his direction changed, but not his dream.

When faced with life experiences, good and bad, maintain the perspective of a life-long student. Learn everything you can from it! The lessons may be incremental or lead you in a new direction that you would never have considered without having gone through it.

Learn to suck the marrow from experiences, good and bad.

Lesson #6
Great Leadership Requires Great Discipline

Whenever I consider the incredible self-discipline Washington exercised in standing on the sidelines while the love of his life, Sally Cary, married his best friend and benefactor, William Fairfax, I can't help but contrast it with the lack of discipline Bill Clinton exercised—and the price he and the country paid—in his Oval Office tryst with Monica Lewinski.

Washington was the ultimate pragmatist, and a paragon of self-discipline. Of all the presidents, none exhibited the inexorable strength of will as consistently and as early as Washington. From the time he began hand copying the 110 precepts from *The Rules of Civility and Decent Behavior* as a boy, Washington—like a great athlete—put himself in training for his dream of becoming a formidable military leader.

Character-driven leaders are always prepared for the contests that life will bring them. For men and women like Washington, self-discipline is not something you exercise prior to a particular occasion. It's a way of life.

Washington also understand that, along with the decision to become a character-driven leader, comes the responsibility of living up to that charge each day because those around him expected no less and—more important—he expected it of himself.

Understand that great leadership requires great discipline. Be ready for success, not just by preparing for it, but by living a disciplined life each day and living up to the responsibilities of a character-driven leader.

Lesson #7
Lead by Example

Washington was the antithesis of Collins' manager from "forty-thousand feet," leading not by theory but through actions and by example as when he courageously charged through a barrage of friendly fire during Forbes' Fort Duquesne campaign, using his sword to "knock up their muskets" and quell the exchange.

He possessed none of the duplicity epitomized by the Hay Group's manipulative manager; rather, he let his own ardent belief inspire others to action as when he candidly disagreed with British General Braddock's strategy during the Battle of the Wilderness asking that he be allowed to "engage the enemy on his own terms." Yet, when Braddock denied his request, Washington dutifully followed orders leading his men into battle, remaining ardent in his efforts to the very end, burying Braddock in a safe place once he had died, and fulfilling his final directive by riding alone to Philadelphia in order to solicit re-enforcements.

Later, as victorious commander, Washington proved that unlike Welch's "ego-driven" executive he saw it as his destiny to lead others toward a vision larger than himself and, in a gesture as pure in its motive as it was elegant in its execution, surrendered his commission to the Continental Congress.

Great leadership demonstrates itself in many ways including heroic actions, sound judgment, inspirational vision, bold decision-making, and discerning diplomacy, but easily the most powerful is leadership by example.

Chapter V

Franklin D. Roosevelt
U.S. President, 1933–1945

Franklin Delano Roosevelt was elected president of the United States for an unprecedented four terms. "I share the view of almost all historians," author William Leuchtenburg stated during a 2002 interview, "when I say that Franklin Roosevelt was the greatest president of the 20th century. His policies were the most imaginative, and he was, in my opinion, the most creative of any president in history."[1]

During the twelve years that he was president, FDR charted the course through the three greatest challenges the United States had confronted since the dark days of the Civil War: the Great Depression, the most severe economic downturn in U.S. history; Pearl Harbor, when at 6:00 a.m. on December 7, 1941, two hundred Japanese aircraft attacked U.S. ships and military installations; and World War II, the most destructive war in history.[2]

When faced with each of these massive challenges, the ever-calm and implacably optimistic Roosevelt rose to each occasion with steely self-confidence, historical grounding, and a mental dexterity matched by few individuals. Nevertheless, Roosevelt's leadership genius, so painstakingly cultivated over his lifetime, wasn't always so evident. For him, becoming a true leader was a hard-won developmental process.

This chapter will explore FDR's leadership with a particular emphasis on one of his greatest achievements: the conversion of America's industrial capabilities from a peacetime to a wartime footing. Dubbed by historians as America's "manufacturing miracle," it was a time when Franklin Roosevelt's creativity and leadership through innovation were never more brilliantly demonstrated.

FDR's upbringing was enviable. Born at Springwood—the family home overlooking the Hudson River in Hyde Park, New York—to James Roosevelt and Sarah Delano, his family was wealthy, socially well positioned, and full of successful relatives (not the least of whom was Franklin's fifth cousin Theodore). The Roosevelt family prospered in Manhattan real estate, dry goods, and the importation of sugar from the West Indies. On the Delano side, Warren Delano II made his fortune as an Asian trader, exporting opium and selling it in China.

James Roosevelt was an instructive father who taught his son how to ride a horse at four and to sail by six. Franklin, whom his immediate family called "Frank," was taught a lifelong respect for music and literature. His mother, Sarah, oversaw piano lessons for him in the mornings and read the classics to him at night. As a teenager, Roosevelt's greatest pastime was the sea. At the time of his death, he'd amassed more than two thousand books about U.S. naval history in his personal library, two hundred fully rigged ship models, and thirty-seven carefully assembled and annotated photograph albums of naval vessels. In fact, no American president—not even his cousin Teddy, who wrote *The Naval War of 1812*—came to office with as much knowledge of ships, the sea, and sea power as did FDR.[3]

At the Groton School, which Franklin attended as an adolescent, the classics, Greek, and Latin were emphasized, as well as French and German (which Roosevelt already spoke fluently). To the sons of old money, however, this thin, wan, handsome teenager seemed "too European." He tried his hand at boxing, discovered that he was too slight for football, and eventually found his niche as a first-class debater, soprano singer in choir, and cheerleader for the football team. Still, he could never fit in as one of Groton's "regulars."[4]

More worldly than his classmates, by the time he was in his mid-teens Roosevelt had already met Germany's Emperor Wilhelm II aboard his father's yacht (he was to keep as a souvenir of the meeting a pencil that the emperor had chewed on), dined with President Grover Cleveland ("My little man, I am making a strange request of you . . . never be president of the United States!" Cleveland had advised him), and was the frequent guest of his cousin Theodore, already the most admired man in the country ("I like you . . . and believe in you," Teddy had encouraged Franklin. "Golden years open before you").[5] Perhaps it was owing to this elevated station and opportunity that, in addition to having a reputation for intelligence and wit, he began to put forth a glib charm that could at times coarsen to manipulative demagogy: "There began to emerge in Franklin certain traits that would become notorious at the height of his public career. His devious tendencies were more evident than ever before in his letters home; his own achievements were exaggerated, his short-comings were never his fault, and reflections on rivals, no matter how narrow the field of competition, become acidulous."[6]

By the time he attended Harvard in September 1900, Roosevelt had developed into a handsome, debonair young man, viewed by peers and professors as affable, well-spoken, and irritatingly superficial. He joined the Republican Club and was appointed editor of the school newspaper, *The Harvard Crimson*, but sailed through the university with Cs. Furthermore, he was disastrously unsuccessful in attempting to gain acceptance into the prestigious Porcellian Club, of which both his father and cousin Teddy had been members. His wife, Eleanor, later claimed that the rebuff gave him an "inferiority complex . . . and was the greatest disappointment of his life."[7]

In truth, FDR was anything but what he appeared to be. In contrast to Teddy's life-and-death struggle with childhood disease and iron-to-steel tempering among the rough-and-tumble cowboys of the Dakotas, Franklin led a pampered life with none of these kinds of experiences. His life was easy and—unlike Washington, Lincoln, or TR, who had emerged stronger for their struggles to achieve self-worth—Franklin was mostly immured from anybody or anything that would seek to challenge, test, or otherwise transform him.

Not gifted as an athlete outside of swimming, he was a male cheerleader, not a Rough Rider. Voluble and quick-witted but hopelessly affected by European culture and clench-jawed Knickerbocker high society, he was seen by his peers not as sophisticated but "strange." Add to this the Porcellian Club debacle and out-of-hand rejection of his marriage proposal by first love Alice Sohier—who responded, "I do not wish to be a cow"—one can discern something less than a wholesome ego in the making of FDR.[8]

Not long after these unsettling experiences, the seemingly unflappable Franklin began dating his distant cousin Eleanor. The product of a family wracked by alcoholism, as a child Eleanor was a disappointment to her mother, Anna, who thought her "plain and dowdy"; further, Eleanor was blatantly abused by her father, Elliot. Though even until her death Eleanor idolized him, the emotions from his side were at best erratic, fueled by alcohol, womanizing, and violent behavior.

Unloved and unwanted, Eleanor was sent to a convent when her family moved to a suburb of Paris. There she became depressed and deeply affected by the cruelty of the nuns, who substituted rigorous discipline for faith and catechism for education. Finally expelled for a trivial infraction, she returned to her mother's residence in Manhattan at the age of eight. With her father having been committed to an Illinois institution for mental illness, she bore up to her mother's hostilities and held her responsible for her father's condition until, at the age of twenty-nine, Anna Roosevelt died of diphtheria. Thereafter, Eleanor and her brothers were sent to live with their elderly grandmother. Tragically and memorably for Eleanor, her youngest brother, Elliot Jr., died less than a year later at age three, also from diphtheria. "My little brother Ellie was simply too good for this world," she would later lament in a diary entry.[9]

Eleanor's adolescence afterward could only be described as "grim" and was made worse when, on August 13, 1894, her father returned to New York on the heels of a sexual imbroglio suffering from violent seizures and delusions. At thirty-two, he was physically and mentally spent when he visited. He shouted incoherently and ran up and down the staircase until he stiffened, then fell backward to his death. Yet, despite the abuse her father had heaped on her, Eleanor never stopped loving him; for all of her life she kept at her bedside a miniature Bible from which he had read to Anna.

Eleanor's luck finally changed in her mid-teens when she was sent to the Allenswood Academy in Manhattan. There she studied under Marie Souvestre, who saw in this shy, tall, and plain young woman an uncommon intelligence, sensitivity, and vision. Eleanor Roosevelt, like Franklin, possessed the chemistry of greatness, though in disproportionate measures. Souvestre took her exceptional student under her tutelage, showing her the great works of art in Florence and exposing Eleanor to the progressive—some would say socialistic—political theories prevalent in turn-of-the-century Europe. During that period Eleanor evolved into a new woman, an individual who, unlike Franklin, had experienced life at the bottom. Admirably, Eleanor pulled herself back up to the top, becoming a well-educated, sincere, and irrepressible champion of the underdog.

By the time that Franklin began attending Columbia Law School, he and Eleanor had fallen in love and were engaged to be married. During their engagement, Eleanor taught immigrant children at a school on New York's Lower East Side. Cautious at first about sharing her experiences there, in February 1905 she arranged for her fiancé to accompany her home from the school. While he was there, a student took ill and Franklin carried the little girl home to the upper floor of a squalid tenement, confessing afterward, "I didn't know anyone lived like that!" Later Eleanor told a friend that it was important to her that her future husband understood the plight of the poor in preparation for when he would hold public office. "It worked," she confided. "He saw how people lived and he never forgot."[10]

To some degree, it was Eleanor's influence throughout their marriage that helped develop the "other side" of Franklin's unique ability to lead Americans of all races, nationalities, and social stripes. Eleanor was "yin" to his "yang." He was handsome, cheerful, and charismatic, she was heartfelt, intuitive, and humane. Like the second piece of a two-piece puzzle, Eleanor was an important part of what would become FDR's public persona as "a patrician that spoke the language of the dispossessed."[11] She complemented the abilities that he already possessed and supplemented those that he did not. They were arguably the most famous couple in American history.

After his graduation from Columbia, FDR took a position with a Wall Street firm, knowing that it was politics and not law that interested him. Still unwilling, or unable, to shake a demeanor best described as flippant, he joined the Democratic Party, claiming that he was disenchanted with the fat-cat complacency of the New York Republicans. Another reason, he breezily explained, was that, like his cousin Theodore, he believed that a man like himself, who came from wealth and power, could accomplish reform and ignite enthusiasm among the poor while also harvesting their votes. In fact, the more plausible explanation for his actions was that, having shrewdly assessed the schism between Teddy's Progressive faction and William Howard Taft's conservatives within the Republican Party, Franklin anticipated a split in the Republican vote that would sweep the Democrats into office.

Even as a twenty-six-year-old, FDR had an uncanny instinct for the momentum of events; after consulting with Teddy, he decided to run for the state assembly. After FDR announced his intention, though, the former Democratic challenger changed his mind about bowing out and Franklin threatened to run as an independent. Party regulars, understanding the power of the Roosevelt name and purse, and recognizing that such an action by Franklin would throw the race to the Republicans by splitting the Democratic vote, suppressed the in-party challenge to FDR's nomination. This freed Franklin to work his magic among constituents and non-constituents alike: Roosevelt campaigned with tremendous energy, and what he lacked in gravitas was made up in exuberance and gregariousness.

Though an underdog in what was traditionally a Republican venue, FDR was aggressive in his attacks on his opponent, Senator John Schlosser, accusing him of being a stooge of Republican Party bosses. Tearing a page from his uncle's campaign book, FDR evoked the Roosevelt name unabashedly and was easy about becoming "*dee-lighted!*" with anything "*bully!*"—and it worked. In his first election to public office, Franklin D. Roosevelt ran ahead of the entire Democratic ticket, wresting the senate seat from the Republicans while piling up 15,708 votes to Schlosser's 14,568.

Roosevelt's time in the New York senate was spent largely on sharpening his own political skills, gathering support among the New York delegation for Woodrow Wilson's candidacy for president, and developing alliances that depended less on personal convictions than on assembling ever-shifting groups of individuals from greatly varied social and cultural origins on the basis of current policy questions. In short, he was a kind of poster boy for the Hay Group's manipulative leader, a man who could be for or against Prohibition, Sunday gaming laws, and women's suffrage, for example, depending on his audience or what popular trends seemed to dictate. It was journeyman *New York Herald* reporter Louis McHenry Howe who saw something indefinably enticing about the sure-footed, mellifluously voiced Roosevelt that thrilled him to the bone. Howe—a veteran of spit-in-your-eye Tammany politics—sensed that this was a man who could someday become president and therefore was the politician whose career he wanted to support and whose coattails he wanted to ride.

Just as Lincoln had Wisconsin kingmaker Carl Schurz to burnish the mythology of his upbringing for public consumption, so too Roosevelt had Louis Howe. Small in stature, chronically humped forward, and with a thin leather face forever clouded by cigarette smoke, the forty-two-year-old Howe was as politically astute as he was physically ugly. In 1912, with FDR running for reelection but bedridden with scarlet fever, the inexhaustible Howe shrewdly managed his campaign, aligning him shoulder-and-hip to Woodrow Wilson's run for the White House. Unfazed by his client's inability to meet voters, he personally took to the road and devised a series of local initiatives to ingratiate his candidate. These included newspaper advertising, freelance articles, and "letters to the editor" lauding Roosevelt's positions written by "anonymous" citizens (often Howe himself).[12] Howe's goal was to so deeply imbed FDR with Wilson's candidacy that when Wilson won, he would feel indebted enough to offer young Roosevelt a position of importance within the administration.

Perceptive people, like TR and Eleanor, saw the personal command and intuitive leadership that the thirty-one-year-old Roosevelt possessed when working crowds, speaking publicly, or chairing working groups within the senate. They could also discern the necessity of a spin doctor like Howe, because, at the root of it, and for all of his skills, FDR was a man with no center. His beliefs were a matter of expedience. His actions were those of a politician, not a leader.

After Wilson trounced both Teddy and Taft for the presidency, TR and Taft added their weight to whatever sense of obligation the new commander in chief might have felt to Roosevelt, and Franklin was offered TR's former position as assistant secretary of the navy. FDR was blessed in his new role with a boss who, as a lifelong newspaper publisher, knew nothing about naval strategy. More to the point, after having spent much of his life either sailing or obsessing over books about naval warfare, Roosevelt appeared a natural for the position.

Yet in his new job he feverishly networked for lasting political contacts at all levels of government; he did this at the expense of a cause like building America's naval power to mitigate Japan's and Germany's ambitions or opening a canal to bridge the world's great oceans. Like Howe, who offered plum jobs and appointments on behalf of the assistant secretary in return for anticipated political favors, Franklin had an ambition that was somewhat crass in nature. Roosevelt personally designed new uniforms for navy officers and campaigned hard for improved ship construction and technology, but he never seemed to hold in his hand or heart "larger" causes. In fact, as soon as he achieved recognition as "the brains" behind Secretary of the Navy Josephus Daniels, FDR began calculating with Howe the tactics necessary to run either for governor or senator of New York in 1914. Up until this point, there was little evidence that FDR would ever have the core values, moral courage, or intensity of character to become a great leader.

We'll leave the perceived importance of manipulative ability to the Hay Group, which would undoubtedly see genius in FDR's ambivalence and dexterity. We'll let Jack Welsh judge whether the ego Roosevelt had thus far displayed was of the kind that would lead him triumphantly down corridors of wealth and power. We'll let Jim Collins measure to which level on the "leadership" pyramid FDR had so far risen with his increasing distance from day-to-day reality and concern for the ever-bigger picture. As a character-based leader, Franklin D. Roosevelt was at this point a political success but a leadership failure, set on an inexorable path toward a U.S. presidency in the mold of Andrew Johnson, James Buchanan, and Herbert Hoover—three of the most detached, superficial, and uncaring chief U.S. executives of all time.

Still, like the perpetually scheming middle manager who expends his talent on Machiavellian schemes to "look good," "end runs" his bosses in an attempt to replace them, or tries to "brownnose" his way to the top instead of simply performing exceptionally in the position that he holds, Roosevelt and his spin doctor, Louis Howe, became victims of their own ambition. The two assumed that FDR's star was rising simply because his name was recognized throughout Washington DC (largely due to Howe's publicity efforts), and they both believed that if FDR ran for senator, flamboyant newspaper mogul William Randolph Hearst would be his opposition and President Wilson would enthusiastically support Roosevelt's candidacy. Therefore Roosevelt decided to run in the Democratic primary for the New York U.S. Senate seat.

These calculations, however, proved inaccurate. It was a fact that FDR was well-known around Washington, but that's not to say he was respected. In actuality, to political elders he was seen as an "over-energetic child."[13] Likewise, the supposition that the easy-to-beat Hearst would be FDR's opposition was also wrong. In fact, it wasn't Hearst that ran, but rather Tammany candidate James W. Gerard, the distinguished former U.S. ambassador to Germany. And finally, President Wilson, who did indeed have warm feelings for Roosevelt, was more concerned with impending world war and his deathly ill wife than supporting any of the candidates. In the end, Gerard won the primary by a margin of three to one, with Roosevelt carrying less than one-third of New York's sixty-six counties.[14]

Chastened by defeat, FDR was beginning to learn valuable lessons about both himself and the nature of political games versus true-life realities. During the next eight years, throughout all of World War I, he would hold his position at the Department of the Navy, demonstrating flashes of political brilliance along with acts that displayed both administrative acumen and personal courage. Never satisfied with the status quo, regardless of his motives, FDR—like Washington, Lincoln, and Theodore Roosevelt before him— soaked up information and experiential lessons with rapacity.

In July and August 1914, after Austria-Hungary declared war on Serbia, the countries of Russia, France, Germany, and the United Kingdom were plunged into hostilities that marked the onset of world war. President Woodrow Wilson, who was loath to enter the hostilities, watched events deteriorating at a rate that even he could not have imagined; ten months later, Britain's Cunard liner RMS *Lusitania* was sunk by a German submarine, killing 1,198 innocents, including 128 Americans. Franklin's childhood acquaintance Emperor Wilhelm II then committed an act of overt hostility that even the idealistic Wilson could no longer countenance. On February 1, 1917, the kaiser announced Germany's new high-seas policy of unrestricted submarine warfare against any ship of any nationality en route to any Allied port. Two days later he made good on the threat, sinking the American ship *Housatonic*. Two months later, on April 2, 1917, President Wilson addressed Congress to demand a declaration of war.

If there had been glimpses of the Roosevelt family's passionate belief in societal responsibility in FDR's coupling with Eleanor, it was Wilhelm's menacing arrogance that raised the hackles of what would become FDR's never-say-die fighting spirit. Upon America's entry into the war, the United Kingdom was already in dire straits. The toll of German submarines on Allied shipping exceeded nine hundred thousand tons in March 1917 alone, and Britain was down to a three-week supply of grain, with the prospect of famine looming. When his boss, Secretary of the Navy Daniels, wilted under the enormousness of the task at hand, Roosevelt took it on himself, without Daniel's or Wilson's authorization, to promise and deliver to the Allies thirty destroyers needed to escort food-bearing freighters. In order to fortify the navy on his side of the Atlantic, he personally negotiated with contractors to build new naval installations for the housing of draftees and the collection of wartime supplies.

While Daniels fretted over the next moves, Roosevelt set out on the destroyer USS *Dyer* to visit the western front, fearing that U.S. strategists would be like "chess players moving their pieces in the dark" if they lacked firsthand knowledge of the battlefield. In London he dined with King George V and met for the first time with Sir Winston Churchill, who would two decades later form with Roosevelt the greatest wartime alliance in military history. During his visit, even as the deliberative Wilson contemplated conscription, FDR publicly called for a draft. Franklin insisted on going to the brink of the battlefront at Verdun, France, where 975,000 French and German soldiers had been massacred in less than two years of ferocious fighting. Later, when his security aide tried to steer him away from the front, fearing for his own life, Roosevelt fired him on the spot.

After he returned to the States, FDR played a vital role in two key naval initiatives. The first was the deployment of 110-foot "sub clearers" to attack, rather than defend against, German submarines. The second was the creation of an antisubmarine "barrage," a network of mines set across the English Channel and the North Sea between Norway and Scotland, where all German vessels made their way into the sea lanes. Satisfied that the addition of American destroyers and an innovative antisubmarine strategy had greatly improved delivery of grain and war materials to Britain and France, and inspired by Clemenceau and Theodore, FDR wrote Eleanor that he'd decided to quit his post at the navy. An admiral had offered him the post of lieutenant commander operating an antisubmarine battery at the front in the U.S. Marines. Of course, Eleanor discouraged his resignation, one of the few times in his life that he acted out of passion rather than calculated reason.

What happened next must have seemed fortuitous to Eleanor and Daniels, with the hand of destiny reaching into some historical continuum. Roosevelt agreed to perform a final assignment in his current position: inspecting the frontline forces with British Commander Marshall Douglas Haig.

During the inspection, both men came under continuous heavy attack; while crossing the Channel, the destroyer that carried FDR was bombed twice by enemy aircraft, and the experience plunged Roosevelt into illness. During subsequent meetings with General Pershing and France's Marshall Foch, FDR ploughed on with a temperature of 102, then traveled to Scotland to oversee progress on the antisubmarine barrage before collapsing from a case of double pneumonia. By the time his ship docked at New York Harbor on September 19, 1917, he had to be carried off by stretcher. In the immediate days following his collapse, FDR still managed—ill as he was—to issue a widely praised report on the status and necessary improvements in waging battle gleaned from his immersion in World War I's most dangerous battlefields.

Clearly, these were not the war heroics of Washington, Teddy, or even John F. Kennedy. Yet FDR's actions seemed to mark the beginnings of an interior evolution, pulling him away from pure self-interest and ambition to something more emotional, indicating that a kind of battle for his character was being waged. One side, the spiritual, would certainly be encouraged by

Eleanor. The other side, the mundane, would certainly be bolstered by Howe and FDR's own proclivity for taking the easy way out, faking the passions, feelings, and internal experiences that a leader was expected to possess. Historian Doris Kearns Goodwin observes: "There was a detachment to FDR, and even those who worked with him day after day wondered what he was really like . . . There were contrasting sides, and one of them desired seclusion . . . for hours he would sit alone with his stamp collection or play solitaire . . . I think that in order to protect himself from his overbearing mother and the responsibilities to the family name he had to hide his real self and it became a habit for the rest of his life."[15]

From strictly an external standpoint, FDR continued to build a fortress of experience for himself. Popular after the war because of his Howe-touted accomplishments as assemblyman and assistant secretary of the navy, Roosevelt was chosen to run as the number-two man on the 1920 Democratic ticket after thrilling the convention with a speech on behalf of Al Smith. The James M. Cox–Roosevelt ticket lost out to the Republicans, but FDR prospered from the experience of traveling by private railcar for over eight thousand miles and stopping in every city along the way. It enabled him to get "to know the country as only a national candidate or a traveling salesman can get to know it."

FDR's externals were strengthened, but what of the building blocks that, when constructed "one by one," form the bedrock character fundamental to enduring greatness as a leader? In the article "Crucibles of Leadership," authors Warren Bennis and Robert Thomas contend that "recent research suggests that one of the most reliable indicators of true leadership is the ability to learn from even the most negative experiences . . . A 'crucible' is, by definition, a transformative experience through which an individual comes to a new or altered sense of identity."[16] Certainly we've seen this in Lincoln, who, plunged into tragedy after tragedy, rose with steely resolve to brave the awesome challenges that he faced. Yet ironically, the most striking parallel for the life-altering malady that was to soon confront FDR was that of his cousin, Theodore Roosevelt, who also battled his way from the smother of disease back to physical health and mental voracity.

On June 6, 1944, Franklin Roosevelt was grim and soulful when he addressed the nation in a radio broadcast with a prayer just before the D-day invasion of France. Yet can anyone imagine the good-looking, smart-alecky Roosevelt of 1920, complete with TR-style pince-nez spectacles and bow tie, articulating this stunningly innocent and guileless prayer to God on behalf of the American people?

Almighty God, our sons, pride of our nation, this day have been set upon a mighty endeavor, a struggle to preserve our republic, our religion, and our

civilization, and to set free a suffering humanity. Their road will be long and
hard for the enemy is strong. He may hurl back our forces. Success may not
come with rushing speed but we shall return again and again and we know that
by thy grace, and by the righteousness of our cause, our sons will triumph. The
darkness will be rent by noise and flame. Men's souls will be shaken by the vio-
lences of war. Some will never return. Embrace these Father and receive them,
Thy holy servants, into Thy kingdom. Thy will be done, Almighty God. Amen.[17]

Franklin Roosevelt's "crucible" experience that transformed him from gifted
politician to great leader happened suddenly, without warning. On August
9, 1921, content in the knowledge that his political future was soaring, he
returned from a swim at a lake near his Campobello, New Brunswick, retreat
feeling "achy." He awakened the next morning to find his feet, legs, and arms
paralyzed by polio.

It was the Italian poet Dante who popularized the notion of one's own private hell, and to FDR at this juncture of his life, there could be no nightmare
more chilling than the one he woke up to on that summer morning. All of his
life he'd idolized his cousin, President Theodore Roosevelt, and dreamed that
someday he would follow his hero into the White House. Yet as he lay in his
room in Campobello, those dreams must have seemed perverse reflections
on what may have been but now never could be. "Polio in those days carried a social stigma like venereal disease," FDR's grandson Curtis Roosevelt
explains. "People were put away when they had polio . . . so to find your
husband, or your father, with polio must have been a huge shock to him and
to his family."[18]

But Franklin D. Roosevelt refused to accept the hand that fate had dealt
him. Perhaps it was the cheerleader in him, the indomitable family spirit,
or other some crackling energy source deep within, but even as the disease
continued to ravage his body, he staunchly maintained that the "cure" was
just a matter of time, patience, and hard work. Curtis Roosevelt remembers:

> He would spend a good part of the day, every day, with his braces and crutches
> trying to walk all the way to the end of the driveway . . . He would drag him-
> self along, back and forth, sweating buckets, and it was not just an impossible
> task in terms of muscles, but it was painful. The sad thing—and I don't know
> how he put up with it—was to recognize that he was not making any progress,
> despite all of the physical therapy he was engaging in. He said to Eleanor just
> once, "I'm a useless person, and I'll always be a burden," and then never again.[19]

It was in his search for a cure that FDR discovered a broken-down rehabilitation center in rural Warm Springs, Georgia. The one-hundred-degree,
mineral-rich water was believed to be the perfect medium for exercising the
weakened limbs of polio victims, and the community provided a haven for

what might now be called group therapy. Immediately taken with the place, Roosevelt withdrew one-third of his trust fund to purchase Warm Springs, turning it into one of the country's foremost centers for rehabilitation. Warm Springs was a place where patients were encouraged to set goals and try for the impossible. It was also the perfect environment—not unlike Teddy's Dakotas—for a man to take himself apart one brick at a time and put himself back together again as someone altered and perhaps even "better."

For nearly two years of the next four, FDR secluded himself with other polio victims—often children and often poor. He took up the role of unofficial physiotherapist and psychological counselor, teaching and encouraging while still himself learning about the nature of pain, poverty, hope, and despair. Forced to use a wheelchair, and often needing to crawl on his stomach to pull himself up the stairs of neighboring cottages to play poker with indigent rural Southerners, he listened to the trials and challenges facing groups of Americans whom he'd never have met, let alone befriend, prior to his affliction.

It was the "transformative" experience of polio, his own indomitable spirit, and Eleanor's inexhaustible devotion that burned the raw ore of his potential to the purified steel of the character-driven leader that would emerge from this, the unlikeliest of locales, Warm Springs, Georgia, four years later. There, too, the creativity and innovation of FDR rose like a phoenix from the ashes of his stricken body. While a "cure" would never come for FDR, his dreams of a successful political career were heartened when, in Houdini-like fashion after months of effort, he developed a method to create the "illusion of walking."

Braced by fourteen pounds of steel strapped around his legs, and supported by a solitary crutch while locking onto the arm of his son, James, FDR would grin handsomely, vivaciously call out salutations, and chat animatedly as he lurched forward, never offering the slightest clue to his audience that it was props, and not his own body, that propelled him. FDR never spoke about his disability, although it was well-known that he had contracted polio. His winning attitude disallowed awkward questions about his health. The brutal regimen of exercise that he'd undertaken for years now had strengthened his chest and biceps to the point that both measured bigger than those of heavyweight champion Jack Dempsey. When one bold reporter did ask him about the effects of his polio, he answered, while grasping a specially built podium that was bolted to the floor, "I have a slight limp." (Unbelievably, the explanation was accepted.[20])

In his book *The Great Deception*, author Robert Nathan describes how Roosevelt campaigned from his private train car—the "Roosevelt Special"—and in political arenas:

> He gave speeches at every town. He had to put on his braces and to do that he had to take off his pants and put on his braces, put his pants back on, have

someone stand him up, and leaning his full weight on a door, he'd step out on
a platform and speak to the crowd . . . The podium had to be bolted to the floor
because the entire time he was speaking he was really holding himself up with
one arm, sometimes he would gesture with the other one, then he would have to
go immediately back to grab onto the podium.[21]

The public was never told that FDR was paralyzed, and the press became
willing partners in the subterfuge through his run for governor of New York
until the final days of his presidency. But why? They could see him being
lifted into his wheelchair. They saw his excruciating expression as he tried to
walk, but they never photographed, filmed, or wrote about his affliction. The
answer is that both the press and the public saw in him a rare kind of courage
and optimism that was contagious and inspirational during periods when both
were in short supply. People wanted to be willingly deceived because they
admired and needed him.

The Franklin Delano Roosevelt who ran for the governorship of New York
in 1928 and the presidency in the fall of 1932 was made mobile by a carefully
choreographed illusion, but it was the resourceful, supremely confident man
and his message of hope—based on hard-fought strength of body, mind, and
character—whom the public chose.

After the stock market crash of 1929, President Herbert Hoover was already
defeated: detached from the public, a poor communicator, and ensconced by
big-business interests, he blamed Europe for America's woes; he was so cal-
loused to the misery of millions of Americans, scourged by 30 percent unemployment, that he once commented on the "charm" of seeing indigents selling
apples on street corners. All across the nation, "Hoovervilles" were being
constructed: self-made camps for homeless families, where cardboard and
scrap metal were used to build makeshift residences set around blazing fires
to provide heat. At the time of Roosevelt's run for the presidency, politicians,
the federal government, and the population seemed paralyzed, incapable of
meaningful action—metaphorically speaking, America was an invalid.

In 1932, however, a man arrived on the scene who was, in fact, a cheerful survivor of a genuinely paralyzing disease. Optimistic, indefatigable,
and totally unlike the aloof president, Roosevelt seemed like an Everyman.
Unafraid and unflappable, he refused to accept the possibility that the great
American experiment was doomed. "Let me assert my belief that the only
thing we have to fear is fear itself," he instructed the people. It was this infec-
tious confidence in himself and his abiding faith in America that he projected
onto the people, and they loved him for it.

FDR took America's economic crisis and declared war on it, allowing
the country to confront its own boogeyman: "Roosevelt was saying to the

country, 'You have a leader now, and you have a leader who is not afraid of exercising power. I am willing to exercise power as though the Great Depression were a war . . . as though we were being invaded by a foreign foe and I'm going to be your commander in chief against this Depression,'"[22] FDR had metamorphosed himself, transforming his shortcomings to strengths so that seemingly overnight his arrogance became gravitas, his calculation became creativity, and his superficiality evolved into a purity of spirit that touched people. Add to this FDR's penchant for action, coupled with his own innate genius for innovation, and by the time he assumed office Roosevelt was as formidable a president as had ever stepped foot into the White House.

The first hundred days of FDR's presidency were carried out, in the words of Musashi, by a man "with his hair on fire."[23] FDR initiated the most prodigious legislative session in American history and became the yardstick against which every president after him would be judged. "He knew there would come a time when Congress and the people would not be so amenable," Eleanor later observed, and he acted accordingly."[24]

One of the first acts he proposed was to repeal the Eighteenth Amendment, making alcohol and beer legal for the first time in thirteen years; once passed, it transformed American society forever. When the banking system seemed on the brink of collapse, he calmed the public with a national radio address, ordered banks to close for four days to avoid a rush, and brought the country's leading bankers and politicians together, demanding that they come up with programs to solve the problem: "'I'm going to lock you in a room and you're not to come out until you come up with a solution to this.' . . . Now that's something that presidents had never done before. This was an insistent leadership for which there is really no parallel in the past," historian William Leuchtenburg asserted.[25]

But that was just the beginning. Recruiting a cadre of stellar minds from Ivy League universities—these became labeled the "Brain Trust" by the media—FDR laid out a blueprint for his assault on the Great Depression: In March 1933 Roosevelt created the Civilian Construction Corps, a group run by the army that employed 250,000 young men and women at one dollar per day, rescuing them from blighted inner cities to perform physical labor outdoors. In the spring of that same year, at a time when agriculture made up 30 percent of America's workforce and desperate farmers were resorting to violence against banks that were foreclosing on their neighbors' mortgages, he established the Agricultural Adjustment Administration to "shore up prices by reducing production," subsidizing the shortfalls with government funds.

On June 16, 1933, FDR proposed and ushered through Congress the National Industrial Recovery Act (NIRA), a compendium of sweeping industrial initiatives that imposed wage and price controls during a time when factories were running at a paltry 15 percent capacity, while scrapping antitrust laws to reduce cost-cutting competition that was driving U.S. manufacturing into bankruptcy. The day that NIRA passed, half a million people marched down New York's Fifth Avenue to show support for the raft of programs that offered average Americans hope and promised to tame disastrous economic cycles by encouraging business and government to work together. Historian Richard Nathan explains: "The best part of that early New Deal was its innovative aspects—let's get after the problem, let's try, let's experiment, even though we haven't had the experience, we aren't sure things will work, and out of that, of course, came tremendously creative, some would say, drastic things."[26]

Of course not everyone was so sanguine about this unprecedented shift of the federal government from the role of laissez-faire observer to active participant overseeing business interests. Early in his first term, FDR forged an alliance with America's most powerful business leaders who, like him, feared the collapse of American capitalism. Once their fears had abated, however, their support receded along with it, and they became his administration's harshest critics. In order to pay for the expanded role of the government—now the largest employer in the country—taxes had risen proportionately, and it was a price that many of the nation's wealthy considered too high. Many charged that FDR had overstepped his role as president, that his programs violated constitutional guarantees, and that he'd taken on a role not unlike the dictatorial ones assumed by Mussolini in Italy and Hitler in Germany.

Nevertheless, the American people had formed a unique bond with the president through Roosevelt's innovative "fireside chats" and Eleanor's weekly newspaper columns. During the Hoover administration, the number of letters received by the White House had averaged fewer than fifty per week: By the midpoint of FDR's first term in office, the average had risen to something on the order of four hundred thousand! As much as his creative ways of delivering his transparent message of hope and action, it was the message and the man himself that so engaged Americans: "My friends, it is high time that we made a clear cut effort to bring about united action, action of labor and management which is one of the high purposes of the Recovery Act," he declared in a "chat" while promoting the NIRA. "I want to tell you what has been done in the last few days, why it was done, and what the next steps are going to be."[27]

By the end of his second term, FDR would have little time to dwell on domestic economic problems because Germany's Adolf Hitler was threatening the borders of half the nations in Europe. After nearly eight exhausting years fighting the metaphorical foe of economic depression, Franklin Delano

Roosevelt, the "fighting president," was the only man Americans believed capable of confronting and defeating Hitler.

Shortly after his speech declaring war on the United States in December 1941, Albert Speer, Hitler's chief architect, wrote a top-secret memo shrewdly assessing the war as a "contest between two systems of organization" for the mass production of military armaments. Fortunately, by April 1945, the United States—initially the least prepared of any of the war's major participants—had, under FDR's leadership, produced an incredible 300,000 aircraft, 70,000 ships, 2.7 million machine guns, and 87,000 tanks and military trucks.

If, in the afterglow of postwar victory, these feats appear foregone conclusions, they seemed anything but that back in May 1940 when Hitler's forces attacked the Netherlands, Luxembourg, Belgium, and France. Not only did Germany possess more planes than all of their opponents combined, but it had, over the decade leading up to war, honed a productive capacity that far exceeded any output their opponents could hope to match. Understanding that the United States would eventually be pulled into war and that American industry would be elemental to any successful outcome, FDR must have rued his comparison of business leaders to "English Tories" during the battle to pass the NIRA. Moreover, at least to Republican business leaders, the president had used "class warfare" as a political tactic to pull votes from the masses while lambasting the business leaders for their social and economic elitism.

For their part, industrial moguls had a dim view not only of the National Industrial Recovery Act, but also of the New Deal's encroachment on capitalism and the president, himself, whom they perceived as a "traitor to his class." With Hitler's troops marching through Europe, the fears of business leaders were heightened at the prospect that FDR, already lionized by Americans, would become something like a dictator himself. So deep was this mistrust that many believed he was personally maneuvering the United States into the war as part of a Machiavellian plan to seize power. If war came, the president of the American Iron and Steel Institute was quoted as saying, "as surely as night follows day," while we are fighting "to crush dictatorship abroad," we will be "extending one at home."[28] Of course, FDR saw it differently, believing that he was serving as a "best friend" to the moguls and reforming "the free enterprise system, in ways that will preserve its viability for generations to come."[29]

Fortunately, Roosevelt was an adroit leader capable of joining disparate constituencies and viewpoints into practical solutions that were acceptable to most. Once having described himself as a "juggler" who was disappointed by people who could "think only in traditional terms," he demonstrated his political dexterity by putting together a seven-person National Defense Advisory Committee (NDAC) composed of both New Dealers and America's most revered business minds. The NDAC was headed by William Knudsen, CEO of General Motors, and also included, among others, U.S. Steel's Edward Stettinius as production director, labor leader Sidney Hellman, and Harriott Elliot, dean of North Carolina University, to represent consumers.

On June 14, 1940, Roosevelt's greatest fears were realized when Nazi soldiers, tanks, and armored vehicles had overrun the defenses of all four of their European adversaries and were entering Paris. Pushing steel manufacturing capabilities to the utmost, Hitler's Germany was producing twenty million tons annually, using it to create forty thousand tanks and more than twenty thousand military aircraft, with many more thousands stockpiled or already in use. By contrast, the United States, then in its eleventh year of the Great Depression, with 17 percent of its workforce still unemployed, was totally unprepared for war. Aircraft production was hampered by paralyzing aluminum shortages owing largely to Alcoa's stubborn market monopoly. Tank production, which took eighteen months from start to finish, required more than a half dozen time-consuming steps. For example, the motors were made by Continental Aircraft, the armor plate by the Diebold Company, the rubber treads by Goodyear, and the weapons by Browning. All of these materials were then shipped to the Rock Island Arsenal in Illinois for the final assembly.

Worse, when just two months earlier Roosevelt had set out to observe the "war games" underway in Louisiana, he was stunned to see firsthand the total inadequacy of American military preparedness. In mock battles, the Red army took on the Blue, but such was the state of the soldiers' conditioning, equipment, and training that by week's end, twelve troops were dead and nearly four hundred hospitalized for injuries and diseases. In contrast to the Nazi's dazzling adoption of high-tech weaponry, FDR was shocked to hear high-ranking traditionalists debate whether the use of horses in the battlefield was superior to that of tanks. The depth of the controversy was supported by the fact that while there were 3,500 horses available for battle, the army could muster no more than 450 tanks for participation in maneuvers.[30]

Secretary of Commerce Harry Hopkins once wrote that FDR "never moves in one direction" but relied on his "innate creativity and powers for innovation" to pursue multiple paths at the same time.[31] After the enormous British losses at the battle of Dunkirk, Roosevelt needed to call on all of these skills in order to accomplish rapid wartime mobilization on a variety fronts. During an emergency address to Congress, Roosevelt boldly challenged the nation to produce military hardware and supplies at levels most believed impossible, while also educating the general population about the new vulnerabilities America faced with the advent of modern air warfare.

In order to effectively mobilize industry, his first job was to engender a public understanding that a genuine threat *did* exist and that the United States had little time to react to it. "We will extend to the opponents of force the material resources of this nation," he pledged in a 1940 fireside chat. "We will harness and speed up those resources of this nation . . . in order that America may have the equipment and training equal to the task of any emergency and every defense . . . We will not slow down or detour. Signs and signals call for speed: full speed ahead."[32]

By the beginning of 1942, revised annual production goals stood at an incredible sixty thousand planes, forty-five thousand tanks, twenty thousand antiaircraft guns, and a million tons of merchant shipping. Convinced of the strategic necessity of supplying Britain with surplus war materials (achieved under the cleverly worded Lend-Lease program), FDR escaped congressional obstructionists but could not elude the practical necessity of granting tangible incentives to stimulate manufacturing productivity. To this end, he passed innovative tax legislation that waived antitrust laws; repealed the Vinson-Trammell Act, now allowing aircraft and shipbuilders uncapped profits; and offered corporations the ability to deduct 20 percent of their capital costs over five years or fewer before arriving at the net incomes on which taxes were paid. Deftly, FDR, the godfather of New Dealers, was also the consummate pragmatist, transforming taxation from a liability to an asset in order to catalyze massive industrial mobilization.

Even in the most fundamental of challenges—national security—a democracy differed drastically from the dictatorships that Hitler and Mussolini led, and organized public dissent from isolationists, communists, and German American Bundists was yet another obstacle that Roosevelt had to master. Chief among these was American aviation hero Charles Lindbergh, who, in a nationwide radio address, accused the president of creating a "defense hysteria." Lindbergh insisted that there existed no threat to America from abroad and that the true threat came from "powerful elements" in America who "seize every opportunity to push us closer to the edge."[33]

Lindbergh was not alone in his view, but history would prove him wrong. Even at that time (and since the mid-1930s), the Abwehr, the Nazi intelligence network, had been sending spies by the thousands into the United States, propagandizing the Nazi cause through the Bundist organization and plotting industrial sabotage on American soil. Thanks to a colossal series of miscalculations, the Nazi terrorist network in the United States failed to be a significant factor in the war's outcome, but after eight German American saboteurs were convicted in July 1942 of plotting domestic bombings, there could be little doubt that America was indeed a piece in Hitler's puzzle for world domination.[34]

Despite all that was going on abroad and on the home front, it was not until December 7, 1941, with the bombing of Pearl Harbor, that America's awesome manufacturing power was awakened and unleashed. "Silly people—and there are many—might discount the force of the United States," Britain's Prime Minister Winston Churchill predicted, "but the U.S. is like a gigantic boiler . . . once the fire is lighted under it, there is no limit to the power it can generate."[35] Churchill, a student of history who marveled at the resolve displayed by the North and South during the Civil War, was proved correct, for within weeks dramatic production improvements were underway. In line with a strategy earlier proposed by labor leader Walter Reuther for conversion of peacetime manufacturing and assembly plants to the production of weapons, a heretofore-unimaginable transformation of American industry was begun.

The automotive industry in Detroit, which once produced 4 million cars annually, would be building 75 percent of the country's aircraft engines, 50 percent of all tanks, and 30 percent of all machine guns eighteen months later. A manufacturer of stoves was making lifeboats. A corset factory was making grenade belts, and a pinball machine maker was producing armor-piercing bullets! In the ever-critical area of shipbuilding, industrialist Henry Kaiser, who had helped construct the Hoover Dam and the San Francisco–Oakland Bay Bridge, translated mass production techniques into the art of shipbuilding using prefabricated bulkheads, decks, and hulls. The resulting productivity gains cut ship delivery time from 355 days in 1940, to 194 days in 1941, to just 60 days in 1942. Crowned "liberty ships," each was capable of carrying 2,800 jeeps, 440 tanks, and 3 million C-rations to aid American, British, and eventually Soviet troops in their death struggle against the Nazis.[36]

If FDR's transformation of the nation was arduous, the personal and philosophical transition that he was forced to undergo must have been as difficult. The prewar America over which Roosevelt presided was one where one-half of the men and two-thirds of the women earned less than $1,000 a year and just 48,000 taxpayers in a population of 132 million earned more than $2,500 a year. In his second inaugural address, Roosevelt had proclaimed that he saw "one-third of a nation ill-housed, ill-clad, ill-nourished."[37] FDR and his New Deal Congress had enacted an unprecedented series of laws, many of which were pro-union, and all of which were populist in nature, beginning with minimum wage, social security, and labor's guaranteed right to collective bargaining. How, then, was this president to reconcile his own pro-labor policies with the need for massive productivity improvements in the face of the Axis threat? Already there were rumblings of a New Deal sellout to big business, and while 1940 was a peaceful year, 1941 saw one of every twelve workers on strike, the highest percentage since 1919.

Given the seriousness of the production gap between the opposing forces and the country's growing discontent with labor, it was a tough and seasoned FDR that rose to deal with a wildcat strike at North American Aviation led by a splinter group with ties to the Communist Party. Sensing that this particular strike had little true backing and seeking to make the point that he was willing to sacrifice ideals for pragmatism in times so desperate, Roosevelt signed an executive order directing the secretary of war to send 2,500 federal troops to take control of the plant. Only two hours after the troops arrived, workers were back to work and the strike was over, once again proving the wisdom of Harry Hopkins's observation concerning Roosevelt's ability to fuse two seemingly opposing viewpoints into a working solution: FDR had calculated the odds and with deft timing sent his first message.

The second came in the form of Executive Order 8802, signed on June 25, 1941, calling on both employers and labor leaders "to provide for the full and equitable participation of all workers in defense industries, without discrimination because of race, creed, color or national origin."[38] Almost simultaneously, the ever-creative Roosevelt had done what was needed in the practical sense while using the identical platform—defense manufacturing—as a mechanism to push forward American social reform.

Perhaps the most concrete example of Roosevelt's innovative leadership came in America's response to his plea for race and gender acceptance. "In some communities," he stated candidly, "employers dislike to hire women. In others, they are reluctant to have Negroes. We can no longer afford to indulge such prejudices."[39] Interestingly, FDR's call for tolerance didn't take on the air of moral superiority, but of pragmatism. He didn't judge, he simply assessed the best course of action to increase the workforce and win the war.

Still, it's not difficult to see hidden beneath the surface of these challenges the hand of Eleanor and the result of FDR's own Warm Springs metamorphosis in his commitment to social and economic mobility. The result of these internal forces was tumultuous. Between 1940 and 1944, more than six million additional women entered the payrolls as welders, blast furnace operators, and machinists. At Boeing, producer of America's most durable bomber, the B-17 "Flying Fortress," no less than 50 percent of the workers were women. As important, the seeds of Roosevelt's vision of an egalitarian nation where every American had an opportunity for education, a good job, and financial security were being sown not by an executive order or congressional act, but by individuals themselves, who sensed their individual strength and understood their personal potential. Such was the case with Inez Sauer, a female aircraft industry worker:

> I started at forty-six cents an hour . . . After I had worked there a few months, Boeing themselves upped my salary to sixty-two and a half cents . . . which was really thrilling . . . I learned that just because you're a woman and have never worked is no reason you can't learn. I had had no contact with Negroes . . . I found that some of the black people I got to know there were superior, and certainly equal to me . . . I learned that color has nothing at all to do with ability.[40]

Roosevelt didn't live to see the consequence of what was the single best example of his own creative genius, and which was America's "manufacturing miracle": the Manhattan Project. Fittingly, it started with an Italian refugee, Enrico Fermi, who first alerted the United States to the potential threat of nuclear weapons. Armed with letters of reference from Columbia University, Fermi, and later physicists Leó Szilárd, E. P. Wigner, and Edward Teller, all found their way to the Naval Research Laboratory to discuss the possibility of turning the atom into a revolutionary explosive device.

They were met with skepticism at first, until Vannevar Bush, director of the Office of Scientific Research and Development, was called in and believed the theory enough to alert Roosevelt in mid-1941. According to these and other sources, nuclear weapons development had commenced in Britain in the summer of 1940, Japan in April 1941, and the Soviet Union one year later. The Germans, it was agreed, had begun serious efforts in April 1939—a daunting prospect when one considered the potential that these physicists had been discussing. With equal weight Bush also opined that development of such a bomb would require "a vast industrial plant costing many times as much as a major oil refinery" in order to separate the U-232. It was an estimate that proved orders of magnitude too modest. On January 19, 1942, Roosevelt wrote a terse reply to Bush's formal request: "O.K.—I think you had best keep this in your safe." And before it was over, what came to be called the Manhattan Project consumed more than two billion dollars, employed 150,000 people, and required equipment, plant space, natural resources, and technical expertise available nowhere but in the United States.

By the middle of 1943 there were multiple factors that contributed to the creation of a U.S. manufacturing transformation of monumental consequence. Munitions production was up 83 percent, aircraft tonnage 140 percent, merchant ships 100 percent, and naval ships 75 percent. The result could be felt by the enemy in far-off corners of the world—including the Soviet Union, where the United States sent to Stalin's war-torn troops 60,000 trucks, 11,000 jeeps, 2 million pairs of boots, 50,000 tons of explosives, and 250,000 tons of aviation gas. In northern Africa Field Marshal Rommel lamented, "The bravest men can do nothing without guns, the guns nothing without ammunition . . . The true battle is fought and decided by the quartermaster before the shooting begins."[41]

There was no question that the tide of the war was turning against the Axis forces. As Hitler's chief architect, Albert Speer, had correctly predicted, the outcome of the war was indeed determined by "a contest between two systems of organization." What Speer failed to recognize, however, was the possibility that the leadership of a president capable of fusing idealism with effective action, and a political system that offered its least-utilized populations opportunity in the face of disaster, could create an American "manufacturing miracle" that would change the course of history.

Beginning on February 4, 1945, Churchill, Stalin, and Roosevelt met in Yalta, Ukraine, for their historic Crimean Conference. With Hitler's dream of building a German Reich that—as he said—would last one thousand years crushed, FDR saw himself as mediator between British colonialism and Soviet communism. There the United Nations was created, a modernized version of Roosevelt's friend and rival Woodrow Wilson's League of Nations, and with it the beginnings of a permanent structure for world peace.

Two months later, on April 12, 1945, Franklin Delano Roosevelt died of a cerebral brain hemorrhage while vacationing at his beloved summer house in Warm Springs, Georgia. The collapse of Germany came less than one month later, with FDR's thoughts on the conclusion of the greatest war in world history preserved in an unfinished speech that he did not live to deliver:

> The issue of this war is the basic issue between those who believe in mankind and those who do not: The ancient issues between those who put their faith in the people and those who put their faith in dictators and tyrants. There have always been those who do not believe in the people, who attempted to block their forward movement across history, to turn them back to servility and suffering in silence. The people have now gathered their strength, they are moving forward in their might and power, and no force, no culmination of forces, no trickery, deceit or violence can stop them now. They see before them the hope of the world: A decent, secure, peaceful life for men everywhere.[42]

Aristotle defined great leadership as "wisdom translated into action for the public good." To be able to do this, he asserted, requires a combination of "moral virtue, practical wisdom, and pubic spiritedness." FDR was a "great" leader because he led with equanimity, a characteristic that answers the question beyond "what are you doing?" which is, "why are you doing it?" Just as Lincoln argued against slavery on economic grounds and moral ones, Roosevelt ushered social justice into the fabric of the United States with New Deal reforms based on World War II's industrial demands. Good managers act pragmatically to solve problems while great leaders, like FDR who are idealists, act pragmatically to solve problems and to help create a more perfect world.

Perhaps more than any other president, Franklin Delano Roosevelt serves to teach us that great leaders are not necessarily born, but are as often self-developed. The great leader he became wasn't the man he started out being. While Washington evolved, Lincoln matured, and Theodore Roosevelt regained his health to channel his energies, F.D.R. truly changed. He transformed himself from what today might be called a "preppy" or a "yuppie"—someone a tad prissy, overly concerned with status, but also someone who was clever to the point of being disingenuous—into the kind of solid and sturdy man that individuals and Americans collectively could count on to "do the right thing." Roosevelt surrounded himself with constructive men and women who had the public's welfare in mind; he used his unique set of talents, creativity, and innovation not to aggrandize his coterie of advisers and himself, but to truly, and sincerely, attempt to move the country and Western civilization forward.

In the case of Hitler, any man's nightmare of an opponent, Roosevelt—who, unlike Washington or Teddy, was not particularly physical or war minded—rose to the occasion. Galvanizing the people of the United States, understanding the consequences of defeat and a strategy for victory, he stood tall, never blinked in the face of monstrous opposition, and did the job. Certainly no longer a country-club, upper-crust, Hyde Parker at the point of his evolution to leadership, Roosevelt became more than a great president. He became a symbol for the possibility of greatness in each of us, at any time, and at any stage of life, proving that we can change to become better—and perhaps even great—simply because we have the desire and determination to do so.

FRANKLIN D. ROOSEVELT'S LEADERSHIP LESSONS

The life of Franklin Roosevelt itself may be the most important leadership lesson that anyone can learn from. The lesson is simple, but profound: Roosevelt became a character-driven leader only after he learned to care about the lives of others. To me, that's the greatest leadership lesson we can draw from his life and presidency, and one that lies at the heart of each of his presidential lessons.

Lesson #1
People "See Through" Situational Leaders

Of the six presidents the most thrilling for me is FDR because it is also the most hopeful. We've all met people like FDR prior to becoming a character-driven leader when his "devious tendencies" were never more evident, his own achievements "exaggerated," his shortcomings "never his fault," and reflections on rival "acidulous."

These are the ones who never stop talking about themselves, their country club, their promotions, the new car they are getting ready to buy. Usually, if that ever ends, they move on to their children—one by painful one—their straight A report cards, their assumed scholarship to an Ivy League university etc., etc., etc.

The above describes what a conversation might be like socially but in a corporate or organizational environment—it's even worse! Could anyone ever trust a fellow employee like this? Would they come to the aid of a subordinate or peer in trouble? Would anyone ever imagine that they were capable of being a character-driven leader? NO WAY!

The fact of the matter is that people "see through" situational people and situational leaders even faster than that. Not only is being a self-absorbed "user" of others a poor moral choice, it is—as Roosevelt and spin doctor Louis Howe discovered during his disastrous run for the U.S. Senate—anathema to upward mobility and an enduring career.

What's so amazing, and heartening, about the life of FDR is that not only does it prove that who you are is a choice, it proves that *it's never too late to make that choice* and become the man or woman you want to be! This is an exhilarating proposition and one that makes the lives we live so enthralling.

Who you are is a choice. Don't let anybody lead you to believe otherwise and character-driven leadership of FDR as president is proof of it.

Lesson #2
Sometimes You Need to See the Floor before You Can See the Sky

One of the most poignant images I have come across is of FDR, paralyzed from polio, driving himself to a shack in a custom-made car, getting out of the car and falling to the ground, then crawling through the dust and up a set of wooden stairs on his belly to play poker with a group of dirt-poor black men living outside of Warm Springs, Ga.

FDR, prior to his polio, was flippant and dismissive, shrewd but not real, calculated but never genuine, a man with "no center." How sad to consider that unlike JFK or TR he never bothered to leave his comfort zone. Or that like Washington, Lincoln, and Reagan—whose backgrounds were not so privileged—he never lived among every day Americans in real life situations.

The image is disturbing, even pathetic, but it is also a leadership lesson and a metaphor. It took the ravages of polio to bring FDR down to a level where he could "see" reality and the people, the suffering, the joys, the sorrows, and the majesty of the human spirit. To him, polio, was a kind of blessing that opened his eyes to a world that may have remained invisible to him.

Don't hide from reality. Don't pay others to keep real people and real experiences away from you because what you are really paying for is not the luxury of a club house but the limitations of a self-imposed exile from learning.

Sometimes you need to see the floor before you can see the sky.

Lesson #3
Develop Your Communication Skills

The best ideas don't necessarily prevail. When communicated poorly, Lincoln's Gettysburg Address can sound like somebody's shopping list! If you're proud of your ideas, why risk failing because your audience didn't understand them or lost interest along the way?

The American people formed a unique bond with Roosevelt through his "fireside chats." During the Hoover administration, the number of letters received by the White House averaged fewer than fifty per week. By the midpoint of FDR's first term the number had risen to four thousand!

As much as his creative ways of delivering his message, it was the concrete nature of the message itself, delivered step-by-step, that inspired the confidence of his listeners. "My friends, it's high time we made a clear cut effort to bring about united action, action of labor and management which is one of the high purposes of the Recovery Act," he declared in a "chat" while promoting the NIRA. "I want to tell you what has been done in the last few days, why it was done, and what the next steps are going to be."

Contrary to popular belief, great speakers like FDR, John Kennedy, and Ronald Reagan were not natural orators. Biographies of each carry the observations of sons, daughters, and spouses who watched each re-writing or practicing before full-length mirrors for hours a day in an effort to get the cadence, verbiage, and intonations of a speech right before delivering it.

Written skills are as important. Capturing the essence of an idea, situation, or plan in as few words as possible is a sign, not only of excellent communication, but also of intelligence. Anyone can make simple things complicated. It takes a discerning individual to condense the essentials of a complex situation into a simple written or verbal communication.

Develop strong communication skills and, like FDR, you'll have an open channel into the minds and hearts of others. Respect your ideas enough to communicate them in the most effective way possible.

Lesson #4
Savvy Leaders Know How to Innovate

After Pearl Harbor, FDR put forward approaches that re-tooled auto plants to manufacture tanks, stove manufacturers to build life boats, and pinball machine companies to make armor-piercing bullets. All of these were game-changing innovations, but they came from labor leader Walter Reuther and industrialist Henry Kaiser, not Roosevelt.

FDR's unique ability to innovate derived in part from his own creative genius, but also from his:

- open-mindedness
- broad circle of creative people with whom he surrounded himself
- eagerness to entertain new ideas
- willingness to change
- unparalleled talent for execution

FDR described himself as "a juggle . . . disappointed by people who could think only in traditional terms" while his closest adviser, Harry Hopkins, marveled at his talent for "fusing two seemingly opposing views into a working solution."

The obstruction most of us face in our attempts to become great innovators is our entrenchment in the reality of "what is" versus what "can be." Roosevelt, as president, had a natural curiosity for the views of others and a genuine desire to overcome America's challenges with effective solutions regardless of who brought them or from where they derived. It was this flexibility, combined with his own resourcefulness that allowed him to couple non-traditional ideas in unconventional ways to see the possibility of a concept as fantastic as the atom bomb and take it from the abstract to the practical with his launching of the Manhattan Project.

If you want to innovate, you must first learn to give up your own paradigms, listen deeply to the ideas of others, *and be willing to change.*

Lesson #5
Lead with Equanimity

Character-driven leaders do what they do for a "larger" purpose.

FDR was originally a smart-alecky rich kid concerned more about social standing than the people who put him in office. It was only after he contracted polio that the plight of indigent whites and blacks, immigrants, and the infirmed became visible to him.

Not coincidentally, it was then, after he surrendered his ego and penchant for self-interest, that he became capable of greatness, and attained the "no fear" attitude necessary to boldly act on plans to make the nation and its citizens more secure, regardless of personal consequences.

Perhaps the most important example of FDR's equanimity came with his signing of Executive Order 8802, banning discrimination in the work place. "In some communities," he stated candidly, "employers dislike to hire women. In others, they are reluctant to hire Negroes. We can no longer afford to indulge such prejudices." Just as Lincoln argued against slavery on economic grounds as well as moral ones, FDR ushered social justice into the fabric of the United States with New Deal reforms based on the industrial demands the war created.

Good managers act pragmatically to solve problems. Great leaders are idealists who act pragmatically to solve problems and help create a more perfect world.

Lead, of course, but lead with Equanimity if you aspire to be "great."

Chapter VI

Theodore Roosevelt
U.S. President, 1901–1909

The leadership exercised by Theodore Roosevelt both in his life and his presidency was perhaps the most unique of any of the six great presidents. To call him a man of action would be an understatement. To say that he exercised a magnetic influence through his own passion, deep-seated beliefs, and superlative communication skills would also seem to miss the more subtle lessons that his leadership teaches us. TR's leadership instructs that total involvement, not detachment; ego bent on moving the lot of others ahead, and not oneself; and purity of motive, not manipulation, are the keys to successful and enduring leadership.

Winston Churchill, a man whose leadership bears some similarities to Roosevelt's, once said, "The man who attracts luck, carries with him the magnet of preparedness."[1] Certainly this is true of Roosevelt. This was a man whose life as a leader proved that an individual is in charge of who he is and what he chooses to make out of himself. His education, his hunger for true life experience, and his natural curiosity in the way people and cultures act and think served him well throughout his later life. He was both a student and a professor. His unbridled passion for life and for the everyday citizens of the United States was a strength tempered by knowledge. He used his penchant for action as a weapon when necessary. He used his deep understanding of human nature to influence all around him, wherever he was, serving in whatever capacity he found himself.

Moreover, if any president's leadership flies in the face of Jim Collins's "managing from forty-thousand feet" executive, it's that of TR. This was an individual of immense energy and vision who, like Washington, was a quintessential "man of action," always in the thick of his own forward-charging history, never detached, and consummately engaged. Also, like John Kennedy and Ronald Reagan, he understood the power of the media—newspapers, and radio at the time—and the influence that the president's bully pulpit could exert on the American public and the world.

Teddy Roosevelt's unique brand of leadership appeared, at times, as eccentric as it was effective. Yet he was a man of his times with a backward and forward reach into world history and American culture that spanned generations and endures to this day.

As with our other great presidents, a panoply of books have been written about TR, but none captures his philosophy of life and penchant for action better than his own words, spoken soon after taking office at the age of forty-two: "Only those are fit to live who do not fear to die. And none are fit to die who have shrunk from the joy of life and the duty of life. Both life and death are part of the same great adventure."[2] Roosevelt would maintain this perspective until the end of his days, but not before making an indelible mark on a palette of disciplines ranging from art to science, from combat heroics to peace promotion, for which he would win the Nobel Peace Prize.

During his eight years in office, Roosevelt transformed the United States from a fledgling nation into a world power, pushing to the forefront of the American conscious an agenda that was, to him, a collection of personal obsessions: the "Square Deal," which promised a government that bettered the living and working conditions of its citizens; the National Parks Program, a forerunner of today's ecological movement; the Panama Canal, which changed the world's trade patterns forever; "The Great White Fleet," whose around-the-world cruise became a showcase for the United States as a global power; and "trust-busting," which expanded executive powers to encompass being steward of the public good and marked the beginning of the "rising tide" of his colossal impact on the people, culture, and government of the United States.

His fifth cousin, Franklin D. Roosevelt, must have had TR in mind when he presented his "New Deal," along with many of the social security, welfare, and public works programs that his uncle touted during his progressive Bull Moose campaign for president three decades earlier. And if author Ernest Hemmingway's "masculine mystique"—African safaris, big-game hunting, and boxing—was borrowed from anyone, surely it was Roosevelt. Into the 1960s, the influence of Roosevelt's family life was emulated, and perhaps even exploited, by the Kennedys of Hyannis Port, where touch football and flinty-eyed competition were not only encouraged, but also widely reported.

If Hemmingway's persona, the Kennedy family culture, and many of the programs put forward by FDR were, in fact, the spidery filament of ideas and ideals spun decades before by Roosevelt, what were the experiences that drove and shaped this remarkable individual?

Theodore Roosevelt was born into wealth along with a prominent position in New York's high society. His grandfather was a multimillionaire. His family name was revered nationally. Yet TR's childhood was anything but easy, and the influences on him were deeply felt. As a six-year-old, TR grimly watched Lincoln's funeral procession from the window of his grandfather's Union Square, Manhattan, apartment. So affected was he by that experience, and his father's personal relationship with Lincoln, that for most of his life he would wear a ring on his finger bearing a lock of the assassinated president's hair.[3]

TR's childhood was stunted by chronic illness, which left him gasping for air and a desperate longing to gain the approval of the father whom he idolized. The battles he waged with his own body were, in effect, a struggle for both survival and personal identity. His bedridden youth made him susceptible to adventure novels filled with tales of romance and heroics. TR was a "natural hero worshipper." Confined to bed , he devoured books about the exploits of others, such as *Ivanhoe, Robin Hood*, and David Livingston's *Missionary Travels and Researches in South Africa.* These books seemed to permeate every pore of his being, and as a result of this reading, he became, by the age of eight, a prodigy in world geography, ornithology, taxidermy, and Charles Darwin's evolutionary theory.

In fact, if there is an observation to be made without stretching one's hand too deeply into the black waters of Freudian psychology, it would be that in their own way each of the great presidents saw their lives as somehow starting from a deficit that each was passionate, beyond words, to overcome: in Washington's case, it was "social status"; in Lincoln's, it was "lack of education"; and in the case of Theodore Roosevelt, it was his abhorrence (and that of his father) for "physical weakness," something that became to him a metaphor for personal failure.

So abiding was TR's obsession with the romantic ideals instilled by his father and the books that he'd devoured as an anemic, oxygen-starved child that even at the age of fifty-five, retired from public life and weighing 230 pounds, he would embark on a dangerous, physically draining Brazilian expedition to chart a body of water known as the River of Doubt. Perhaps an insight into Roosevelt, and his childhood influences, is given to us in Kathleen Dalton's *Theodore Roosevelt: A Strenuous Life*: "He carried with him two classic texts of chivalric romance, 'The Chanson de Roland' and Sir Walter Scott's 'Quentin Durward.' TR's hero Roland chose heroic death over asking for help, and Quentin, an emissary for a foreign king, saved the monarch's life by killing a wild boar with a spear . . . When the Roosevelt-Rondon expedition stopped at Sao Paulo, TR saw his chance to duplicate Quentin's feat . . . and so he borrowed a spear from Dom Joao and used it to kill a 'valiant and truculent' boar."[4]

If we continue to look at abiding influences on the young TR, we must look more closely at his father. Called Thee, Theodore Roosevelt Sr. was tough-minded progressive in many of his ideas and was molded by strict Victorian principles. He represented a lineage that had "provided New York with leadership for generations." Since the Revolutionary War, the Roosevelt family had held large landholdings—property that Thee's father had parlayed to become founder of Chemical National Bank in New York. His father's brother, Judge James I. Roosevelt, had been a prominent Democratic congressman before he was appointed to New York's highest court, and Thee himself founded a manufacturing enterprise that supplied plate glass for much of the world.

Despite, and perhaps owing to, the onus of that family status, Thee spent the better part of his life wrapped in mano a mano contests against ineffective government and corrupt politicians while his wife (who suffered from neurasthenia); his daughter Anna (who suffered from a spinal injury); and his son Teddy (who was plagued by asthma) drifted deeper each day into the confines of invalidism. Thee believed, as a matter of religious faith, that it was the Roosevelt family's noblesse oblige to move civilization forward in something akin to social Darwinism. In New York, a city plagued by wholesale murder, prostitution, and gang rapes, men like Thee felt compelled to take on Tammany Hall bosses who used the Democratic patronage system as a catchall for block votes within the city's immigrant neighborhoods. When Democratic politician Boss Tweed populated New York's fire department with unqualified firefighters, Thee publicly demanded that professionals take their place, eventually forcing reform. Not long after, it was the anti-Tweed Citizens Association—funded by Thee—that modernized Manhattan's government by creating a Metropolitan Board of Health that enforced new sanitary codes and street-cleaning regulations.

The social construction to which the morally rigid Thee adhered was uniquely American, encouraging economic opportunity and social mobility to those smart and hardworking enough to climb their way to the top. To help the poor man in his climb, Thee lent financial support to the Young Men's Christian Association and the Children's Aid Society. As a world traveler, he wanted to share the wonders that he'd seen in the great European cities with New Yorkers, so he founded the American Museum of Natural History and helped plan fledgling collections at the Metropolitan Museum of Art. Philosophically, he supported Charles Kingley's "muscular Christianity," a movement that saw Jesus not as a weak victim, but as a spiritual warrior literally battling Satan in the same way that earthbound Christians needed to battle the evils of society in a moment-to-moment struggle for the souls of men.

So it was that TR, crippled by life-threatening asthma, bore witness to his father's labor, in which he selflessly performed household chores at the behest of his neurasthenic wife; tended to the needs of his crippled daughter; walked the floor with his son, who struggled to breathe; and upheld the Roosevelt name with public service and the running of an international business enterprise.

On the surface, Thee's son "Teedie" was bright-eyed and funny, a natural entertainer who mimicked his aunts' and uncles' idiosyncrasies at the dinner table. Yet his letters, diaries, and recorded conversations are rife with references to the withering feelings of "shame" and "inadequacy" he endured, for he desired desperately to be like his robust and selfless father. The anguish TR suffered, however, was not just psychological. Because no cures for asthma existed, young Theodore was subjected to torturous regimens by those who would surely today be categorized as "quack" physicians.

At first when he suffered from respiratory ailments that caused swollen lymph glands on his neck, they were massaged, but when that proved ineffective they were lanced—without anesthesia. Leeches were used on him for "bloodletting" during severe attacks, along with "medicines" that included ipecac, quinine, magnesia, strong coffee, and cigar smoke. In 1868 Dr. Alphonso D. Rockwell began administering electrical charges to his ten-year-old patient's temples, abdomen, and feet in an urgent move to thwart the progress of what was diagnosed a constitutional weakness caused by "over-civilization." All the pain and humiliation young Teddy suffered as a result of these "treatments" was, of course, to no avail. The "treatments" from the "trained" physicians proved hopeless, and instead it was his father's take-the-bull-by-the-horns approach that ultimately saved him.

The depth of TR's dread at the prospect of disappointing Thee by becoming a "permanent invalid" is perhaps best summed up when he wrote as an adult, "The only man whom I told everything . . . the only man to whom I believe I was inferior . . . and the only man of whom I was truly afraid . . . was my father . . . The thought of him now and always has been a sense of comfort. I could breathe. I could sleep, when he held me in his arms. My father, he got me air, he got me lungs, strength—life."[5]

There are, of course, multiple ways to interpret the awe that TR felt toward his father, but one that I favor has to do with the inspiration Thee offered young Theodore by insisting that he stand up to his affliction. Thee had a propensity for translating spiritual disease—that couldn't be warred against—into physical opponents that could be taken on and defeated; he encouraged his son to see his asthma as an enemy whose defeat could only be achieved by the strengthening of his own physical self. Simple as it may seem, the metamorphosis that transformed the invisible and untouchable into something physical and within his grasp must have been a revelation to the young Teddy. If he could strengthen himself physically, that strength would, in direct proportion, weaken his disease.

From the moment that equation registered, a new child was born—as well as a new identity and path for the young Roosevelt. In the logic of the muscular Christian and Thee, he accepted that if Satan could be crushed by religious individuals performing good deeds as they marched to the hymn "Onward, Christian Soldiers," he too could be a soldier and "kill the invalid within him." Once Thee reframed his son's illness from curse to challenge, a huge weight was lifted, miraculously transforming young Teddy from a victim to a hero engaged in his own epic battle to become, in reality, the man he'd always envisioned.

With the personal control Thee began to exert over Teddy's physical health, TR practiced rigorous physical regimens, including running, boxing, weightlifting, and hunting. To each, this was tantamount to undertaking the Reverend Charles Kingsley's soul-strengthening program of muscular Christianity, saving one soul at a time through evangelical work, chopping away at the Devil's spiritual stamina while Christian soldiers enhanced their own.

Later, when TR's asthma flared up, Thee had him shipped by stagecoach to Moosehead Lake, a boys' camp, to recover alongside healthy young boys instead of invalids and "delicate" women at the posh health resort that his mother wanted to bring him to. To young Teddy this must have been a dangerous undertaking because he had never before gone anywhere unescorted by a bevy of protectors. Indeed, while there, he was verbally tormented, abused, and humiliated by the others. When he tried to fight back, he discovered that his gymnasium boxing lessons had less to do with real brawling than therapeutic exercise. Roosevelt's autobiography alludes to his disillusionment when he writes, "I was ashamed . . . and hated myself for being a sissy."[6]

Possibly more than any other, it was this Moosehead Lake experience that galvanized Theodore's iron will around the need to physically confront and defeat his enemies, both within and without. Later in life he would claim that he "remade his body" and "defeated asthma"; however, others, like his wife Edith, knew that he suffered until his last days with the disease, though he was careful to conceal future flare-ups from friends and the media. Still, if TR's asthma wasn't totally eradicated, it is a fact that by the time he entered Harvard as an undergraduate he was an inordinately strong, athletic, and focused in the way he approached competition.

If the Moosehead Lake experience registered in TR's mind as just one more debt he owed to Thee's head-on approach to progress, two painful incidents that he watched his father endure also duly registered in the scorecard of his psyche. The first was Thee's defeat at the hands of corrupt Tammany Hall officials who rigged vote counts against him when he ran for public office in New York. The second was that, as a young man, Thee had capitulated to the wishes of his wife, Mittie, and paid two proxies to serve in his place when he was drafted to fight in the Civil War. The first of these "failures" was blamed on the institutionalized corruption that Thee, and later Teddy, spent much of his career uprooting. The second was blamed on himself, an error in judgment of operatic proportions that he regretted for his entire life.

No wonder TR would burst from the gates onto the political scene. Can anyone imagine the psychological Vesuvius that must have been building beneath the surface of Roosevelt as an adolescent? Each of us who has ever suffered from flu, fever, or an illness that keeps one in bed for even a week understands the physical exhilaration experienced when the flu symptoms pass, the fever breaks, or the suddenly healthy body emerges from the shackles of illness and repair. If not objectively stronger, one still imagines the ability to lift mountains. If not physically more fit, one experiences a psychological surge that sets the pulse pounding. Imagine, then, the emotional forces at work here as day after day, week after week, this young man, surrounded by family invalidism and inspired by his father and the epic heroes he idolized, not only discovers a perceived road to health and athleticism, but actually "cures himself."

The Teddy Roosevelt that enters Harvard is captured, in both physicality and spirit, in an early photograph of him: barefoot and sitting with his arms crossed over a substantial bare chest, the bearded freshman with the glowering eyes and bandana tied over his scalp is suggestive more of a pirate than a future president. This was a young man who had a score to settle with life, a fire in his belly, and a political and wartime record he wanted to set straight on behalf of the Roosevelt family.

With regard to the penchant for action and influence that burgeoned in Roosevelt during those years, there is no better example than his courtship of the fetching, and well-appointed, Alice Hathaway Lee. Simply put, she wanted nothing to do with him. Her social standing presented obstacles to TR's marital plans, owing to the fact that the Lee family was "exceedingly English" and Boston Brahmin to the bone. Additionally, a more incalculable challenge were the problems presented by TR's own bumptious inelegance. Like a lovesick pit bull he proceeded, visiting her home continuously, professing his love at the drop of a hat, and pressing his suit in a vein more akin to Mike Tyson at Madison Square Garden than Romeo at the foot of a balcony.

When his action in courtship proved to be less than effective, Teddy did not stop his pursuit but opened a new front in his battle for Alice Lee's hand by using a second weapon—influence. His understanding of its importance, and his ability to wield it, perhaps developed while wheedling favors from caring women while he lay in his childhood sickbed:

He brought more originality to his fight to win Alice than her other beaux. He campaigned by encirclement, winning his way into her family's heart by being

himself. He made himself a boon companion to her uncle Leverett Saltonstall
. . . When Theodore played lawn tennis with Alice . . . he made a point of including her plain-looking cousin Rose Saltonstall . . . He also roughhoused with
Alice's nine-year-old brother, Georgie, and told the boy and his sister Bella tales
of bears and wolves, and brought them into a dark room to scare them with ghost
stories, which they adored.[7]

As demonstrated in TR's methodology for gaining Alice's hand, pairings
of temperament that appear contradictory today—action and influence,
soldier-warrior and gentle father, hunter and conservationist, realist and
idealist—seem to have sprung from the same reservoir of boyhood influences: first, the idealistic fantasy world he lived in as the funny, brainy,
invalid child depending on the kindness and aid of others; and second, the
hard-hitting, super-real world of his father, where cause and effect reigned
supreme. While it was the individual residing in the second of these two
worlds that made headlines for Roosevelt as president, the first's charming and vulnerable "Teedie" never died. He simply showed himself less
frequently—usually during intimate moments, or at times when his father's
straightforward methods proved ineffective.

For every story about Colonel Theodore Roosevelt charging up San Juan
Hill, there's a more frivolous anecdote about "Teddy," as president, assailing
his Secret Service men with a surprise jiujutsu attack from behind. For every
tale concerning President Theodore Roosevelt facing down financial mogul
J. P. Morgan, there's a more convivial report of him running on the White
House lawn—his children in hot pursuit—during a game of touch football.
For those who hold he was a gunboat imperialist subjugating natives of the
Philippines and Cuba to expand America's empire, others contemplate the
fact that he was a man of peace, having helped negotiate an end to the Russo-
Japanese War.

By the time he took office after the assassination of President William
McKinley on September 14, 1901, TR had evolved into a broad-thinking,
hands-on leader, but raw energy and vaulting ambition wouldn't be nearly
enough to prepare him for the new century ahead. And if great leadership is a
matter of *internal* rather than *external* development, this fledgling personality would need to pass through many a dizzying corridor of pain, failure, and
emotional challenge in order to attain the tempered strength and deep-seated
confidence that great leadership demands.

When Teddy was nineteen years old, Thee died of cancer. To TR it was
a blow felt more acutely than most children feel over the death of a parent
because he had idealized his father as more than a man. The effect disturbed
what must have been a delicate balance within him as he felt his way along

the path to becoming the adult he wanted to be. This devastation, however, was offset by his newfound love for Alice, who finally agreed to marry him after his graduation from Harvard. Soon they settled into married life while he attended Columbia Law School in New York, where in addition to studying law, he would kindle the fires of his new love for the American West.

The parallel lives Theodore Roosevelt was leading then were almost comic in their juxtaposition. As soon as he and Alice settled in New York, TR became active in the local Republican organization in their "silk-stocking" district. While hobnobbing there with the patriarchs of millionaire families who resided near their Fifth Avenue home, he was his father's son, bedecked in dark Brooks Brothers' three-piece suits. When living out west, life was nothing like that, and try as he might he couldn't shake either his upper-class Harvard affectations or his predilection for dressing up like the romanticized cowboys he'd encountered in novels. It's not difficult to imagine the behind-the-back grins that Teddy's outfit—complete with Stetson hat, fringed buck-skin shirt, holstered six-gun, and leather chaps—inspired among the weather-hardened men he rode alongside. One anecdote has him attempting to lead a gang of cowhands into the prairie at dawn with a high-pitched, taut-jawed cry of *"Hasten forward, there!"* only to find them locked in their place astride their horses, laughing too hard to follow.[8]

Yet, while one course at Columbia Law School broadened his understanding of America outside of New York and toughened him up for political battles that lay ahead, the second had him gaining enough support among his family's equals to run for the New York State Assembly. On November 8, 1881, he won the seat, 3,502 votes to 1,974, and it was in this role that the two parallel worlds began to coalesce.

Riding hard with the tough men of the Dakotas, TR conquered any remaining pangs of self-doubt and learned the importance of quick decisions and self-reliance. As important, his time there shattered many of his early precepts about the intrinsic goodness of the rich versus the presumed depravity of the masses who worked every day for a living. "Everybody worked and everybody was willing to help everybody else with no favors asked," he observed, taking that same iconoclastic notion along with him into politics.[9] He added to his list of family friends men like Jake Hess, a German Jew; and Joe Murray, an Irish Catholic immigrant who took him to working-class bars and even a cockfight on the Lower East Side.

More to the point, it was Roosevelt's craving for reality that compelled him to expand the breadth of his acquaintances. As a surge of European immigrants began to change the face of American life, he came to understand, as few men in his social circles could, that the country was evolving. Emblematic of this transformation, he took up union leader Samuel Gompers's challenge to accompany him on a tour of the "other" America. TR witnessed firsthand the squalor of homes where fathers, mothers, and children worked day and night in their tiny apartments, amid the taint and odor of curing tobacco, for wages from cigar manufacturers that entitled them to nothing more than starvation.

Appalled at the way these immigrants were forced to live, TR became the assembly's most vocal proponent of a "tenement house" bill that exposed this exploitation, arguing that regulating home cigar rolling was a public health measure. Later, he was elated when the bill passed, only to discover something Gompers had understood all along: big business was as ingrained in New York's corrupt political system as the Catholic Church was in immigrant neighborhoods. The bill was voted into law but ruled unconstitutional by the New York courts—longtime beneficiaries of the cigar industry.

At twenty-three years of age, Roosevelt had learned much about the difference between the way systems operated in theory versus the way they worked in the real world. Perhaps because he'd been helpless as a sick child himself, he took particular interest in causes that affected society's most vulnerable citizens: women and children. He railed against organized liquor interests, which he believed exploited immigrant families, and fought hard to restrict the growing clout of saloons by the implementation of licensing fees and regulation. After learning about the abuse many women faced at the hands of their husbands, he launched a campaign to pass a law punishing wife beaters by whipping them in public. When evidence surfaced that financier Jay Gould had bribed Judge T. R. Westbrook to rule against a public interest bill, TR demanded an investigation. When Westbrook's powerful friends in the assembly rose up to defend him, Roosevelt courageously stuck to his guns and moved for the judge's impeachment, only to become enraged later upon finding that all the charges had been dismissed out of hand.

During those early days, TR's fortitude was tested often as he brought to the assembly a new style of patrician reform: one shaped by true-life situations that he learned from, and made part of, the leadership he exerted. Still, no amount of experience could prepare him for what happened on February 14, 1884.

On February 13, while in Albany, New York, TR received an urgent telegram about his pregnant wife, who had suddenly been taken ill. The next morning, he was shocked to learn, from a second telegram, that doctors had diagnosed Alice with Bright's disease and that her condition was dire. Catching the first train back to the city, he rushed to his wife's bedside, where he found her insensible with fever and in labor. That same night, only hours after giving birth to a baby daughter, Alice died quietly, locked in her husband's arms. But Roosevelt's sorrows were not yet over. Soon after the clock chimed midnight on Valentine's Day 1884, his mother Mittie, who was recovering in the same house from what was thought to be a passing fever, also died unexpectedly. "As a young flower she grew, and as a young flower she died . . . A light went out of my life forever," a forlorn Roosevelt would later write about his wife.[10] Abandoning life in New York and his political career, TR left his newborn daughter in the care of his sister and retreated to his ranch in North Dakota.

If nearly every one of our six great presidents experienced a "wilderness" period where political defeat, illness, or personal failure caused them to flee the ebb and flow of everyday life and define who they truly were, this period was surely Theodore Roosevelt's time to reevaluate everything he'd done and all that he wanted to do. Once the wealth and family name was stripped away, as was the love he received from Alice and his mother, *who was he*? What did he stand for, now that his father, too, was no longer alive to give him counsel and help set the direction of his life?

These rueful questions must have swirled through his bloodstream like shards of broken glass. Yet he did have his family's history, his education, and a first-class mind cultivated by studies in a wide variety of disciplines. Beyond that, he possessed fortifying personal experiences derived from his forays into the West and the slums of New York City. Finally, he had his own approach to life, his own perspective, based on the principles he'd learned from Thee and the lives of the heroes he so admired, both real and fictional. From out of these not-insubstantial raw materials, Teddy Roosevelt knew he had to build a new man: the tough, self-confident visionary who would become one of America's most important presidents.

During the next two years, TR devoted the incredible energies that his depression had catalyzed to live the life of the pioneer West. He wrote incessantly about it for book publishers and magazines. In Western books like *Hunting Trips of a Ranchman* (1885), *The Wilderness Hunter* (1893), and the four-volume *The Winning of the West* (1889–96), he idealized the bold, action-oriented men he had come to know, using them as a blueprint for his own construction. He saw the desolation of the prairie as a stage on which brave men and women survived—like the heroes in his childhood books— through their basic values and ardent acts. These were American heroes who could be easily contrasted with the lawyers, financiers, and industrial moguls who had put a stranglehold on the East, virtually enslaving whole masses of individuals. "[Western life] is patriarchal in character," he wrote at around that time. "It is a life of men who live in the open, who tend their herds on horseback, who go armed and ready to guard their lives by their own prowess, whose wants are very simple and who call no man master."[11]

In 1896, two years after leaving New York, a transformed Roosevelt married long-time friend Edith Carow in London, returned to New York City and ran for mayor. The marriage, which came as no surprise to family members who had watched them grow up together, was a success. His run for mayor was not, although the defeat stirred something deep within him that altered the way he viewed the nature of politics forever.

Much as his father had reframed his childhood illness from curse to challenge, TR came to see a political career not as a job, but as an opportunity. To him, politics became not an activity, but an arena where, like knights of old, men—both good and evil—battled for the right to lead others and shape the world around them. As with Thee's revelation about his asthma, this simple switch in perspective was rich in reward. In politics he could test himself and his ideas, avenging his father's political loss at the hands of corrupt Tammany officials while putting forward the social reforms that his father had come to personify. Like the stolid cowboys he'd known, he could stand up like a man, taking on the criminals, corrupt politicians, and corporate bullies who exploited the weak and vulnerable. Moreover, he might someday embark on the much larger task of recreating America, from the urbanized, have-and-have-not industrialized society it was to the idealized world power and beacon of individual liberty that he knew it could become.

One question about leadership concerns whether there exists, in fact, the possibility to lead from a middle-of-the-pack position: "How can I lead if I am not the president, or the CEO, or boss in any positional sense within my organization?" A phrase used to capture this ability is "360-degree leadership," meaning that the person in the middle (middle manager) or in the field (sales rep), or individuals performing a function that may seem devoid of the possibility of leading (administrators), can in fact lead without possessing the positional authority that traditional leaders might enjoy. I heartily endorse the 360-degree concept, and Theodore Roosevelt would too. In fact, that is exactly what he illustrated while working his way up the political ladder to become president of the United States. From the time he took his first position in the New York State Assembly, making a name for himself as the hands-on reformer who raided the Lower East Side tenements where children labored in the cigar industry, Roosevelt's leadership credo was unambiguous: "Do what you can with what you have, where you are."[12] His was a call to rally the internal nobility of each individual to push society forward and to make a difference.

On May 6, 1895, Republican Mayor William Strong appointed former state legislator Theodore Roosevelt president of the board of New York City Police Commissioners. At first, like a daunted middle manager, he wondered whether it was a dead-end job. Devoid of any historical authority and smothered by a pervasive corruption, TR nonetheless eagerly embraced the mayor's mandate for reform, calling it "a man's work." With visions no doubt of a noble, steely-eyed sheriff cleaning up a small Western town—despite the fact that New York had two million inhabitants—Roosevelt set out to make merit replace bribery in the system of job assignments and to compel police officers to enforce the laws without regard to wealth, race, or social status. This he did, in his own inimitable style: "To see whether patrolmen were walking their beats, he began making the same rounds late at night and incognito—though at times in the company of a newspaper reporter. Once, Roosevelt, found three bluecoats loitering outside a saloon at 2:30 a.m. 'What are you men doing here?' he asked abruptly. 'What the %$@&# is that your business?' snapped one of them, in vintage New Yorkese. Roosevelt, spectacles glinting, then introduced himself and lectured them on performing their duty."[13]

While on these midnight rambles, TR frequently took with him newspaper man Jacob Riis, who'd written an influential book entitled *How the Other Half Lives.* Much like union leader Samuel Gompers, Riis, a Jew familiar with the ugly plight of immigrants, suggested that Roosevelt accompany him into the slums about which he'd written. Once there, TR was again shocked to see how laws concerning alcohol, opium, and prostitution were laxly enforced—or not enforced at all, if the practitioners had the money to bribe police. It was on one of those excursions that Roosevelt made one of the toughest decisions of his political career. Understanding that alcohol and drugs were the root cause of much of the suffering he had witnessed, particularly among women and children, he decided to enforce both the "Dry Sunday" law, which prohibited bars from opening on Sundays, and the Raines Law, which decreed that only hotels with ten or more rooms could serve alcohol with a meal on the Sabbath. Beyond that, utilizing contacts he'd cultivated within New York's Board of Health, he used his influence as police commissioner to tear down rat-infested slums where landlords made fortunes while their immigrant tenants sweltered in squalor in the summer and froze, sometime to death, in winter's cold.

This broadening of the traditional authority of his position made TR few friends and a plethora of enemies. Bad cops were now discharged from the force. Saloon keepers, hotel owners, and corrupt local politicians who'd made a second living "on the pad" by overlooking violations of the "Dry Sunday" and Raines laws were now deprived of that illicit income. New York City was indeed being cleaned up—but Roosevelt paid a huge price for his public righteousness, one reminiscent to him of the suffocation his father's own political career endured under corrupt Tammany Hall forces.

Two years after taking the position of police commissioner, Roosevelt had accomplished most of what he'd set out to do, introducing bicycle squads to police the city's worst areas, offering professional training for law enforcement officers, and creating an independent commission that monitored the behavior of its public servants. Rates of violent crime and police brutality against New York's poorest citizens dropped, along with incidents of wife and child abuse, but for Teddy it seemed to be the end of his chance to parlay local success into national prominence. "He is a fighter, a man of indomitable pluck and energy," wrote the *Washington Post*. "A field of immeasurable usefulness awaits him. Will he find it?"[14]

In 1897, based on Roosevelt's seminal 1883 book about naval warfare, *Naval History of the War of 1812, or the History of the United States Navy During the Last War with Great Britain*, and his success as president of the board of New York City Police Commissioners, President William McKinley appointed him to a national, though seemingly dead-end, position: assistant secretary of the navy. A die-hard navalist who found it "sickening" that Congress refused to authorize funds for the construction of a world-class fleet of warships, TR was anything but acquiescent in his new position. "We are actually at the mercy of a tenth-rate country like Chile!" he told the president, secretary of defense, and anyone else who would listen.

TR moved to Washington DC in early October, believing that even in a position subservient to Secretary John Long he could convince Congress to follow a "large policy" with regard to naval expansion in order to gain America influence over the shape of the twentieth century. Lobbying with Congress for more defense spending, he used the time when his boss was out of town to make and put forth his own decisions on naval technology and construction. TR was a fighter, and throughout the mid-1890s he wanted to fight, not only against the forces of corruption, but against the Spanish "bullies" whom the press reported had been committing atrocities against the Cubans in their struggle for independence. During the two months that his boss John Long vacationed, he promoted his views to President McKinley, dining and taking carriage rides with him whenever the opportunity presented itself. TR urged the president to make the U.S. Navy as strong as that of the Japanese, sharing with him his own strategic military plans for war with Spain. In order to extend America's reach into the Pacific, he encouraged the annexation of Hawaii not only as an economic frontier, but in order to "use empire and war to revive the nation's vigor and manhood."[15]

On February 15, 1898, after the U.S. battleship *Maine* exploded under mysterious circumstances in Havana Harbor killing 266 sailors, TR became convinced that hostilities with Spain could break out at any moment and therefore prepared for war. During that same month, as Long dragged his feet, he took advantage of yet another of his boss's absences to telegraph Commander George Dewey to coal up and be ready to take Manila if war came. Some historians have criticized Roosevelt's actions as "impetuous," but Long didn't countermand the order, and on April 11 the president sent a war message to Congress, giving Dewey the opportunity to defeat the Spanish Pacific fleet just three weeks later.

Within days, TR—who had been secretly gathering friends from Harvard, Princeton, Yale, and the Dakotas who possessed "the fighting edge" for recruitment into his Rough Riders—resigned his post at the Department of the Navy to enlist in the cavalry. When he was officially given the commission to lead his division into combat, he called it the "happiest day of my life," thinking no doubt about his father's "mistake" in avoiding combat in the Civil War thirty-five years earlier.[16]

Roosevelt didn't have to wait long to have his obsession about putting his "body on the line for his beliefs" gratified.[17] On June 24, 1898, Teddy and his Rough Riders—which comprised men like ex-sheriff Bucky O'Neil, Andover-Yale athlete John Greenay, and horseman Bob Ferguson—saw intense combat for the first time when Spanish troops fired at them in the jungles of Las Guasinas. It was hard to see the enemy, and two of his best soldiers, Hamilton Fish and Allyn Capron, were killed immediately. Still, TR and his men advanced steadily through the dense jungle terrain, finally forcing the Spanish fighters into retreat.

One week later, on July 1, he would make the newspaper headlines about Las Guasinas seem a distant memory with the exploits of the Rough Riders at the Battle of San Juan Hill. With indecisive commanders preventing them from attacking, TR and his Rough Riders were huddled at the foot of Kettle Hill, at the mercy of both Spanish artillerymen who lobbed shells and riflemen who picked off TR's personal friends, like Bucky O'Neil. When orders for a cautious advance finally came, TR took matters into his own hands, mounting his horse and charging up the hill, his Rough Riders following behind. When he saw soldiers from the Tenth Division retreating, he scolded them, "Why will you refuse to stand your ground when I am on horseback charging alone?"[18] As he rushed toward the hill's crest, heavy rifle fire and artillery shells exploded around him and a piece of shrapnel wounded his wrist. The Spanish, stunned by the force of his unexpected assault, finally fled, surrendering the hill.

From there, Teddy and his Rough Riders moved on to support General Hamilton Hawkins at a second military target, San Juan Hill. Here again Roosevelt demonstrated his propensity for action, charging with his men through a withering barrage of fire to capture their objective. Casualties among the Rough Riders were the highest of any division engaged in the Spanish-American conflict, but soon it was realized that defeating Spanish defenses on the low hills was the key to controlling Santiago de Cuba. Once the Spanish lost the high ground they couldn't defend the city. They surrendered on July 17, 1898.

Proclaimed the hero of the war, Theodore Roosevelt ran a successful campaign for governor of New York four months later. For him, the state would become a microcosm of the policies and vision he had for America. Unlike his campaign for mayor, he used the experience to perfect his skills as a public speaker. As he told author Rudyard Kipling, he reached out to voters through an "appeal to their emotions."[19] The public's response was overwhelming. It was not unusual for twenty thousand people to come out to hear "Teddy" as he launched the ideas and ideals he'd learned from his father to enthusiastic crowds the likes of which even Thee could not have imagined:

> TR campaigned to enthusiastic throngs . . . He praised unions, state factory inspection laws, and the closing down of sweat shops; he pledged a strong commitment to reform. As his campaign train traveled all over New York, one Rough Rider blew his bugle from the back of the caboose, bands played "There'll Be a Hot Time in the Old Town Tonight," and fans climbed aboard . . . TR calmed down his raucous crowds by joking with them: "I want to ask you to let this be as much of a monologue as possible." They laughed and then they listened.[20]

During that period, haunted by the ghost of his father's humiliation and his own election defeat, TR campaigned like a man possessed, giving as many as forty speeches in two days. He won the election by just 17,794 votes. The first thing he did upon moving into the New York State Executive Mansion was remove the billiard tables and install mats on the floor for wresting and *jiu jitsu*, where he'd personally grapple with friends and foes alike. Called the "boy governor" by enemies like William Randolph Hearst, Roosevelt used his youthful exuberance to propel the progressive reforms both he and his father believed in. Soon labor leaders, women's rights advocates, and urban reformers realized that this was a politician unlike any other. In his first six months as governor he pushed through an eight-hour-workday law for all state employees and was a proponent of the Costello Anti-Sweatshop Act, which regulated home work conditions. Consumer protection was high on his agenda, so he signed pure food laws that required labeling and a health quality guarantee. Roosevelt's early childhood fascination with wildlife had taught him the importance of a clean environment, a predilection that led him to declare the Adirondacks and Catskills protected state parks. "When I hear of the destruction of a species, I feel just as if all the works of some great writer had perished; as if we had lost all instead of only part of Polybius or Livy," he wrote.[21]

Spurred by his own childhood experiences at Moosehead Lake, Roosevelt never liked "bullies." When he was asked to pardon murders, rapists, and child molesters, it offended his moral sensibilities to the point where he came to favor the death penalty. When asked to pardon a woman for throwing sulfuric acid in her stepdaughter's face and then smothering her to death, Roosevelt would not yield to the pressure of public sentiment against the execution. But it was the awesome financial and social power of politically connected monopolies, and not criminals, that created TR's knottiest conundrum regarding the balance between pragmatism and his own personal ideals.

In a time when less than 10 percent of the population controlled more than 70 percent of the country's wealth, it was difficult for Roosevelt, who considered himself a friend of honest business, to overlook the fact that U.S. Steel had within months swallowed up 138 competitors. Who was it that suffered? The "little man," whose job was lost and whose income, despite the vast wealth being accumulated by men like Andrew Carnegie, John D. Rockefeller, and J. P. Morgan, was shrinking to the point where by 1900 three-quarters of the American people qualified as poor.

In these business giants, however, TR wasn't fighting Spanish soldiers or Tammany Hall politicians, so when he sought advice on how to control the trusts, few were willing to help him. To control the working poor's spin into abject poverty, he offered New York City armories as shelters during the winters and worked hard to pass the Ford Franchise Tax Bill, only to have its legitimacy challenged in court by the trusts, thereby blocking its implementation. *"What to do with this madman?"* the moguls wondered aloud, until someone suggested that he be "kicked upstairs" as the vice presidential candidate on the McKinley ticket. The joke among them went something like this: "A woman has two sons—one goes to sea, the other becomes vice president—neither was ever heard from again."

And so it was done. In rousing stump speeches, imbued with "motion and action," Roosevelt slammed the opposing candidate, William Jennings Bryan, and exhorted supporters of the McKinley-Roosevelt ticket, "I would expect any one of you, Good Citizens, to act as in a football game: Don't flinch! Don't foul! Hit the line hard!"[22] A dominant theme in these speeches was TR's concern with opportunity for all citizens—a sentiment not all Republicans could embrace as willingly.

After the election though, Roosevelt greeted his new position with resignation, understanding its limitations and concluding that ice water rather than blood ran through the veins of the stodgy President McKinley. The lack of passion in the one man, and the surging emotions of the other, made for something less than total compatibility. But TR's worries about being cubbyholed came to a startling end on September 6, 1901. While the Roosevelts vacationed in the Adirondacks, President McKinley visited the Pan-American Exposition celebrating turn-of-the-century technological progress. While there shaking hands with the crowds—something he had been warned against—the president prepared to greet Leon Czolgosz, an anarchist whose hand was wrapped in a handkerchief. In the meteoric second before their hands touched, Czolgosz shot McKinley twice at point-blank range. McKinley would recover from the surgery that followed but ultimately die from his wounds on September 14.

When Roosevelt entered the White House in 1901, he took control of a federal government that had generally aligned itself with big business. More of a centrist than the iconoclast that men like Mark Hanna (influential Republican senator and party chair) took him for, TR restrained his progressive leanings and wisely avoided a shakeup on Wall Street, where jittery investors saw him as, at best, a wild card when it came to future domestic economic policies.

Anyone familiar with Roosevelt's background knew that whatever restraint he exercised was based on ascertaining the political landscape he'd inherited before moving on to the economic, social, and foreign policies he felt that he had been born to push forward. Consider the fact that in 1878, when Roosevelt was twenty years old, clerical workers constituted less than 1 percent of the workforce. By 1900 their ranks had swelled to 4 percent and would rise to more than 6 percent by 1910.[23] During that same period, titanic corporations arose with incredible swiftness: Standard Oil, U.S. Steel, American Telephone & Telegraph, and the Pennsylvania Railroad, to name a few. Through intense mechanization, division of labor, and "scientific management," industrialists endeavored to departmentalize all aspects of production to reduce workers' bodies to components of a great machine. Henry Ford, in articulating his vision of maximum industrial efficiency, declared, "In the past, the man has been first; in the future, the system must always be first."[24]

In his first annual message to Congress, TR made his first pointed remarks on the subject of trusts, saying that while he opposed banning monopolies, he preferred that the federal government "assume power of supervision and regulation over all corporations doing an interstate business."[25] Despite his generally pro-business outlook, TR despised the "bullying" ways of the new class of superrich over the working poor. If his carefully worded message to Congress didn't demonstrate the force of these emotions, his decisive action in the anthracite coal strike would certainly give America's moguls pause.

In May 1902 fifty thousand United Mine Workers (UMW) of northern Pennsylvania walked out in a strike, demanding a 10 to 20 percent raise, recognition of their union, an eight-hour workday, and fringe benefits. For six months, the union professed its willingness to negotiate, but the owners refused, attempting to starve the workers back into the mines. Finally, with the scarcity of coal threatening to close schools and hospitals in several cities, Roosevelt called the union and its owners to the White House for a meeting: "I wish to call your attention to the fact that there are three parties affected by the situation in the anthracite trade," he began the meeting, "the operators, the miners, and the general public. I speak for neither the operators nor the miners, but for the general public."[26]

Union leader John Mitchell offered to meet with the owners and accept binding arbitration by a commission that TR had appointed. The owners, in contrast, as represented by George F. Baer, were indignant at the president's involvement, railing that he was forcing them "to deal with outlaws" (they had accused the union of more than twenty murders). When Roosevelt looked to Mitchell for an explanation, he answered deferentially, "The truth of the matter is, as far as I know, there have been seven deaths . . . three of these were caused by management's private police, and no charges have been leveled in the other four cases."[27] Ignoring the verity of Mitchell's response, Baer's contingent refused to participate in negotiations or third-party arbitration and went on to suggest that a stauncher chief executive, like former president McKinley, would send in the U.S. Army to break the strike—violently, if necessary.

Unimpressed with the owners' arguments, TR told Attorney General Philander Chase Knox to use federal troops not to force workers back to the mines, but to confiscate the mines *from* the owners. If negotiation became impossible, the troops would produce coal for the country, he added, ordering Secretary of War Elihu Root to put a force of ten thousand army regulars on instant alert. The threat of the mines' confiscation rattled the owners to the core, but it was as much *influence* as *action* that would throw the dispute into the jurisdiction of a presidential commission. Acting on the advice of the well-connected Root, TR sent his secretary of war to meet with business mogul J. P. Morgan to see if he could convince the mine owners that negotiation was the only way to avoid federal intervention.

The "Corsair Agreement," crafted aboard Morgan's yacht, the *Corsair*, settled the dispute over a presidential commission, which was finally accepted by the owners and the UMW. On October 13 a temporary settlement was finalized. The workers went back to work, and TR appointed an arbitral board to craft a settlement. Several weeks after the strike was resolved, George Baer and TR's longtime confidant Owen Wister encountered one another in a crowded restaurant. "Tell me," the furious railroad executive roared at Wister, "does your friend ever think?" Wister thought for a moment and then answered, "He certainly seems to act."[28]

A savvy man in every sense of the word, Roosevelt understood Adam Smith's theory, put forward in *The Wealth of Nations*, that free-market capitalism would bring prosperity for all by finding new ways for workers to divide their labor. Smith viewed wide-open competition as the driving force of a free-market system, but competition often resulted in price wars, wasteful duplication of production, and bankruptcies. Profit-minded business leaders had discovered that the way around the instability of competition was to dominate the market by creating cartels and bigger industrial organizations. Once its competition was gone, a firm could charge and pay whatever it chose.

While seeking to resolve the anthracite coal strike, Roosevelt coined the phrase "Square Deal" in reference to his fair treatment of the participants in the crisis. Like many of his catchphrases, the term stuck in the imagination of the American public. Soon after, the phrase Square Deal would come to represent more than just a balanced approach but also a progressive agenda founded on the belief that it was the government's function to serve all the people—not just big business or special interests. As significantly, it became an escutcheon for a new kind of activist chief executive, one engaged and vigorous in the definition and shaping of America's future.

Unlike the Buchanan-Taft vision, which "took the . . . narrowly legalistic view that the President is servant of Congress rather than of the people," TR's definition of leadership was simple yet profound: "Leadership is how you can use the power you have to accomplish the things you believe in," he wrote in his autobiography. "My belief was that every executive officer . . . was . . . bound actively and affirmatively to do all he could for the people."[29]

In 1901 James J. Hill, E. H. Harriman, John D. Rockefeller, and J. P. Morgan made a secret deal to combine their railroad stocks in a "holding company," another type of trust. Their new company, the Northern Securities Company, controlled all the major railroads in the Northwestern states. Soon afterward, a cartoon drawn by Edward Kemble for *Life* magazine illustrated the growing perception in the minds of the American public that "robber barons" like Morgan had taken control not only of the economy but perhaps the government as well. In it, TR, like Jack, climbs a beanstalk high into the sky, ax dangling from his belt. As he reaches the top, the squinting, myopic president can barely make out the image of a grinning giant gorging himself from a silver platter. Upon closer inspection, TR is shocked to see the giant feeding from dishes filled with helpless, trussed human beings.[30]

So it was that on Thursday, February 20, 1902, the federal government brought suit against the Northern Securities Company, citing the all-but-forgotten Sherman Antitrust Act of 1890. The news of Roosevelt's lawsuit sent shockwaves through financial circles. J. P. Morgan, furious that he had not been given advance warning, sat by, stubbornly watching the panic spread at stock exchanges throughout the world as stockholders rushed to sell. Within the first hour of trading more stocks fell off the board than during a full day of normal activity. Inspired perhaps by a sense of responsibility—but as likely by profit motive—Morgan finally instructed his men to counter-buy stocks en masse so that, by closing time, prices had actually begun to rally.

Roosevelt had made his point, not just about trusts, but about himself, his office, and the validity of his Square Deal. His action won support from both sides of the political field and was regarded as a much-needed check on the runaway power of trusts and the men who ran them. Liberals welcomed a blow struck by authority against monopoly. Conservatives were sure that the Supreme Court would reaffirm that holding company combinations were legal. In keeping with the premise of his Square Deal, TR didn't boast nor did he make predictions about the outcome of the court battles to follow. Rather, he determinedly moved forward his domestic and foreign agenda, understanding that whether the government won or lost, his action had excited public optimism at a moment in the country's history when few saw a way out of the corporate stranglehold everyday citizens felt powerless to escape.

"I think that to make up his mind to take this first step, to declare this war, on the captains of industry, was a stroke of genius," TR's longtime friend Owen Wister would later write, "and . . . it marked the turn of a rising tide for both Roosevelt and the country."[31] Northern Securities lost in the lower courts and went on to appeal to the Supreme Court, claiming that the Sherman Act violated the freedom of contract. In 1904, in a stunning opinion for the Court, Justice John Marshall Harlan declared that "every combination" that eliminates interstate competition was illegal. The Court included combinations of manufacturing companies and railroads, asserting that all monopolies tended to restrain trade and "to deprive the public of the advantages that flow from free competition."[32] The Court therefore ordered the breakup of the Northern Securities Company into independent competitive railroads.

Before his second term concluded, the Roosevelt administration would launch forty-five lawsuits against the largest monopolistic corporations in the country based on the Sherman Act. Most of them proved successful. If Owen Wister sensed that these acts of bold assertiveness marked "the turn of a rising tide" for Roosevelt and the country, he was correct in that a beaten-down and skeptical American population was witnessing with their own eyes the ardor and basic morality of the man who, in his own words, "spoke softly but carried a big stick." TR's progressivism meant a Square Deal for the American people *and* American business—a society where businesses profited through fair competition and not at the expense of the average citizen.

In a larger sense, too, by taking on America's most powerful business leaders and their trusts before any other individuals or issues, Roosevelt showed that he wasn't afraid of a good fight or its consequences, if he believed in the cause—which, in this case, was the fundamental fairness of American society. "Look at this man," any working person could say. "He comes from money, but he is fighting against his own for us!" To average citizens then, this was a president who was establishing a country of laws and ideals.

Roosevelt's antimonopoly actions played out along lines much broader and deeper than the issue itself. In many ways, his rejection of the Buchanan-Taft view of presidential authority redefined the role of the president from a narrowly responsible executive to a broad-based leader. For him, the Square Deal represented more than a collection of programs. It was a vision and a unique approach to the exercise of power and presidential effectiveness.

It was his effective, energetic, hands-on leadership that resulted in what TR himself called the "greatest achievement of my presidency." For years both military and commercial leaders in the United States had talked about building a canal across the isthmus of Central America to link the eastern and western coasts of the United States. The original plan was to work with the Colombian government, which controlled Panama—where the canal was to be constructed—but when that proved futile, Roosevelt was among the first to recognize it and change direction. Understanding that the Panamanians had wanted their independence for generations, he sent battleships to support their cause, with the caveat that when their independence was won, a canal would be built. Roosevelt had sent American support without the consent of Congress because he believed he had the power to do so. "I took the isthmus, started the Canal, and left the Congress to debate me . . . While the debate goes on the Canal does, too!" he happily announced to newspaper reporters.[33]

Between the years 1904 and 1914 labor continued on the construction of the largest canal ever undertaken. The project was completed, under budget, at a cost of $380 million. When, midway through the project, workers fell ill with malaria and the successful completion of the canal was in jeopardy, TR traveled to the construction site himself and operated a bulldozer alongside the workers. Finally, after a decade of effort, the Panama Canal began operations, a feat that few historians believe could have happened without the hands-on leadership of Theodore Roosevelt.

On an entirely different plane, during his presidency Roosevelt revealed a predatory intelligence that grappled with diverse issues of interest to him and the future of the nation. Clearly, his conservation stemmed from his early childhood interest in nature and ecology, a term that didn't even exist yet. "I recognize the right and duty of this generation to use the natural resources of this great country, but I do not recognize their right to waste them or abuse them for future generations," he lectured industrialists from the bully pulpit he enjoyed as president."[34] But to TR these were not just words. During his nearly eight years as president, he doubled the number of national parks and designated 125 million acres as national forests. Typical of his use of presidential powers is the question he posted to his attorney general when a conservationist alerted him to the impending doom of birds on Florida's Pelican Island: "Is there any law that prevents me as president from declaring it a federal bird preserve?" "Mr. President," Attorney General Knox answered, "there is no such thing as a 'federal bird preserve.'" "Very well," answered Roosevelt, "then I shall declare it!"[35] The creation of the Pelican Island National Wildlife Refuge led to the set-asides of fifty-one additional sites and was the beginning of the United States Fish and Wildlife Service.

The breadth of TR's experience, education, writings, and reading gave him a purview unlike any other world leader with the possible exception of Winston Churchill. While his experiences in New York and the Dakotas provided a sound foundation for domestic policy, his international travels; extensive reading and writing on military matters, geography, and other cultures; and personal relationships with world leaders gave him a strong working knowledge and insight into foreign policy matters. Roosevelt believed that nations, like individuals, should pursue the "strenuous life" and do their part to maintain peace and order. He also believed that a strong military, especially a navy, was necessary as deterrence against foreign aggression—and, therefore, the key to peace. Every year he asked for larger appropriations for the army and navy. Congress usually cut back on his requests, but by the end of his presidency he'd built the U.S. Navy into a major force at sea and reorganized the army along efficient, modern lines.

Understanding the German interest in controlling Latin America when they threatened to intervene in Venezuela—ostensibly to collect debts owed to them—TR framed a policy statement in 1904 that became known as the Roosevelt Corollary to the Monroe Doctrine. It stated that the United States would not only bar outside intervention in Latin American affairs, but would also police the area and guarantee that countries there met their international obligations. Roosevelt backed up the establishment of the policy with a show of military might, thus short-circuiting future German initiatives.

Citing the African proverb "speak softly and carry a big stick," Roosevelt again showed an uncanny ability not to promulgate war, but to avoid it through strength. Much in the manner of future president Ronald Reagan's dealings with the Soviet Union, Roosevelt put a halt to talk of Japanese aggression in the Pacific by sending the U.S. Navy's "Great White Fleet" around the world in a display of naval power. It demonstrated that the United States was indeed able to bring a military presence to bear anywhere in the world. Moreover, it sent a strong message to Japan that the United States—which included Hawaii and the Philippines—was a Pacific power capable of defending itself.

Roosevelt's African proverb also speaks about "speaking softly," and that is exactly the kind of breadth and restraint TR was capable of exercising—even as the fleet's presence was meant to give Japan pause, the president sent his secretary of war to negotiate agreements that appeased Japanese interests in Manchuria and diffused a dispute over Japanese immigration into the United States. Despite popular opinion to the contrary, TR was actually anything but bellicose when it came to diplomacy, understanding as few others could the delicate balance between strength and effectiveness, as well as sensitivity and restraint. It was this juxtaposition of virtues and the timing of their use that made him such a devastatingly effective leader.

In 1905 Roosevelt displayed his own diplomatic skills and the U.S. coming of age as a world power when he used both public and private channels to mediate a peace agreement between Japan and Russia in the Russo-Japanese War. With in-depth knowledge of both cultures stemming from his father's travels, his boyhood reading, and his own personal relationships with the leaders of those nations, he not only possessed the knowledge, sensitivity, and reputation to facilitate such a knotty dispute, but had credibility enough with the governments of both countries, and the world, to be entrusted with the job. Understanding the economic reasons why Japan—which was winning the war—would want to put a halt to hostilities, and the political reasons why Russia would want to do the same, proved the key to a successful mediation of peace. One year later, with the peace agreement settled on, President Theodore Roosevelt became the first American to be awarded the Nobel Peace Prize.

Teddy Roosevelt made his last appearance as president in February 1909. It was a joyous occasion for him, the return of the Great White Fleet to New York Harbor from its triumphant world cruise. Stepping down from office at the age of fifty, he was younger and more vibrant than most presidents had been upon assuming office. At first he was enthusiastic about his successor, William Howard Taft, and consigned himself to scholarly adventures involving nature studies in Africa and a spectacular tour of European capitals. Ultimately, however, he came to see Taft as a weak man whose adherence to Roosevelt's own passions and policies, such as conservation, were tenuous or nonexistent.

In 1912, upon his return from abroad, TR assumed command of the progressive movement. He advocated far-reaching social and economic reforms, many of which would form the basis of cousin Franklin's New Deal agenda. After winning most of the primaries, Roosevelt and his constituents felt cheated when party politics prevailed at the Republican National Convention and Taft received the nomination. Breaking off into a hastily formed Progressive Party, TR ran for the presidency.

Campaigning in Milwaukee, Wisconsin, in October 1912, he was wounded in an assassination attempt. TR had been shot point-blank by a Colt revolver to the left of his lung. A speech Roosevelt had been carrying in his suit jacket had slowed the bullet's progress, as had the inches of thick musculature that ran through TR's unusually developed chest, the result of decades of weight-lifting. Aides and doctors were unanimous in their opinion that this was a critical injury, of the kind that had claimed President McKinley's life, but Roosevelt would have none of it. Seeing this as his chance to push forward the progressive agenda he believed in so strongly, Roosevelt said, "This is my big chance, and I am going to make that speech if I die doing it."[36]

Despite pain, the loss of blood, and a bullet lodged near his lung, TR went to the hall where he'd been planning to campaign and spoke for an hour and a half to a stunned audience. Roosevelt showed his blood-stained shirt and explained that he had been shot, but added, "It takes more than that to kill a Bull Moose."[37] Reiterating that he "would not speak to you insincerely within five minutes of being shot," he said he was running "to stand for the sacred right of childhood and womanhood . . . to see that manhood is not crushed out of the men who toil by excessive hours of labor, by underpayment, by injustice and oppression."[38] In the end, Roosevelt outpolled Taft—a tribute to his abiding popularity—but his hopes of winning and establishing a viable third party were thwarted: Democratic nominee Woodrow Wilson—who also appealed to progressives—carried the election.

After the 1912 defeat, TR found that his effectiveness was limited, owing to the fact that Wilson enacted many of his reform programs, and also because Wilson was reluctant to invite opinions, particularly those regarding America's neutrality after the outbreak of World War I. Although Roosevelt continued to advocate domestic reforms, he increasingly devoted himself to calling for a strong pro-Allied foreign policy and greater military preparedness. All four of TR and Edith's sons fought in World War I, and the death of his youngest son, Quentin, in combat proved a heavy blow to both TR and his wife. Frustrated by his inability to instigate the bold changes he saw as necessary to keeping the United States at the cutting edge either domestically or in foreign military matters, TR, with his health deteriorating and weighing 230 pounds, decided to explore Brazil's uncharted River of Doubt with his son Kermit.

It was a tough journey, with TR coming down with a high fever and malaria. Teddy and Kermit survived the forty-eight-day ordeal, eventually discovering and charting the end of the River of Doubt, which was renamed Rio Roosevelt in honor of the former president. The reality was, though, that Roosevelt would never physically or mentally be the same man again. During the expedition, he'd lost more than fifty pounds; afterward, he never completely got over the malaria he'd contracted, suffering for the remainder of his life with chronic fever. On January 6, 1919, Theodore "Teddy" Roosevelt died at his home of natural causes in Oyster Bay, New York.

THEODORE ROOSEVELT'S LEADERSHIP LESSONS

Sometimes it seems we live in a world so weighed down by convention and the fear of making a mistake that significant change or radical improvement somehow gets smothered along the way. Well, have no fear, Teddy Roosevelt is here! At least that's the way it must have seemed to those who were touched by the life of this true-life action hero. What I admire most about Theodore Roosevelt is the "no fear" attitude that permeates each of his presidential lessons in leadership. I hope you feel the same.

Lesson #1
It's Not Where You Start but Where You Finish the Race That Counts

TR's childhood was stunted by chronic illness that left him gasping for air and a desperate longing to gain the approval of the father he idolized. The battles he waged with his own body were, in effect, a struggle for both survival and personal identity.

In fact, each of the great presidents saw their lives as somehow starting from a deficit that each was passionate, beyond words, to overcome: in Washington's case, it was "social status;" in Lincoln's, it was "lack of education;" and in the case of Theodore Roosevelt, it was his abhorrence (and that of his father) for physical weakness," something that became to him a metaphor for personal failure. Each started his journey toward character-driven leadership at a different point in his life, but once they began "to see" the world around them and their mission within it, decided to do something about it.

Boxer "Irish" Mickey Ward, who achieved his life-long dream to become middleweight champion of the world at the age of thirty-seven, had it right when he said "Good things happen to guys that don't quit." Ward was a fighter, not a president, but nevertheless captured the essence of an abiding characteristics of great leaders possess: tenacity. If you want to achieve a goal as estimable as character-driven leadership you must be prepared to sweat, fight, and "never give up."

The starting point for your climb toward leadership excellence will vary. As with TR, your awakening might be early, or like his uncle, FDR, it may come later in life, but—like "Irish" Mickey Ward—it's important to understand that it's not where you start the race that counts but where you finish.

Never give up your quest to become a character-driven leader!

Lesson #2
Crave New Experiences and Go Out of Your Way to Get Them

Riding hard with the tough men of the Dakotas, TR conquered any pangs of self-doubt and learned the importance of quick decisions and self-reliance. As important, his time there shattered many of his early precepts about the intrinsic goodness of the rich versus the presumed depravity of the masses who worked every day for a living.

When TR took up union leader Samuel Gompers' challenge to accompany him on a tour of the "other" America, he witnessed firsthand the squalor of homes where fathers, mothers, and children worked day and night in their tiny apartments for starvation wages. Finally, after the death of his wife, and a "wilderness" period of soul-searching, he developed his own approach to leadership based on the principles he'd learned from Thee and his own true life experiences.

Roosevelt, like John Kennedy, could easily have lived in a cocoon surrounded by trust-funded Ivy Leaguers but shunned the comfort of those environs for Black Hills hard-riders, tenement-locked immigrants, abused women and children, and grim-lived laborers because he wanted to make a difference.

The reason TR, and every genuine leader, is compelled to feel the feel, and smell the smell, of reality is that they recognize new experiences expand who they are. Real life experiences, like Kennedy's on PT Boat 109 and TR's legendary forays into the reality of others, test a leader's metal, toughen them for the challenges ahead, and broaden their sensitivities to the plight of others.

Crave new experiences and go out of your way to get them.

Lesson #3
Learn to Lead from the Middle of the Pack

A question I found myself asking early in my career was, "How can I lead if I am not president, CEO, or even the boss of my department?"

A phrase that captures this ability is "360-degree leadership," meaning that the person in the middle (middle manager) or in the field (sales rep), or individuals performing a function that may seem devoid of the possibility of leading (administrator), can in fact lead without possessing the positional authority that traditional leaders might enjoy.

TR was a 360-degree leader.

If ever there was a president who proved a man or woman can lead from the middle of the pack, surely it's TR. From the time he took his first position in the New York State Assembly, making a name for himself as the hands-on reformer to the day he died, Roosevelt's leadership credo was unambiguous: "Do what you can with what you have, where you are."

As one of four police commissioners in New York, he didn't get bogged down in politics or bureaucracy but went out into the streets, exposed the wrong doers, and got rid of them. As Assistant Secretary of Navy, the power of his ideas and the level of his conviction could not be contained by a title or his boss, John Long's lassitude, and his vision of a world-class U.S. Navy became reality.

One of the biggest "cop-outs" in life is the phrase "it can't be done" and one of the most common reasons given is that we lack the "power" or the "authority" to lead change.

Great leadership, I've learned, isn't about the title we have, it's about the person we choose to be and the talents we have to offer.

Lesson #4
Have a Bias for Action

With indecisive commanders preventing them from attacking, on July 1, 1898 TR took matters into his own hands, mounting his horse and charging up the hill, his Rough Riders following behind. Roosevelt, wounded by shrapnel, rushed toward the hill's crest, through waves of rifle fire and exploding artillery shells, forcing the Spanish to finally surrender the hill.

Proclaimed the hero of the war, he ran for governor of New York four months later.

In his first six months as governor TR pushed through an eight-hour-work-day law for all state employees, was a proponent of the Costello Anti-Sweat-shop Act, signed pure food laws that required labeling and a health quality guarantee, and declared the Adirondacks and Catskills protected state parks.

A business maxim to which Roosevelt certainly would have subscribe says, 'If you know you're at least 70% right, do it!' The point here is well taken: TR believed in "motion and action."

The most dangerous situation employees of a company, members of an organization, or the population of a country can face is a vacuum. Vacuums are generally filled by people's worst fears. Inaction, paralysis, and mixed signals are anathema to sound leadership.

Great leaders lead, and while the action itself is the tip of a very large ice berg, the net result is action, always decisive and often bold, that compels a true leader to ask, as Roosevelt asked a member of the Tenth Division on his way to taking Kettle Hill, "*Why will you refuse to stand your ground when I am on horseback charging alone?*"

Like TR, have a bias for action.

Lesson #5
Understand the Power of the "Bully Pulpit"

Sun Tsu, in *The Art of War*, makes the point that "compromise is preferable to war." Interestingly, TR and Reagan, both reputed to be aggressive, even war-like, in their domestic and international postures, were far more prone to "influence" their opponents than to confront them.

TR's handling of the UMW strike, along with business mogul J.P. Morgan, and the resulting "Corsair Agreement" is one example. His mediation of the Russo-Japanese War is another, but the most salient example of Roosevelt's power of persuasion was his use of the "Bully Pulpit."

The leadership lesson Roosevelt's "bully pulpit" teaches is this: we all enjoy a bully pulpit of some kind, whether as an executive, teacher, parent, or just plain self-empowered individual. Great leaders use their bully pulpit to influence but also to create dialogue between themselves and the people their leadership embodies. The "bully pulpit" TR used so effectively was never his own but was a conduit that belonged to the American people.

Using one's position, such as president, to influence others was not anything new for world leaders ranging from Caesar to Napoleon. But TR, in using public speeches, whistle-stop addresses, and the printed media to win popular support for his Square Deal programs, re-defined what it meant to be a modern president.

Just as any man or woman can "lead from the middle of the pack," so too they can use their position as an executive, teacher, supervisor, or parent to influence others.

As TR's presidency instructs, understand the power of your bully pulpit and use it to influence rather than confront both those that oppose and follow your leadership.

Lesson #6
Develop Yourself on Multiple Levels (or risk becoming irrelevant)

Theodore Roosevelt used every available moment to expand the breadth and depth of his knowledge, even prolonged hospital stays when near death! Confined to bed as a child, he devoured books about the exploits of others such as *Ivanhoe*, *Robin Hood*, and David Livingston's *Missionary Travels and Researches in South Africa*. These books seemed to permeate every pore of his being, and as a result of this reading, TR became, by the age of eight, a prodigy in world geography, ornithology, taxidermy, and Darwin's evolutionary theory.

The net result of TR's "natural curiosity" about the world around him— geography, history, other cultures, the sciences—is that it kept him relevant. The problem with a narrow, or non-inclusive, education is that it limits a leader's capabilities allowing his or her enemies to cubby-hole them as a "one trick pony."

Without Roosevelt's knowledge of naval warfare, there would have been no Great White Fleet. Without his expertise in geography and world trade, there would have been no Panama Canal. Without his intimate knowledge of global affairs and Asian and Germanic cultures, he would never have been trusted to mediate an historic peace accord.

Like TR, learn to be a life-long student. Develop yourself on multiple levels for the curve balls challenging times will undoubtedly throw your way, or risk becoming irrelevant.

Lesson #7
Pursue Your Passions with a "No Fear" Attitude

TR was an expert in *jiu jitsu* who understood and practiced one of the major tenets of the art which is to "control the fear within."

The way to accomplish this in *jiu jitsu* is the way a man or woman can accomplish it in their own leadership development: by continuously challenging, testing, and strengthening one's "inner self," freely acknowledging weaknesses, and—like a muscle in one's arm or leg—working diligently to develop it.

Campaigning in Milwaukee, Wisconsin in October 1912, TR was shot point blank in the chest by an assassin. Aides and doctors were unanimous in their opinion that this was a critical injury, but Roosevelt would have none of it. Despite pain, loss of blood, and a bullet lodged near his lung, TR went to the hall where he had been planning to campaign and spoke for an hour and a half to a stunned audience. Roosevelt showed his blood-stained shirt and explained that he had been shot, but added, "It takes more than that to kill a Bull Moose."

An example of a developed "inner self" and how it was developed is my son, Greg. Just a White Belt in *jiujitsu* at the time, and going into a tournament against others, older and more experienced, I asked him, "Are you nervous?" "Why would I be nervous?" he replied. "I do this every day."

Like TR, Greg—just 15 at the time—had it right. What is there to be afraid of if you've had the foresight and strength of character to "do this every day?"

Pursue your passions with a "no fear" attitude, not because you are foolish, but because you understand the nature of fear.

Chapter VII

Ronald Reagan
U.S. President, 1981–1989

In August 2007 Chris Matthews, host of the political talk program Hardball, commented that since the publication of Reagan's diaries one month earlier, critics would have to "reconsider" many of the preconceptions they held about him. One assumption that Matthews was referring to was the belief that Reagan was intellectually lazy and led with a dependence on delegation that was tantamount to abrogation of responsibility. In other words, his management was anything but hands-on.

Beyond the diaries, which show him to have been astonishingly engaged, the recent release of hundreds of speeches and more than one thousand radio addresses, written in his own hand, demonstrate the depth of that misperception. In fact, Ronald Reagan is shown to have been a deeply religious, unswervingly persevering man whose presidency was founded on a political ideology cultivated since early childhood: a leader who, as historian Richard Reeves defines great leaders, "broke the historical continuum."[1]

As was the case with Lincoln and Franklin D. Roosevelt, Reagan's current status among the pantheon of great American presidents followed a rocky reception. In 1981 revered presidential adviser Clark Clifford called him an "amiable dunce"; even former secretary of state Henry Kissinger wondered, "How did a man like this come to be elected governor, much less a president?" Yet, through an innate ability that Eugene Jennings, a professor at Michigan State University College of Business, calls "maze smart"—the talent to "get out of the briar patch without all those briers on your pants"—Reagan's two terms in office are now commonly referred to as the "Reagan Revolution."[2]

During an interview with former speechwriter Peggy Noonan, our nation's fortieth president reflected on his tenure in office: "I never thought of myself as a great man, just a man committed to great ideas. I've always believed that individuals should take priority over the state . . . There's no question I'm an idealist, which is another way of saying I'm an American."[3]

Others would go much further in their praise of Reagan's effectiveness in accomplishing the short list of crystal clear objectives that he came to office vowing to achieve:

Lower Taxes. The day he took office in 1980, the top income tax rate was 78 percent—lowered from 90 percent by John Kennedy—with the tax code based on eleven brackets. By the time Reagan left office in 1988, the top rate was 35 percent, with three brackets, and eight million people off the tax rolls.

Smaller Government. From 1979 to 1984, the annual rate of growth in federal outlays slowed from 17 percent to 5 percent. This, was accomplished while the United States embarked on the greatest military buildup since the onset of World War II.

Economic Recovery. In 1980 and 1981, the United States was in the midst of the worst economic depression since the 1930s. During Reagan's two terms in office, the economy grew by more than one-third, producing a $15 trillion increase in America's wealth; unemployment dropped 30 percent, interest rates fell from 18 percent to 6 percent, the rate of inflation decreased from 15 percent to under 4 percent, and the Dow Jones index soared from 800 points to 2,400 points.

U.S.-Soviet Relations. Reagan believed that during the 1970s America had abdicated its role as leader of the free world; he decided on a "new realism." Understanding that the Soviet economy was a shambles, he confronted them directly in the Caribbean, Southeast Asia, and Latin America. By the time he left office, his dream of turning strategic arms "limitation" (SALT) into strategic arms reduction (START) would be realized, and within his lifetime a stunned world would witness the dissolution of the Soviet empire.

Perhaps the most elusive aspect of the Reagan persona is the complexity of his character vis-à-vis his perception among some as an "intellectual lightweight." It is a misconception that Reagan not only tolerated but tacitly encouraged. For example, when *Fortune* magazine interviewed Reagan for its September 1986 story "What Managers Can Learn from Manager Reagan," the cover photo of him was captioned with his quote "Surround yourself with the best people you can find, delegate authority, and don't interfere." More to the point, when confronted by ABC's Sam Donaldson at a White House news conference about rumors that he worked only four hours per day, Reagan jauntily answered, "I know hard work never killed anyone, but I figure, why take a chance?"

When word spread that Attorney General Ed Meese chose not to wake him in the middle of the night during a foreign affairs crisis, Reagan's response to the media frenzy was "I've laid down the law to my staff, to everyone from now on about anything that happens: No matter what time it is, wake me—even if it's in the middle of a cabinet meeting." Similarly, White House advisor Drew Lewis reports that when pressed for a statement on the economy, a sudden act of aggression by the Soviets, or a voice of support for a disgruntled NATO ally, it was not uncommon for Reagan to mock critics who accused him of being detached from the job, "Well, Drew," he would say pleasantly, "tell me what to say, and then tell me how to say it. And by the way, when you're done, tell me what I said."[4]

Clearly, Reagan—the former movie star, wizened survivor of the Hollywood "blacklist" days, successful governor, and at seventy the oldest person ever to be sworn in as president—was jostling the media with the wit and wisdom of a man who had in his lifetime led multiple lives. Nevertheless, critics would do well to contrast that lighthearted, if slightly world-worn, personality to the one who imbues nearly ever written word of his personal diaries with the kind of deep, soul-searching probity unseen since the days of Lincoln.

Here is Reagan's diary entry for Monday, March 30, 1981, handwritten shortly after assassin John Hinckley Jr. laid him down with a bullet to the lung:

My day to the Bldg. & Construction Traders . . . at the Hilton ballroom—2 p.m. Was all dressed to go & for some reason at the last min. took off my really good wrist watch and wore an older one.

Speech not riotously received—still it was successful. Left the hotel at the usual side entrance and headed for the car—suddenly there was a burst of gun fire from the left. S.S.

Agent pushed me onto the floor of the car & jumped on top. I felt blow to my upper back that was unbelievably painful. I was sure he'd broken my rib. The car took off. I sat up on the edge of the seat almost paralyzed by pain. Then I began coughing up blood which made both of us think—yes, I had a broken rib & it had punctured a lung. He switched orders from W.H. to Geo. Wash. U. Hosp.

By the time we arrived I was having great trouble getting enough air. We did not know that Tim McCarthy (S.S.) had been shot in the chest, Jim Brady in the head & a policeman Tom Delahanty in the neck.

I walked into the emergency room and was hoisted onto a cart where I was stripped of my clothes. It was then we learned I'd been shot & had a bullet in my lung.

Getting shot hurts. Still my fear was growing because no matter how hard I tried to breathe it seemed I was getting less & less air. I focused on that tiled ceiling and prayed. But I realized I couldn't ask for Gods help while at the same time I felt hatred for the mixed up young man who had shot me. Isn't that the meaning of the lost sheep? We are all Gods children & therefore equally beloved by him. I began to pray for his soul and that he would find his way back to the fold.

If the comedic Reagan gleefully tweaking the noses of White House reporters was in full bloom during the former passages, than the other Reagan, amazingly complex, spiritually grounded, and eminently self-knowing, is at least as present in the latter. Even to this day, with landmark speeches such as the "Evil Empire" address now favorably compared to Churchill's "Iron Curtain" speech and a list of accomplishments that even early critic Henry Kissinger calls "nearly incomprehensible," Ronald Reagan is still perhaps the least understood president of the last fifty years.

To many, notably neoconservatives, he's been lionized and frequently holds the position among them as the greatest president of the twentieth century. To others, chief among them liberal Democrats, he's been demonized, a symbol of intellectual superficiality, detached leadership, and gross uncaring for minorities, the poor, and those physically or mentally disadvantaged. In some ways, the truth is in the eye of the beholder. Yet several points cannot be argued: Reagan wasn't a stupid man, nor was he a genius. He was someone of above-average intelligence who possessed an awesome belief in the historical importance of the American democratic experiment, who persevered personally to attain a position in the world to declare his bounding faith in it, and who—on the scale of Lincoln, Washington, TR, FDR, and Kennedy— took the reins of leadership to alter the direction of the United States, and the world, with an impact that is still being felt today.

Why does Ronald Reagan remain so enigmatic, his motives obfuscated, and his historical weight so disproportionately measured? Like the other great presidents we've studied, the answer lies as much in his background and evolution as a leader as it does in facing his greatest challenge—helping to bring about the dissolution of the Soviet Union and ending a cold war that dominated the second half of the twentieth century.

To understand Reagan, the man, and the leadership lessons his presidency can teach us, we must first understand how "a man" was defined for someone born into an indigent Irish American family on February 6, 1911. Today's commonly accepted descriptions of a background like his might be "impoverished immigrant family" or "son of a man who struggled with alcoholism"; among hardened survivors of Ireland's potato famine, however, each would be considered a weak excuse for not stepping up to the plate "like a man" and stoically moving ahead with your life, while cautioning curious neighbors to "mind your own business."

In fact, Ronald Reagan—who liked to be called "Dutch"—and his brother, Neil—who liked to be called "Moon"—did grow up in a small-town Illinois home like that. His father, Jack, was a shoe salesman in Tampico whose frequent bouts with alcohol forced the family to move every two years or so, supposedly to "find work." Jack Reagan was a chain-smoking, back-slapping salesman who wore his smashed dreams on his sleeve. He was cynical, pessimistic, and abusive when he drank.

As with many of the other great presidents—such as Washington, Teddy Roosevelt, and Kennedy—Reagan, as a child, understood deeply the feelings of withering shame that came along with his dad's alcoholism. The stories of it are multiple, but none so stigmatizing as the morning he found Jack passed out on the sidewalk in front of the one-bedroom apartment the family rented over a bank building. Reagan later wrote about seeing his father sprawled out, "as if he'd been crucified," lying in the snow.[5] At first he felt like leaving him, until the tug of his mother's religious instruction called him to duty. "It's a disease, Ronnie," she told him. "You know he can't help it." And that's when Dutch turned back and began wordlessly dragging him back into the house, as neighbors and bank customers passed them by, the dutiful son with the "sick" father.

Reagan would later remember only the better qualities of Jack and his circumstances, the old saw "if you can't say something good about somebody don't say anything at all" no doubt smothering any of the bad thoughts. "Jack was the best raconteur I ever heard, especially when it came to the 'smoking-car' sort of stories," Reagan would later rave.[6] About his childhood, possibly the most "unhappy" of any president of the past one hundred years, his memories seem to have passed through some prism of optimism that left him talking like a boy from Mark Twain's *Huck Finn*, so earnest was he about exchanging the modest material possessions he had for intangible ones—most notably his dreams for the future.

Certainly his mother, Nelle, a devout Christian Evangelical, contributed to the foundation on which his early character was built: "My brother and I were truly influenced by my mother, who was deeply religious but also possessed great kindness. We were a rather poor family, and yet my mother was always finding people worse off than we were that she could bring help to."[7] A passionate believer in the instruction given in her favorite book, *The Christian's Secret of a Happy Life*, she taught both him and Moon the salient lesson that dominated her existence: Jesus is present in all that you do. Because He loves you, and is involved in your life moment to moment, you can live your life confident that your destiny is linked directly with God's. You may not always understand why something is happening, and it might seem bad, or even hopeless, but Jesus wants you to be yourself and never be afraid of doing the right thing.

In one of the hundreds of handwritten letters he left behind, Reagan offers testimony to the depth of his mother's Christian belief: "I now seem to have her faith that there is a divine plan for each one of us, and while we may not be able to see the reason for something at the time, things do happen for a reason and for the best. One day what seemed to be an unbearable blow is revealed as having marked a turning point or a start leading to something worthwhile."[8]

Later in life, after Reagan was elected president, people like William Bennett would observe an uncanny inner peace that could be, and often was, misperceived as lassitude. "Reagan was a man in possession of his soul," Bennett observed. Longtime friend and former cabinet member Michael Deaver explained it differently: "Reagan was a humble man of supreme self-confidence. He never second-guessed himself. Once he made a decision that was it." Others, such as his son Ron Jr. and his wife, Nancy, frequently cited Reagan's unflappable belief in divine providence and what he described as his "rendezvous with destiny."[9]

Long before anyone observed Reagan's bounding self-assurance, there were within him diametrically opposed forces mixing like the constituents of an exotic elixir to determine the kind of man he would become. In the tradition of George Washington, the first force was an honest belief that he was destined for greatness. The second, equally influential, were the realities of poverty, a bleak home life, and shame of his family's societal standing. In another individual, these forces could easily negate each other, but not in the case of someone with Reagan's burning determination and vaulting imagination. Within him these forces never met for one simple reason: Reagan never acknowledged the second force. By imagining his circumstances differently, he had nothing to overcome. It was in this way that Ronald—a name he never liked—became "Dutch" Reagan transforming himself *internally* in the way he saw himself and *externally* in the way others perceived him, to change his future prospects forever.

One sign of the future he dreamed about came at age eleven when he read Harold Bell Wright's *That Printer of Udell's*:

> The story is eerily similar to Reagan's own, opening with a scene of a boy standing over the expiring body of his alcoholic father in a scene similar to what Reagan experienced with his own father at roughly the same time he read Wright's book. The boy in the story grows up, moves to the big city, overcomes hardship and poverty to become a tradesman, and then becomes politically active, urging his fellow citizens in a speech to make provisions for the poor among them. He finds religion and a loyal wife along the way, and the story ends with the city voting to send him to Washington, D.C.[10]

Long before Dutch Reagan's "inner self" concretized, the two forces that threatened to subsume the eleven-year-old could not have been more ominous. Here was an insecure youngster reading about the exercise of great human potential in the character Udell, while during that same year picking up his unconscious, alcohol-sodden father from out of the snow. While the flames of his dreams for upward mobility were being stoked by novels with heroic protagonists, such as the Rover Boys and Frank Merriwell series, another part of him must have agonized over the fact that his personal development, even beyond familial encumbrances, was missing the mark horribly.

Despite every effort, young Ronnie seemed to have only average abilities in school and no talent at all in sports such as baseball, football, or tennis. When a ball was thrown to him, pathetically, he couldn't even make contact unlike his idol, Babe Ruth, swatting it out of the park. In football, he couldn't seem to catch a pass like the other boys. *More shame.* Instead of celebrating Dutch, the self-created hero of his imaginings, he was forced to acknowledge the fact that his schoolmates didn't want him on their team!

One day, while playing with his brother, Moon, Reagan put on Nelle's glasses and, suddenly, the world appeared different to him. It was as if someone had just turned on the lights in a dimly lit room. Objects that were no more than blurs all at once became visible to him—chairs, sofas, even the faces of family members—so that when he later stood at the plate, not only could he see the baseball, but suddenly he could count each stitch, if he chose, while it was spinning toward him.

To Reagan, this was a life-altering event. Like one of his heroes in the Rover Boys, he too had found a happy ending. Sports, literally overnight, became easy for him, and soon other kids, their parents, and coaches called him a "natural" athlete. He began to play varsity football and baseball and became a lifeguard that summer—and for the six that followed—earning fifteen dollars a week. It was good money for the times, but more importantly, he had truly become Dutch Reagan.

It was his job to protect the lives of swimmers at Lowell Park on the Rock River, where currents were swift and often dangerous. It was work he took more seriously than the other young men because to him saving lives was the job of heroes. In the seven years he worked at Rock River, Reagan not only developed his swimming abilities, but used the God-given talents he had cultivated to save seventy-seven lives. "Ronnie "Dutch" Reagan," he must have imagined others commenting, "here's a young man who, unlike his father, Jack, is highly regarded within his community, reliable and daring, a "heroic" individual."

Reagan's son Ron Jr. reflected on this aspect of his father's character shortly after his dad's passing:

My father saw himself as a kind of savior—not in a religious sense—but somebody who could save the day, ride in on a white horse with a white hat and do

that . . . In Sacramento [when he was governor of California] my parents had a
party for the legislature in a backyard with a large pool. He was mingling, doing his thing, but always had an eye on the pool because there were kids in the
pool so he was watching, watching, while talking to someone and one little girl
went down but she didn't come up, I mean, she's just not coming up. "Excuse
me," my father says mid-conversation, dives to the bottom of the pool, scoops
this little girl up, and puts her on the side of the pool. I have a photo of him
standing in the water with her, asking if she's all right. That was my Dad . . .
really something.[11]

Aside from his unique ability to formulate imaginative solutions (call them
"alternate endings") to real-life situations—such as his invention, like Teddy
Roosevelt, of a new self—Reagan's character was built on an intrinsic belief
in the God-given dignity of each individual. His parents were great influences
in this arena. In the case of Jack Reagan, who despised discrimination, it was
a practical matter because he was himself a victim during the days when
signs in factory employment offices read, "No Dogs or Irish Need Apply."
For Nelle, it was a matter of faith. Each person is a "child of God," she would
instruct her sons. But Reagan's parents didn't just say it. They lived it.

When a blizzard overtook Jack Reagan on a business trip and the only
room available was in a "No Jews Allowed" hotel, he gave the owner a stern
lecture, then spent the night in his car. In his memoir, *Where's the Rest of
Me?* Reagan makes frequent reference to such accounts, but perhaps the most
telling story came when Dutch was on the road playing football at Eureka
College and the coach was told that Burghie, a black player, couldn't stay
with them because the hotel was restricted. "Come along with me," Reagan
told him. "My folks live less than an hour from here. They'll put us both up."
Knowing he couldn't call Jack and Nelle to tell them they were coming because his parents didn't own a phone, the two just showed up unannounced,
and both were welcomed with open arms.

There were other characteristics, some positive, others negative, that
Reagan picked up from Jack and Nelle, many of which would have bearing
on the man he became and the leadership he exercised as president. One of
those, surprising to many, was that his father was suspicious of established
authority, and his son felt similarly. Reagan made note of his father's distrust
in an unpublished personal letter: "Jack was always suspicious of established
authority, especially the Republican politicians who ran the Illinois state government, which he considered as corrupt as Tammany Hall."[12] As it turned
out, Reagan also was never the friend of big business that many supposed him
to be. As governor and president, he expressed a surprising disdain for the
mighty corridors of finance and economic gurus like John Kenneth Galbraith,
whom he considered "a brilliant stupid man."

As a candidate during his runs for governor and president, Reagan frequently cited the fact that he'd voted for FDR four times in his life, was a member of the AFL-CIO, and served as president of the Screen Actors Guild (SAG). As the union's president during the height of the "Red Scare" in Hollywood, he refused to cooperate in FBI investigations of members and was vocal in his defense of civil liberties concerning communist "witch hunts" targeting James Cagney, Humphrey Bogart, and others he felt were being railroaded by overzealous Washington bureaucrats.

In his single most poignant stand as president—the one most often used to validate his big business leanings—against PATCO, the air traffic controllers union, it was never, to him, about the "system" versus the "worker." It was, rather, about a virtue that Reagan was brought up to cherish—honor. The air traffic controllers had taken an oath not to strike and they were breaking that oath while putting public safety and national security at risk. They were breaking their word. To him, it was that simple.

With Reagan, it was always about the individual. In keeping with his times and the way that "a man" behaved, he never bragged, never wore religion on his sleeve (as did Jimmy Carter), and rarely talked about his beliefs, his background, or his innermost feelings. He simply did it, much as he rescued the little girl from the pool. He quietly excused himself, saved the girl, deposited her poolside, checked to see if she was comfortable, and went back to his guests with a smile and a shrug.

In one way, we see Reagan like Theodore Roosevelt. Roosevelt invented "Teddy," the swashbuckling, sword-wagging hero charging on horseback up San Juan Hill. Like other great self-promoters—boxing champion John L. Sullivan and magician Harry Houdini come to mind—he then wouldn't let anyone forget about it. With Reagan, we see a similar self invention in the creation of "Dutch," but Reagan wouldn't brag about it anymore than would the film heroes of the late 1940s and 1950s—actors Gary Cooper and Robert Taylor come to mind—because a real man, steel tempered by World War II, let his actions speak for him.

Even the way Reagan, as a twenty-year-old, got himself admitted to Eureka College was like the plot to a 1940s film. After having read F. Scott Fitzgerald's novel *The Great Gatsby* and another of his favorites, Young and Coleman's *Brown of Harvard*, two realizations were apparent to him. First, he wanted to participate in the ivy-covered-walled sophistication of a college campus because he knew it was his ticket into a world beyond Tampico. Second, he was a C student, without a dime to his name excepting his meager lifeguard savings, which wouldn't come close to covering tuition, meals, and expenses. In keeping with his unique ability to reinterpret his obstacles and find imaginative solutions, however, Reagan arranged a private meeting with the college dean. Bringing with him his athletic credentials and a folder filled with accounts of his lifesaving heroics, his plan worked and Dutch Reagan was admitted to Eureka College on a needy-student scholarship with a job washing dishes in the girls' dorm to help pay for books, meals, and a dormitory room.

In sophomore year Reagan was selected spokesman by his peers for a student strike against deep faculty cutbacks proposed by Eureka's board of directors. Dutch Reagan, now acting in school theatrical productions, playing varsity football, and representing his class in the student senate, was immediately seen by fellow students as passionate about decisions affecting student life. As spokesman he made a rousing speech calling for a vote on whether to call for a student strike. The audience responded in the affirmative, giving him a standing ovation. Reagan was thrilled; the cuts were rescinded and the dean resigned. Dutch Reagan, athlete-actor-activist, was proclaimed hero of the confrontation and elected student body president.

Given his knowledge of football and trained voice as an actor, after graduating Reagan decided to try his hand at radio broadcasting in a newly created role within the industry, play-by-play sportscaster. He traveled to Davenport, Iowa, where he convinced the station manager at WOC to hire him. It was not his dream of acting on the big screen with the likes of Spencer Tracy and Errol Flynn, but he understood intuitively that it was one step closer. As significant, the job tapped many of the innate talents he'd later call on in his role as governor and president: writing, elocution, and vivid description. "When Reagan was doing a broadcast, it was like you were there," a fellow announcer remembers. "He had the ability to get you excited, like the game, or play, or whatever it was, was really important. I mean important to you personally."[13]

Within the year, Reagan got laid off and traveled to Des Moines, where he parlayed his meager credentials into a job as sportscaster at WHO, an NBC affiliate. From there it was on to Chicago, where he did play-by-play for a big city audience, persuading the station manager to let him follow the team to California to cover spring training. In an interview Reagan later explained that he finagled the move to "get out of the cold weather," but as clearly drawn as an architect's blueprint, Dutch had angled his way to California to be nearer his dream of becoming a Hollywood movie star.[14] While in Los Angeles, he met a young lady who sang at the Biltmore Hotel. He shared his dream of becoming a full-time actor and she introduced him to a film agent who frequented the hotel. The two met and the agent was immediately taken with Reagan's rugged good looks, imposing voice, and stage presence. On the spot, he called a casting director at Warner Brothers: "You may or may not believe this but I have another Robert Taylor sitting in my office." Within the week, Ronald "Dutch" Reagan was signed to a seven-year contract with a salary starting at two hundred dollars per week. It all happened that way, just like in the movies.

Reporter Lou Cannon writes about the illusory aspect of Ronald Reagan's life: "Reagan already lived in a world of illusion before he arrived in Hollywood . . . He used his optimistic imagination to transform his difficult childhood into an 'idyll.' Later, he would invent an America that never was and share with his fellow citizens a bright, shining vision of our nation's greatness founded on an imagined version of the past. The vision would be accepted because of Reagan's belief in it. But it was not a vision that thrives on close encounters."[15] Historian Richard Reeves is equally derisive in his assessment of Reagan's grasp of reality as president, suggesting that he got the idea for the Strategic Defense Initiative (aka SDI or Star Wars) system from a 1950s science fiction movie he had acted in. This may or may not be true, but Gorbachev believed the concept possible, as did prominent scientists on both sides. Reagan's belief in it, coupled with the Soviet's belief in it, did—in fact—change the rules of the game in the nuclear arms race.

To truly understand Reagan, described by former secretary of state James Baker as the "principled pragmatist," one must also understand Reagan "the artist" and the way his mind worked. In conceptualizing Star Wars (a proposal to use ground- and space-based systems to protect the United States from attack by strategic nuclear ballistic missiles), Reagan undoubtedly saw SDI not as an illusion spinning in space, ungrounded, but as an extrapolation of a life-saving invention, framed in the reality of a different but similar time, operating in the most dire of circumstances—world war. Here is Reagan explaining his rationale for SDI, putting on display his unique ability to collapse history, pooling the past and present to anticipate the future: "You know, before World War II, the British were developing a new defense system, it was called radar. And without radar, it's possible that the Royal Air Force wouldn't have been able to beat back the Nazi air assault on England . . . well [during negotiations with Gorbachev] I couldn't help but think that giving up SDI would have been like Chamberlain giving up radar, as well as Czechoslovakia, at Munich—a tragic blunder that might have spelled the end to freedom in Europe."[16]

The true issue when we consider whether a leader is great is not whether one lives in, or believes in, something that doesn't yet exist. The issue is, Does the leader who has this "vision" possess the powers of persuasion, grasp of the future, and perseverance to convince others that it is important and worth doing? Moreover, can he or she compel others to devote themselves to its achievement and turn the "illusion" into "reality"? Ronald Reagan was able to do all of this.

In his book *Greatness*, Steven Hayward uses philosopher Isaiah Berlin's analysis of FDR's imaginative leadership to shed light on Reagan's ability to see past obstacles that could easily confound a more traditional mind: "Franklin Roosevelt, who as much as any man altered his country's inner image of itself, its character and history, possessed it [imagination] to a high degree. This kind of imagination if filled with sufficient energy and force and, it may be added, fantasy, which is less frightened by the facts and creates ideal models in terms of which the facts are ordered in the mind, sometimes transforms the outlook of an entire people and generation."[17]

Reagan's perseverance, optimism, and energy did not dessert him in his pursuit of political office, nor did it fail him in Hollywood, where he was immediately swept into the whirlwind of Tinsel town glamour. In his first eighteen months, he made thirteen movies, including *Santa Fe Trail*, in which he played Custer; and *Knute Rockne All American*, in which he played Notre Dame's inspirational football player George Gipp, rubbing elbows with stars like Ida Lupino, Katherine Hepburn, and Erroll Flynn, and becoming close personal friends with Robert Taylor and William Holden.

The roles usually had him playing who he was—or had become—a quietly heroic protagonist unafraid of what perils the future might hold: ready, willing, and able to take control of a bad situation and find a way out. When told he had to join a union (SAG), he wasn't sure he wanted to until it was explained that noncontract actors needed the union to get social benefits. When presented that way—as helping others—he enthusiastically joined. Three years later, he wasn't only a member of the union but also a member of its board of directors.

On January 26, 1940, Reagan married actress Jane Wyman, a beautiful girl-next-door type, loaded with talent and considerably more sophistication than the young actor-athlete from Tampico, Illinois. While Reagan could act, Wyman was an actress of distinction, landing roles in classic films like *The Yearling* and *Johnny Belinda*, for which she earned an Academy Award. The disparity in their respective talents and roles must have created some tension even before pressures from his burgeoning political career entered their marriage, though, even into their eighties, neither ever spoke about it.

In the August 1942 edition of *Photoplay* magazine, Reagan, with more than thirty feature films to his credit, wrote an article entitled "How to Make Yourself Important." Meant to give the rising star a venue to tell his fans that he'd been drafted, today it offers students of Reagan's leadership a glimpse into the future president's character and values, unvarnished, if a little bit corny by today's standards:

A fancy storyteller holds his punch for the story's end, but as I'm a plain guy, I may as well write accordingly. I hold that all of this business about making yourself important by means of externals is no good. Clothes, being seen in the Right Places, show, swank—No! Nor do I believe that you have to be a standout from your fellow men in order to make your mark in the world.

Lots of kids write and ask my advice about how to make their mark on an indifferent world . . . So what I'd like to tell them is this: Look, you must love what you are doing. You must think what you are doing is important because if it's important to you, you can bet . . . that other people will think so, too. It may take time, but they'll get around to it.

I've just been told, here at the studio, of two very important parts that were to have been mine. But I won't be doing those pictures. Uncle Sam has called me and I'm going off to war . . . As for believing what you are doing is important— well, if fighting to preserve the United States and her Allies isn't important, you name it.

And who knows—maybe when I get back again, "when the world is free," there will be other good parts waiting for me and my buddies.

The thirty-one-year-old Reagan wanted to be an air force pilot, but because of his poor vision he was rejected and became a second lieutenant in army air force intelligence. Significantly, Reagan took what he knew about filmmaking and extrapolated it into an innovative new method for training pilots prior to bombing missions. Using a soundstage, cameras, and special effects, he taught his unit how to put detailed replications of Japanese cities and targets on film. Pilots then viewed the footage in a simulated cockpit, allowing them to practice the actions they'd later be performing on missions. The technique was eventually used for pilot training throughout the Pacific.

Reagan's unit also received raw footage of classified films to edit and duplicate, among them the Allies' first encounters with Nazi death camps. His exposure to the atrocities was shocking to him and left an impression about the evils of totalitarian governments that would greatly affect his later views on the Soviet Union: "It [the film] showed the interior of a huge building. Our troops had just taken over the camp and had entered the building. It was cavernous, like a warehouse. And the floor was covered with bodies. Then, as we watched in horror, one of the bodies rose up on an elbow and a hand reached up—a hand rising out of a sea of bodies, as if it were pleading for help."[18] Could there be a more horrific metaphor for the Nazi regime than a man buried in bodies holding his hand out into the empty air? Probably not, but the events that followed Reagan's discharge from the military would soon put him squarely in what authors Bennis and Thomas have called the "crucible" of leadership. Here his lifelong views about Soviet communism would be crystallized and a seething political ideology formed.

When the war ended, Reagan returned to Hollywood, but after a four-year absence there were no "good parts waiting for him." Never a star of the Gable, Bogart, or Stewart echelon, what work he got was in B war films like *That Hagen Girl, Stallion Road*, and *The Voice of the Turtle*, and then—nothing. Suddenly, the near-miraculous good fortune he'd lived with and come to expect deserted him. Without work in films, he parlayed his growing interest in dinner-table politics into making speeches to army veteran associations, film studio conferences, and churches. "I wanted to save the world," he later remembered. His speeches centered on support for FDR's New Deal, the role of post–World War II American democracy, and a very personal evocation of his disdain for neo-fascism, which he believed "steals a man's dreams."[19]

One can sense in Reagan's early speeches a struggle to get into focus something deeply felt that was then forming and needed desperately to be expressed. In 1948, while speaking at the Beverly Christian Church, something inexplicable happened. Reagan attempted a modest expansion of his themes of faith in democracy, for the first time contrasting "American values" with "Soviet communism," and suddenly the room fell into icy silence. He finished his speech, puzzled by what happened until several days later he received a letter from a woman in the audience confiding her fears that the church had become a "front for Communism."

To Reagan, who considered himself a liberal democrat, the beliefs of others were their own affair, but this was different. In the guise of one reality—say, a church or civic organization—a covert political party with ties to a foreign government was luring people in to support their agenda. To him, what they were doing seemed dishonest and un-American. Soon after, when a Hollywood strike against movie studios was contemplated, Reagan was asked by SAG to study the issues, most of which involved jurisdictional disputes. When he returned with findings that didn't support a strike and was ready to announce them during a speech at the Hollywood Bowl, he was confronted by an unidentified man. "*If you show up tonight, your face will never be in pictures again,*" the man threatened. That night Reagan called the Burbank police, who put him under twenty-four-hour protection.

Despite the threats, Reagan made the speech and, on the spot, called for a vote, which supported his view (2,748 votes to 509). But it wasn't over. In the days to follow, SAG became a battleground for control of the film industry. Cars were firebombed, people beaten, bones broken. For the next seven months, after a plot was uncovered by police to throw acid in his face, Reagan carried a .32-caliber pistol in a shoulder holster for self-protection. Finding himself thrown into the middle of the fray, Reagan did what Reagan does. He personally investigated allegations that the strike was part of a Soviet plot to gain influence over Hollywood studios and the content of their movies—a suspicion later confirmed by the California Senate Commission on Un-American Activities—tenaciously holding his ground in speeches that decried the strong-arm tactics being used to gain control of the union.

Yet when the FBI came to his home asking him to participate in sting operations to lure communist infiltrators out of SAG, Reagan refused. He wasn't a "red baiter" he told them. But on his own, working with Jimmy Roosevelt—Franklin's son—actress Olivia de Havilland, and actor William Holden, he presented his views supporting American values, the importance of the film industry, and an actor's right to choose whatever politics he or she favored. During speeches he was assailed by catcalls of "fascist" and "capitalist scum" from fellow members of the Hollywood Independent Citizens Committee for the Arts, many of whom were aggressively anti-American. For some Ronald Reagan became a hero while, suddenly, for others he was a hated enemy.

The catalyst for Reagan's activism was not coercion but the "bullying" of a friend, actor John Garfield. During a political gathering at actress Ida Lupino's home, he was asked to speak. As soon as he began, shouts from the opposition threatened to prevent him from continuing until Garfield stood up and said, "Why don't you listen to what he has to say? Maybe he has information that you don't!" More than a decade later, Reagan recalled what happened in vivid detail, such was the impact of that evening on him:

> I saw a well-known character actor take John to the back of the garden . . . I could see him back John up against a tree and, with one hand holding him by the shirt front, he read an angry riot act, punctuated by a jabbing finger. While I could hear nothing of what was said, I was so fascinated by the tableau I almost forgot to parry the hostile shots coming my own way. John stayed back there, leaning against the tree, hands deep in his pockets, after the actor left him, and finally he edged his way to a back gate and left . . . [Later, after Garfield died of a heart attack] like a voice from the grave, the press carried the story of his last forty-eight hours. He had gone to the FBI and the House committee and poured out a story of fourteen years in which the Communist Party had turned him on and off like a hot water faucet.[20]

If his battle with communists in Hollywood deposited Reagan squarely into the crucible of leadership, his response to the challenge reveals much about his character. On the one hand, he became a virulent anticommunist; on the other, he was keen to discern the political demagoguery that surrounded the issue in Washington DC and was outspoken in his defense of fellow actors whom he believed were being targeted by the House Un-American Activities Committee.

Owing to this basic sense of Midwestern fairness and ability to stand tall in the face of moral ambiguity, Reagan was nominated for and won the

presidency of the Screen Actors Guild during one of the most politically uncertain periods that Hollywood, and the United States, had ever experienced.
In taking the post, and handling it objectively as opposed to becoming an
instrument for either side, he put his name, career, and life on the line. Peggy
Noonan in her book *When Character Was King* captures the combination of
principles, idealism, and perseverance that epitomized Reagan's leadership
of the union during that period: "In a time of malice he was not malicious;
in a time of lies he did not falsify; in a time of great pressure he didn't bend
or break; in a time of disingenuousness he was clear and candid about where
he stood and why. And in a time when people just gave up after a while and
changed the subject, he remained in the field through all the long haul."[21]

During this time period, Reagan expressed his unease not only with the
totalitarian governments that had risen to power during his lifetime, but also
with the threat to individual liberty posed by more benign, modern bureaucra-
cies. Here is an excerpt from a 1982 precedent-shattering speech delivered
before the British Parliament: "There is a threat posed to human freedom
by the enormous power of the modern state. History teaches the danger of
government that overreaches: political control takes precedence over free
economic growth; secret police, mindless bureaucracy—all combining to
stifle individual excellence and personal freedom" (Address to the British
Parliament, June 8, 1982). Perhaps this was what Reagan meant when he
proclaimed during his run for California governor, "I am not an echo, I am a
voice!" Safe to say these words were not what Britain or the rest of Europe,
already steeped in socialism, wanted to hear. But these insights into the nature
of government—based on beliefs instilled as strongly in him by his mother's
religious teaching and books like *Udell's Printer* as Lincoln's beliefs concerning social justice were instilled by childhood readings of the Bible and
Aesop's Fables—would become the epicenter of a lifelong political ideology.

The bottom dropped out of Ronald Reagan's life between 1947 and 1950.
His transformation from actor to political activist, work as union president—often tedious and sometimes ugly—and a miscarriage suffered by
his wife all contributed to her quietly filing papers for divorce. To Reagan,
who was taught and believed that marriage was forever, it was a devastating personal defeat. In addition to his career in movies hitting rock-bottom,
the stress of dealing with a factionalized union membership, McCarthy's
Senate hearings, and marathon contract negotiations with studio heads left
him psychologically drained and now without the one woman in the world
he believed he loved.

Shattered emotionally and physically spent, Reagan for the first time in his
life showed weakness, even collapse. For months after the divorce, he struggled, confiding his fears and loneliness to friends Robert Taylor and William

Holden—memories of his father, Jack, and the shame he had put their family through no doubt cascading through his mind. Was he ultimately no different from his father? Had he traveled four decades and thousands of miles to the pinnacle of fame—only to discover that he, too, was a failure?

It was during this "wilderness" period that Reagan realized he was being tested, and that he had to reinvent himself or fade into oblivion like the vast majority of actors returning to Hollywood after the war. If his worst fear was becoming his father, his hope for the future came in a pretty, young actress raised much like him who would support him with the same intensity and devotion as his mother. The woman was Nancy Davis, a newcomer to Hollywood, worried that she might be mistaken for another actress with the same name who'd been "blacklisted." Hearing about her concerns from friend Spencer Tracy, Reagan agreed to help the young actress with her problem. From out of that meeting came one of the greatest love stories of the second half of the century: Ronald Reagan and Nancy Davis were married on March 4, 1952, fifteen months after they first set eyes on each other.

After his breakup with Jane Wyman, Reagan made it a point never to share intimacies as he had with Taylor and Holden during those lonely times. As governor and while president, few, if any, of his colleagues felt that they knew him intimately, which for critics was a sign of superficiality. More likely, Reagan's reserve was a cultivated discipline that prevented what was undoubtedly a deeply feeling man from appearing to be an overly emotional one. Former Reagan cabinet member, Michael Deaver, observes, "With Reagan it was like you never got to see all of him, what he was thinking, what he was feeling . . . In that sense, he was remote, emotionally . . . friendly, charming, yes, but there was always that elusive 10% that I don't think any of us [in the administration] ever got to see."[22] Whatever reserve Reagan maintained in dealing with others after his divorce vanished when it came to Nancy. The artistic, romantic side of Reagan was in full bloom from the day they met and during their entire marriage. There is no detachment, emotional or otherwise. He held back absolutely nothing, as evidenced in one of the hundreds of love letters he wrote to her over their nearly fifty years of marriage:

July 13, 1954

My Darling,

The first day of shooting and like all first days I can't tell you good, bad, or indifferent . . . Most of the morning was spent getting the trucks unloaded and equipment straightened out . . .

However there is one golden glow warming my soul in this first sunset—I'm twenty-four hours closer to you. Last night was another one of those nights—just too beautiful to stand. So tonight I'll probably be looking at the Moon which

means I'll be looking at you—literally and figuratively because it lies far to the South of this mountain top and that's where you are. That takes care of the "literal" part—the "figurative" part requires no direction. I just see you in all the beauty there is because in you I've found all the beauty in my life.
I love you,
Ronnie[23]

The turnaround in Reagan's emotional life and his career were nearly simultaneous. In 1954 he was asked by General Electric to host a weekly anthology called *General Electric Theater*, shown at eight o'clock on Sunday nights. Hesitant at first to embrace the new media, the steady work was alluring, but even more so was the additionally responsibility of traveling to GE's 139 plants in 39 states delivering pro-American and pro-GE speeches to its more than 250,000 employees.

One can sense that in considering GE's proposal, Reagan was driven by the same calculated determination that brought him to Hollywood in the first place. One can easily imagine Reagan "connecting the dots" to see in their proposal the possibility to fulfill an unarticulated ambition that he quietly carried within his bosom and held secret from all but his mother for more than forty years. Like Udell—the fictitious hero of his favorite novel as a child—GE was offering him the chance to become a citizen-politician sent, by the people, to Washington DC.

The job as host would afford him television exposure to millions of American families each week during prime-time hours. It also gave him the opportunity to personally meet hundreds of thousands of working Americans and share with them his uniquely reasoned beliefs about the future of the country. To Reagan, a man who conscientiously believed in the power of an individual to shape his own destiny, there was just one final consideration that would position him at the starting line to undertake yet another career. In order to accept the offer he needed the freedom to broaden the topics of his speeches to issues of importance to all Americans, not just employees. After GE agreed to that provision the deal was sealed and with it the first breath in the political life of Ronald Reagan was drawn.

General Electric Theater was an instant hit. Overnight Reagan, the B movie actor, became one of the most recognizable faces in America. For eight years the show was rated among the nation's top twenty programs, but it was in his secondary role, as public speaker, that he began to change the public's perception of him. Taking full advantage of nonstop encounters with large gatherings of Americans from a large cross section of the country, he studiously elicited the concerns of working men and women. Equally important, plant visits offered him a venue to hone his craft as a speaker. What made people laugh in Georgia as opposed to California or New York? What were people's regional concerns? What common thread bound Americans together?

For Reagan, it was heartening to find that the political themes that consumed him—higher taxes, government encroachment into the private lives of citizens, the rise of Soviet power around the globe—seemed to resonate no matter where he was speaking. When standing before hundreds, and often thousands of workers, he was no longer the all-American athlete, the Hollywood movie star, the stubbornly principled union activist, or the spokesman for one of the world's leading corporations. He was Ronald Reagan, the nononsense citizen-politician convincing enthusiastic audiences that progress on these issues could only come if it was insisted on, democratically, by "We, the People." It was a political theme that he'd brandish like a fiery sword from those fledgling days as a public speaker through to his election as governor of California and on to the White House.

The clarity of Reagan's message and the deep-seated passion with which he clung to these principles is no surprise to anyone familiar with the "Reagan Revolution," but what's not commonly understood was the implacability of his nature—at once blithe in the ease with which he achieved his objectives, but at the bottom amazingly consistent and persevering. Like Washington, Reagan, even as an adolescent, believed that he was destined for greatness, and he attempted to translate every situation into a lesson in preparation for the challenge ahead. In Washington's case, from surveying expeditions in the "wilderness" to gleaning all he could absorb about the ways of "high society" from the Fairfax family, America's first president understood that in order to become the great man he envisioned he needed to use every available experience to build himself into a more capable and worthy individual.

Strikingly similar to the status-obsessed Washington and intellectually voracious Lincoln, Reagan was forever expanding his horizons, however modest his beginnings or circuitous his path. As a young man, he used his lifeguard experience to gain the idealized self-image of Dutch—athletic, strong, and heroic. Later, he took his college acting skills and football experience and parlayed them into work as a sportscaster, all the while nurturing his improbable dream to become a Hollywood movie star. When drafted into the military, he was able to translate what he had learned about moviemaking into breakthrough aviation training for American pilots. When work as an actor dried up, he had the intuitive sense to move from movies to television; as GE public speaker, he possessed the foresight to insist on the freedom to write about themes of his choosing, thus setting the stage for a political career.

Reagan's ability to take seemingly unrelated life experiences and extrapolate them into specific skill sets was so stunning that many historians attribute his effectiveness in negotiating with Gorbachev at the Reykjavik nuclear arms summit to the experience he gained settling SAG contacts with Hollywood moguls Jack Warner, Sam Goldwyn, and Louis B. Mayer forty years earlier: "Ronald Reagan learned how to negotiate from these men. He learned how to play tough and be tough, how to feint, stall, and vamp for time . . . He used the skills he learned in Hollywood in every negotiation of his presidency, including at Reykjavik."[24]

If Reagan believed that he was destined to become a great leader, and that "the presidency seeks the man," the events that he shaped and that shaped his path to the presidency played out like a textbook on the subject. By 1960, with his ideological evolution complete, he officially registered as a Republican, explaining to friend A. C. Lyles, "I didn't leave the Democratic Party, the Democratic Party left me!" And there was some truth to that, at least in the mind of Reagan and millions of others who drew a sharp distinction between FDR's "safety net" for those who needed public assistance during a time of crisis and an entrenched class of individuals who subsisted, generation to generation, on government "welfare." The divergence between the trends of those times and Reagan's homegrown conservatism couldn't have been starker, and on this score he was prescient. What had begun as JFK's forward-looking technological revolution, epitomized by NASA's moon project and the radical concept of supply-side economics to accelerate economic growth, had morphed into LBJ's raft of "War on Poverty" programs that, to Reagan, smacked of socialistic entitlement guaranteed to undermine everything JFK had tried to accomplish.

By 1962 Reagan was an unabashed economic conservative, so much so that GE felt compelled to rethink his responsibilities. Yes, they wanted him to continue hosting their successful television anthology, but his public speaking needed to be restricted to the corporation and its products. His political views were interesting, GE management explained, but not helpful to their corporate image, as he had become what some were calling a right-wing extremist. Reagan argued that his speeches had never been more enthusiastically received, memories of his father, the failed shoe salesman, no doubt dredging up the question from the backwater of his mind, have I come all this way to sell refrigerators? He refused and GE cancelled his contract.

His mother's religious instruction about "good coming from bad" couldn't have been far from Reagan's thinking when he made the decision to reject GE's directive and, soon after, an opportunity presented itself that would become a milestone in his political career. Arizona Senator Barry Goldwater's headquarters contacted him to ask if he'd become cochair of the candidate's presidential campaign. Reagan, who had read the senator's book *The Conscience of a Conservative*, immediately accepted.

Goldwater, a blunt and ineloquent man, believed in many of the same principles that Reagan did. What's more, like him, Goldwater believed that the federal government was out of step with ordinary citizens who worked hard each day but spent thirty-seven cents of each dollar they earned in taxes while watching welfare rolls swell, street crime escalate, and college campuses foment with unrest against the unpopular Vietnam War. Government, both believed, had become hopelessly bureaucratic and inefficient.

With logic unique to his innate capacity for illuminating the darkest recesses of dense political conundrums, Reagan asserted that the middle class that FDR had fought to preserve during the Great Depression had become estranged from the party that had saved them. More important, he maintained that a window of opportunity existed to create a new Republican Party made up not of Wall Street capitalists but of ordinary citizens like the ones he'd come to know during his GE days. There was, he believed, an opportunity, founded on need and principle, to—like Udell—become a "man of the people."

From the time he accepted the position as cochair of the Goldwater campaign, Reagan stopped using the labels Democratic or Republican in speeches and began describing a new political movement, neither "right wing" nor "extremist"; though it was called "conservative" by many, that movement—like Reagan himself—defied labels:

> It seems to me impossible to legitimately debate the issues of the day without being subjected to name-calling and the application of labels . . . Today we are told that we must choose between left and right or, as others suggest, a third alternative, a kind of middle ground. I suggest to you there is no left or right, only up or down . . . The New Republican Party I envision will not and cannot be limited to the country club big business image that, for reasons both fair and unfair, it is burdened with today. The New Republican Party I speak of is going to have room for every man and woman.[25]

The difference between Goldwater and Reagan was simple. Goldwater understood what being a conservative meant but could only define it by what it was not. Reagan understood what a conservative was and could articulate it in terms founded on deeply rooted American values such as freedom of choice, economic liberty, and vigilant defense of democratic principles. This oneness with the essence of what it meant to be an American was never more clearly demonstrated than in the electrifying speech he delivered at the Ambassador Hotel, where he officially endorsed the presidential hopeful—an address that later became known simply as "The Speech": "This idea that government is beholden to the people, that it has no other source of power except the sovereign people, is still the newest and most unique idea in all the long history of man's relation to man. This is the issue of this election: whether we believe in our capacity for self-government or whether we abandon the American Revolution and confess that a little intellectual elite in a far-distant capital can plan our lives for us better than we can plan ourselves" (Goldwater Endorsement Speech, October 27, 1964).

Following the Ambassador Hotel endorsement, Reagan was swarmed by ecstatic Goldwater supporters encouraging him to do the speech on television. Soon after, a group of California businessmen offered to buy thirty minutes of NBC airtime at 9:00 p.m. on the eve of the election. On October 27, 1964, with Reagan about to speak, Goldwater's headquarters phoned, telling him that they'd decided to cancel because the speech was "too incendiary." But Reagan, sensing it was the decision of Goldwater's handlers and not the candidate, refused to comply, firing back that Goldwater, himself, would have to call it off. As it turned out, Goldwater hadn't seen the text, but once he read it he contacted Reagan to "endorse it thoroughly." Finally, the speech was made.

The Reagan family went to bed that night not realizing the seismic impact his words had made on the American public. At 3:00 a.m., the switchboards at Goldwater headquarters were still lit up like a Christmas tree. Thousands of contributions poured into the candidate's coffers, and though Goldwater went down in defeat, a new political star was born—personally complex, ideologically profound, and eminently in touch with a vast cross section of the American public.

In the winter of 1964, the same businessmen who paid for his NBC airtime saw the fifty-four-year-old former actor as the best chance the Republicans had at defeating popular gubernatorial incumbent Pat Brown. Reagan, still amazed at the impact his speech had on the electorate—or at least acting that way—begged off, saying, "I'm just an actor!" But all involved knew better. Reagan, battle hardened by his Hollywood experiences, had established a resonating dialogue between himself and the American people, along with a leadership persona that was at once commanding in its sensibility and unassuming in its approach.

By the beginning of the year, Reagan agreed to crisscross the state making political speeches. Significantly, he identified himself neither as a Republican or Democrat, but simply as Ronald Reagan, the "citizen-politician." What political genius we have here. Reagan is at once audacious and modest, radical in his proposals but incredibly familiar in his manner: a conservative-revolutionary. The audacity he displays in this life-altering episode illustrates an important leadership lesson. Reagan's success can be attributed to the fact that in overcoming the challenges of his early life, he retained his optimism and creativity. At every point where his progress might have ended, he made for himself a new story line. What he saw as a real potentiality, conventional political thinkers saw as a flight of fancy. A critical element of great leadership consists of discerning the difference between the two and capitalizing on hidden opportunities unrecognized by others around you.

On January 4, 1966, Reagan announced his candidacy. Labeled an "actor mouthing words" and "extremist" by Pat Brown, the California Democratic Party saw Reagan as an easy mark. But both the governor and his party grossly underestimated their opponent. Taking a page from the book of his hero, FDR, Reagan reversed the tables, not only attracting huge crowds of Republicans at his rallies, but also California factory workers, teachers, and laborers—mostly Democrats—tired of high taxes, high crime, and the declining quality of state services.

He did this by promising what Brown and the Democrats had not delivered: competence and accountability. He would accomplish this, he vowed, by running the government like a business with the help of a new breed of public servant—professionals from the private sector who worked the job because they wanted to contribute their expertise, not because they had career ambitions. Like JFK before him, he emphasized sacrifice, telling voters that he'd set a philosophical framework, establish specific and measurable objectives within that agenda, and require that they be achieved, no different than what a top executive in a corporation would expect.

The extent of Reagan's success among ordinary citizens must have astounded the overconfident Brown, who until the last week of his campaign believed Reagan to be an "amateur" capable of attracting only a "radical fringe." When the votes were counted, however, Reagan won by sixteen percentage points and more than one million votes. More impressive was the fact that when the election results were analyzed, political pundits were shocked to discover that his support came from middle-of-the-road voters of all ethnic backgrounds, races, and economic levels, drawn from both parties. "It was," Reagan accurately stated during his inaugural address, "a rebellion of ordinary people."

On January 1, 1967, when Reagan was sworn in as governor of California, the upheaval of the 1960s was in full fury. He saw it on the street, where African Americans rioted, and on college campuses like Berkeley, where student protests had become violent and deadly. In addition to social unrest, San Francisco lawyer Caspar "Cap" Weinberger, who Reagan had put in charge of budgeting, discovered that California was in the deepest debt since the Great Depression, spending one million dollars per day more than it was taking in.

After having based much of his campaign on lowering taxes, the notion of covering the gap with a tax increase was anathema to Reagan. He immediately put a hiring freeze into effect and cut state spending by 10 percent across the board. But even these draconian measures couldn't right the imbalance because the deficits, unknown to California voters, had been accumulating for more than a year prior to his taking office. And it was then that Reagan's knowledge of history and strength of character swung into action, putting on display yet another leadership lesson.

First, like FDR, he faced the brutal facts and "took it to the people" in a televised statewide speech that outlined the crisis. Second, instead of stubbornly holding to his campaign promise, he told them that he would be forced for a period of time to raise taxes by the highest margin in California history in order to mitigate the problem but would begin reigning in the state's runaway spending immediately so that the fiscal imbalance would be corrected during the coming year.

Reagan was roundly criticized for the decision and was so upset by the predicament that by February he developed a bleeding ulcer that permanently threatened his health. Clearly, he knew that his decision would be unpopular, but he was a pragmatic leader who understood that politicians come and go but principles endure. "The challenge of leadership is to have the vision to dream of a better world," he told voters, "and the courage, persistence and patience to turn that dream into reality."[26]

And that is exactly what "Manager Reagan" did, using the challenges he faced as governor as a testing ground for his beliefs and their practical application—much as Theodore Roosevelt did as governor of New York—in order to later apply them nationally. First and foremost, he applied his belief that a smaller, less expensive government, run efficiently, could be more effective. Second, he applied "supply-side" economics, which maintained that lowing taxes stimulated investment, productivity, and consumption of goods in the private sector, thereby growing the economy and, ultimately, increasing state revenues. Third, he applied a realistic "get tough" approach to violent crime, whether in the inner-city streets of Watts or on university campuses.

A final aspect of Reagan's governorship and its application to his time as president was the much-vaunted—and highly overestimated—degree to which he delegated authority. On the subject of his management style, Reagan wrote, "I don't believe a chief executive should supervise every detail of what goes on in his organization. He should set broad policy and ground rules, tell people what he or she wants them to do, then let them do it; and make himself available so that members of the team can come to him for direction if there is a problem."[27]

Clearly, this statement, often used by critics to confirm their opinion that he was "out of touch," is a long way from subscribing to anything like what author Jim Collins calls "Level 5" leadership from forty thousand feet. Harvard presidential scholar Roger Porter, speaking in a 1986 interview with *Fortune* magazine, explains: "He does not devote large chunks of time to peripheral issues, but focuses on his major initiatives. That is one of the keys to his success . . . Reagan's predecessor, Jimmy Carter, read reams of Treasury documents on tax reform, which got nowhere . . . Reagan, on the other hand, has a high tolerance for hearing competing views argued very intensely among members of his Cabinet."[28]

Reagan was anything but detached. Rather, in keeping with his approach, both to life and elected office, his management was far more personal and discerning than simply reading internal staff memos or abrogating executive responsibility: "I use a system in which I want to hear what everybody wants to say honestly. I want the decisions made on what is right or wrong, what is good or bad for the people. I encourage all the input I can get . . . And when I've heard all that I need to hear, I make a decision, I don't take a vote. I make the decision. Then I expect every one of them, whether their views have carried the day or not, to go forward in carrying out the policy."[29]

Reagan's personal diaries, published posthumously in May 2007 as *The Reagan Diaries*, demonstrate that—especially during his first term as president—he was involved, moment to moment, not only in policy making but also in gaining support for his programs. The entries are not grandiose, but they are powerful in their cumulative effect as we witness a very engaged president wooing congressional leaders for votes, meeting with experts daily, and committing to paper not only his rationale for decisions, but also his justifications for them with references to historical context and statistical data. In fact, in addition to being a hands-on leader, he may well have possessed a photographic memory. More generally, the Reagan diaries reveal not nearly so much about his management style as about the individual himself. A man who was, as described by *Diaries* editor Douglas Brinkley, "principled, confident, happy, free of ego, and devoted to his wife . . . a man who understood instinctively that . . . leadership is not as it's described but how it's performed."[30]

In 1970 Reagan was reelected governor by a margin of 53 percent to 45 percent. By the time he left office in 1975, he had dramatically reduced the size of state government, cut taxes twice, balanced the budget, and rebated more than one hundred million dollars to the people of California. As early as January 1966, however, when he first announced his candidacy, it was obvious to anyone who understood him that his interests went far beyond Sacramento and California politics.

Fast becoming the leading Republican conservative in the country, Reagan would mount two unsuccessful presidential campaigns. One in 1968, when he was testing the waters to see if Richard Nixon would fail, and another, in 1976, when he challenged President Gerald Ford for the GOP nomination.

There is perhaps no better example in modern presidential politics of a candidate with a sense of mission—save Richard Nixon—than Ronald Reagan. In 1976, when he challenged President Ford, he lost the first five state contests in a row and, as primary day in North Carolina approached, his campaign was virtually bankrupt. Convinced that his powerful personality would split allegiances within the party and hurt Ford in the general election, Republican governors as well as eleven past chairs of the party signed a document demanding that he "get out of the race." Reagan refused. Some, at the time, called him stubborn, others a stalwart ideologue hell-bent on "making a point." Yet doggedly, and with a quiet sense of purpose set ablaze by the ignition of a childhood dream that he'd always believed could become reality, he persevered.

By the time he went into the convention, Reagan had won twenty-three primaries and was within striking distance of Ford. Once there, deeply tanned and dressed in a solid white suit, sitting in the convention center's balcony beside Nancy and other family members, Reagan didn't look like a future president so much as an American political savior. His sense of theater and ability to capture the drama of the moment was impeccable, elevating the crowd and the convention's final moments to a state of political pandemonium.

Ford desperately needed Republican unity, and after the delegates' votes were counted, allowing him to hold onto the nomination, he waved his adversary up to the podium to join him. There, like Kennedy after Kefauver beat him for the second slot on the Stevenson ticket, Reagan stole the show, solidifying his bona fides in national politics. Martin Anderson, policy adviser for the Reagan campaign in 1976, remembers:

> And what happened was when Ford was speaking, the Reagan delegates were screaming "Come down Reagan!" There was so much noise he [Ford] couldn't talk even with the microphone. So he looked up and with his arm waved Reagan down . . . So Reagan got up, buttoned his coat . . . and suddenly he was at the podium. And the entire convention was standing. Tens of millions of people were looking at him . . . and now he was beaming with confidence . . . radiant with dignity as he vowed support for the President and the party.[31]

Significantly, while Reagan put forward a message of party unity for the general election, the underpinnings of his impromptu address bolstered three of his most enduring beliefs regarding nuclear proliferation, America's need to be proactive in dealing with the Soviets, and his abiding faith in the ability of the American people to determine their destiny: "We live in a world in which the great powers have poised and aimed at each other horrible missiles of destruction, nuclear weapons that can, in a matter of minutes, arrive in each others' country and destroy virtually the civilized world that we live in . . . [But] the campaign trail is no place for the cynic . . . I am more than ever convinced of the greatness of our people and their capacity to determine their own destiny."[32]

Afterward, despite his popularity, at the age of sixty-five and with Carter—the winner of the general election—as president for at least four years, most political analysts assumed he wasn't going to run for president a third time. But Reagan was not a man who parceled logic and circumstances into neat packages. Rather, like Theodore Roosevelt, he was a man of large ideas that dwarfed common speculation and arithmetic rationale. Clearly, he knew he'd run again but shared his ambitions with no one, methodically giving eight to ten speeches a month, editing a newspaper column twice a week, and writing commentary for radio each day.

What even Reagan could not fully comprehend at the time was the level of decline that the U.S. economy, geopolitical situation, and morale would experience during the next four years. By 1980, when Reagan launched his campaign, the country was demoralized and in crisis. Americans were coping with gas lines, rampant inflation, and their fellow citizens held hostage in Iran. Compared to Carter, and his rival candidates for the nomination, Reagan's strength and optimism was a stark counterpoint.

On his road to the White House, Reagan would prove to be unstoppable. This was no Johnny-come-lately to the political arena, but a man of full measure who possessed a uniquely American blend of humor, insight, strength, flexibility, and confidence. The reason for this harkened back to what is the most salient of our lessons in leadership: *Ronald Reagan lived his life.* He welcomed challenge. He learned from his failures. He adhered to a clear set of principles that he lived each day. His leadership was character-driven.

As his rival for the nomination, George H. W. Bush, discovered during a New Hampshire debate when the sound engineer turned off his microphone, Reagan acted like a president before he became one. "I'm paying for this microphone!" he roared, stealing the moment and the nomination from Bush. During the presidential debates Jimmy Carter learned the same bitter lesson. "Are you better off now than you were four years ago?" Reagan asked Americans, and they responded by carrying him to a landslide victory, beating Carter by eight million votes out of the eighty million cast for both men.

For those who, even today, consider Reagan "superficial" or "not serious," his inaugural address demonstrates that like an iceberg with seven-eighths of its bulk beneath the surface, the weight of his ideological beliefs, though not always visible, was most assuredly there. America was in crisis, and like Washington, Teddy Roosevelt, and FDR before him, Reagan was determined to aggressively act with programs to help:

> It is no coincidence that our present troubles run parallel to the insinuation and intrusion into our lives that result from unnecessary and excessive government.

It is time for us to realize that we're too great a nation for us to limit ourselves to small dreams. We're not, as some would have us believe, doomed to an inevitable decline. I do not believe in a fate that will fall on us no matter what we do. I do believe in a fate that will fall on us if we do nothing. So, with all the creative energy at our command, let us begin an era of national renewal. Let us renew our determination, our courage, and our strength. And let us renew our faith and our hope. (Inaugural Address, January 20, 1981)

The day he walked into office, every aspect of Reagan's ideas, management philosophy, and character was tested by the quagmire he inherited. On the economic front, the budget deficit was eighty billion dollars and growing, with interest rates at 21 percent and inflation at an astounding 17 percent. Internationally, an emboldened Soviet Union was spending 50 percent more a year than the United States on weapons while running roughshod over the globe with military adventures in South America, the Middle East, and Africa.

To Reagan, the dilemma was clear. In order to affect the economy he needed to cut taxes, along with nonessential government programs, and put money in the hands of those that could stimulate the private sector. In order to stem the tide of Soviet aggression, which he believed would ultimately lead to nuclear confrontation, he needed to engage in a military buildup that the United States could ill afford. His choice was both creative and character-driven. Though he could have cut taxes and slashed military expenditures to stimulate the economy without deficits, he put his own credibility at risk by aggressively pursuing tax cuts while engaging in the largest military buildup in U.S. history. The short-term result, he understood, would be record deficits that would appear contradictory to the balanced-budget agenda he'd campaigned on; like FDR, however, he believed Americans would understand his decision and rally around him once it was explained. On this score, Reagan was both right and wrong.

On the night of February 18, the new president unveiled his economic program to Congress, proposing cuts to eighty-three major programs, a 30 percent tax decrease to all Americans, and an unprecedented increase in military spending: "We're in control here. There's nothing wrong with America that together we can't fix. The taxing power of government must be used to provide revenues for legitimate government purposes. It must not be used to regulate the economy or bring about social change. We've tried that and we must be able to see it doesn't work."[33]

The media reaction to Reagan's initiatives was slow to gather. Though most analysts were impressed by his speech, and a *Washington Post*/ABC News poll showed that two-thirds of the electorate agreed with him, it was the *New York Times* that picked up on the revolutionary nature of Reagan's programs in their front-page headline the next day. "TRYING TO REPEAL KEYNES," it read. "President's Plan Considered as Revolutionary as Those Espoused by the New Deal in the '30s."

The *Times* chief economic correspondent, Leonard Silk, offered a detailed explanation in the analysis that followed:

> He is urging tighter eligibility rules and reduced spending in food stamps, student loans, welfare, free school lunches, aid to the arts, humanities, sciences, public-service jobs, and much else . . . But in economic terms, something even much larger is afoot. The most remarkable aspect of Mr. Reagan's program is his effort to repeal the so-called Keynesian revolution . . . The Keynesian doctrine sough economic growth and stable prices through the manipulation of Government budgets . . . In crisp contrast, President Reagan has declared new guidelines for public policy that stress stimulating not demand but production and supply, mainly by lowering business taxes, while relying on other measures—budget cuts and tight money—to rein in inflation. And, more fundamental, the President's overriding purpose is to bring about a permanent shrinkage of Government's place in the American economy.[34]

It took a week for the magnitude of what Reagan was proposing to settle in, but once it did, key members of the Democratic Party, along with voters from both parties affected by the spending cuts, became outraged.

While Reagan put forward his economic agenda to Congress, he was equally aggressive in putting into action his strategy regarding the Soviet Union. During a meeting with Richard V. Allen, his first national security adviser, Reagan began their discussion of the cold war by saying, "My idea of American policy toward the Soviet Union is simple, and some would say simplistic. It is this: 'we win and they lose.' Now, how would we go about achieving that?"[35]

At his first news conference as president in January 1981, Reagan denounced the Soviet leadership still dedicated to "world revolution and a one-world Socialist-Communist state." In May the following year, he again talked about communism at a commencement address at his alma mater, Eureka College, this time offering an insight into the U.S. assessment and strategy that would eventually lead to its demise. "The Soviet Union is faltering," he declared, "because rigid centralized control has destroyed incentives for innovation, efficiency and individual achievement . . . The Soviet dictatorship has forged the largest armed force in the world . . . but this military buildup combined with the preemption of the human needs of the Soviet people," he predicted, "will undermine the foundations of their system" (Eureka College Graduation Address, May 9, 1982).

Almost immediately, the Reagan administration, in addition to its revolutionary economic policies, began pursuing a multifaceted foreign policy offensive that included covert support for pro-democracy groups in South America, Afghanistan, Africa, and Poland; a global campaign to reduce Soviet access to Western technology; and a drive to further squeeze the Soviet economy by driving down the price of oil and limited natural gas exports to the West. "We adopted a comprehensive strategy," Secretary of Defense Caspar Weinberger would later recall, "that included public as well as private diplomacy including new media outlets like Radio Marti, TV Marti, aimed at Cuba, and WorldNet, Radio Free Europe, and Voice of America, aimed at Eastern Europe and Latin America."[36]

Yet in all of these initiatives—both in economic and foreign policy— Ronald Reagan the idealist was always in the company of Ronald Reagan the pragmatist. While his rhetoric was often blunt and purposefully dramatic, a more studied observer would see in his leadership style a constantly recalculated balance between the two that demonstrated his understanding that the kind of goals he sought to achieve would only be realized gradually, year by year.

With regard to the economic program he presented to Congress and later compromised on, he told a senior adviser, "I've never understood people who want me to hang in there for 100% or nothing. Why not take 70% or 80%, and then come back another day for the other 20% or 30%?" So he did, again and again, on defense, taxes, budget cuts, and most of his major initiatives. Warren Bennis, professor at the University of Southern California's Marshall School of Business, observes, "Reagan was a master of compromise. Like Abraham Lincoln, he temporized, but never lost sight of his vision."[37]

Similarly, while no modern president played hardball more convincingly than Reagan, there was within him an overwhelming need to personally engage world leaders in diplomacy in an effort to foster nation-to-nation harmony and thereby world peace. While Reagan's reputation among many is as a military "hawk," he was in reality both conciliatory and ambitious in his approach to arms negotiations. Reagan scholar Professor Kiron Skinner, who has been studying his handwritten documents from the late 1970s, observes: "This is Reagan's draft of a speech he gave in 1979 criticizing the Strategic Arms Limitations Treaty [SALT], he opposed the treaty because he felt it did not address the real problem . . . What is really significant about it is that it shows he was not a war monger, that he want arms 'reductions,' not arms 'control,' the way it was being presented in the SALT II treaty. He wanted real reduction, and that's what he's saying here."[38] Interestingly, more than "control" of nuclear weapons, Reagan wanted "reductions" leading to obsolescence, even as demonstrators throughout the world protested against the military buildup he had called for in an effort to move the Soviets toward that goal.

The Reagan presidency was launched, but it nearly came to the end with the crackling reports of gunfire from a pistol held by John Hinckley Jr. on the afternoon of March 30, 1981. The president had just finished a speech to AFL-CIO representatives at the Washington Hilton Hotel. As he was leaving the building, just two miles from the White House, Hinckley opened fire, critically wounding him and James Brady, his press secretary. In the immediate aftermath and the weeks that ensued, the president demonstrated the meaning of the word *hero* while guaranteeing overwhelming public support for the pending legislation he'd submitted to Congress.

Former Reagan cabinet member Michael Deaver remembers that fateful afternoon and Reagan's composure after having been shot:

> I will never forget Reagan when he arrived at GW hospital not having been able to talk in the limousine . . . to find out if he'd been hit . . . The door opens and he gets out of the car, pulls up his pants like a cowboy in a western movie, buttons his jacket, and then walks into the hospital . . . and then he hit the doorframe and the minute he hit the door, he went down, but you talk about the movies . . . to him that door was the curtain and once he got past the curtain, he was no longer on stage.[39]

Thirty minutes after Reagan entered the hospital's emergency room, he was fighting for his life. The wound was a unique and dangerous one because the bullet that hit him had first struck a car and traveled along the side of it, distorting its shape so that it resembled something like a jagged dime. The result was more like a knife wound that sealed, leaving no hole but causing serious internal bleeding that initially went undetected.

Nancy Reagan will never forget that day and the terror and confusion that followed:

> I'm running into the hospital and Mike Deaver was waiting outside and he said "the president was hit." And they put me in a little room and all I wanted was to see Ronnie and they kept saying "he's all right but you can't see him just yet." And I said "if he's all right, why can't I see him?" Then when I finally saw him he had that mask over his face and he was absolutely white. I'd never seen anything like that and he pushed it up and whispered, "Honey, I forgot to duck." I put the mask back down and I said, "I love you."[40]

Immediately after surgery to remove the bullet, which had entered under his left armpit and lodged dangerously near his lung, the president was pronounced to be in "good condition" by the doctors who performed the surgery. But his condition soon took a frightening turn for the worse when he contracted a bacterial infection, that put him back on the tenterhooks of a life-and-death situation.

Only those who were closest to him understood how tenuous his condition had become. One of those was the Reverend Dan Moonmaw, the family's minister and Reagan's spiritual adviser, who rushed to the president's bedside upon hearing the news: "I asked him if he was ready to meet God and he said, 'No, I've got so much I want to do for the United States and the people of the world.' And I said, 'No, that's not what I mean. I mean, if the bullet would have taken you, or if you're current condition takes you and you die, are you ready to meet God?' And then he said, 'Yes.' 'How do you know?' I asked. 'I'm ready to meet God because I have a Savior,' he answered."[41]

As much an account of the spiritual faith that Reagan had kept since early childhood, Moonmaw's encounter highlights Reagan's enduring belief that he was a man of destiny and would be spared because he was meant to accomplish deeds important to the world. "I think there's a reason I've been saved," he later told his daughter, Patti; while still in the hospital recovering, he wrote a personal letter—over the objections of Secretary of State Alexander Haig—to Soviet leader Leonid Brezhnev requesting a dialogue to try to find a way for lasting peace between the two superpowers.

Less than one month after he was shot, Ronald Reagan plunged back into the thick of the fray in Washington over his pending economic proposals as he addressed a joint session of Congress. That night he was given a hero's welcome, and after hearing the thunderous standing ovation, he quipped, "You wouldn't want to talk me into an encore, would you, Mr. Speaker?" Then, with a mixture of persuasion, charm, and wit, he proceeded to make the case for his economic package before Congress and tens of millions of Americans watching his speech on television: "These policies will make our economy stronger . . . and with your help and your Congressman's vote, we'll make it happen" (Address on the Program for Economic Recovery, April 28, 1981). Reagan, like Teddy Roosevelt, used the bully pulpit that night and all through the legislative process to push his proposals through Congress. Even as he was recovering, his diaries reflect the moment-to-moment management he exercised on the phone and in face-to-face meetings with senators and congressmen from both parties, doing his best to convince them that his legislation was correct and necessary.

In the end, he didn't get everything he wanted. The tax cut he eventually signed was for 25 percent, not 30 percent, and though that victory paved the way for other successes, economic recovery was not around the corner. Over the next twelve months, the unemployment rate rose to more than 10 percent, the recession deepened, and his approval rating dropped to 35 percent, the lowest of his presidency. His political opponents were scathing in their criticism. Protests among everyday citizens spread across the country, and even David Stockman, his closest economic adviser, publicly questioned the validity of his programs.

But Reagan stayed the course, never losing faith—in the tradition of FDR, he stood tall through the adversity. After two torturous years, the economy finally turned. Reagan's economic policies—based on tax cuts (supply-side economics), tighter currency supply (sound money), less bureaucracy (deregulation), and emphasis on open markets (free trade)—suddenly appeared magical to many. The inflation rate plunged to single digits for the first time in six years, interest rates dropped to record lows, and the stock market began soaring; before it was over, "Reaganomics," formerly labeled "voodoo" economics by George H. W. Bush, was credited with helping to create the most enduring wave of economic prosperity in U.S. history.

In his interview with *Fortune* magazine, "Manager Reagan" explained the success of his administration, shunning Jack Welch's ego-driven model for a sound and pragmatic character-driven one: "Maybe part of it [my success] is dictated to me by a little plaque on my desk that says there's no limit to what you can do if you don't mind who gets the credit."[42]

By 1984, when Reagan ran for reelection, Americans enjoying the fruits of Reaganomics rallied around their triumphant president. During their second debate in Kansas City, when Democratic challenger Walter Mondale implied that at seventy-two he was too old to lead, Reagan again used humor to leave his opponent gasping for breath: "I want you to know that I also will not make age an issue in this campaign," he fired back. "I am not going to exploit, for political purposes, my opponent's youth and inexperience." Mondale afterward laughed as hard as anyone in the audience, but the president had won the moment and the debate. On November 6, after gaining the endorsements from 218 major newspapers versus just 69 for Mondale, Reagan was reelected in one of the greatest landslides in American history, carrying forty-nine states and winning the popular vote 54,455,472 to 37,577,352. It was a victory later described by historian Thomas Cavanaugh as one of the two most important of the twentieth century, the other being the election of Franklin D. Roosevelt.

Despite his stunning successes and overwhelming popularity, there was something subtle but pervasive creeping into Reagan's life and management of the office that Mondale and others close to him may have begun observing: a growing distance between himself, his vision for the country, and the accountability of his staff. Former Canadian prime minister Brian Mulroney remembers meeting with Reagan after his reelection and discussing his leadership style: "He said: "Brian, I have good people. I put them in place and I tell them to enact my programs . . . I then give them carte blanche to do their thing. I'm not interested in details, on how they get from point A to point B. I want them to get to point B.""[43]

But there had been significant changes in Reagan's staff. At that point, James Baker, Ed Meese, and Michael Deaver, all longtime confidants from his days as California governor, had left for jobs in the private sector. Those closest to him afterward, like White House Chief of Staff Donald Regan, may have understood what he wanted but not his vulnerabilities. Reagan's later diary entries as president reflect his distancing from facts and statistics in favor or anecdotes and truisms. His intentions are as clear and forceful as ever, but evidence of his hands-on involvement become rarer by the month, suggesting that he'd begun the treacherous practice of "managing from forty thousand feet." It was this change, along with his personal passion for coming to the aid of a group of Americans whose lives were at risk overseas, that sucked him and his administration into the maelstrom of Middle Eastern violence and the greatest political crisis of his presidency, the Iran-Contra affair.

The president had told Americans that he would never negotiate with terrorists, but when the prospect of gaining freedom for hostages by trading arms with intermediaries was proposed to him, he made the decision to do it. Compounding the problem was the fact that the arms-for-hostage scenario was being carried out by White House staffers unknown to him, military and intelligence operatives whose actions far exceeded the program Reagan had approved. Not only were arms shipments being traded for the hostages' release, but the profits were being channeled to Nicaragua's anticommunist rebels, the Contras, in violation of a congressional ban. By December 1986, after repeated denials, it was clear to most that the administration had been caught breaking the law.

Reagan—the master politician, visionary, and unabashed American patriot—had been stung by exactly the type of "delegation" style that he'd vaunted to Mulroney. Ken Duberstein, Reagan's deputy chief of staff at the time, explains how his boss fell victim to the crisis: "It was a very tough time but we [his immediate staff] became convinced that Reagan, perhaps by benign neglect, had let others run away with the store . . . Was this a case where delegation and trust worked to his detriment? Yes, absolutely, it was."[44]

Perhaps of all the episodes in each of the presidencies we have studied, Reagan and the Iran-Contra scandal is the best case for one of the key tenets of the *Presidential Lessons in Leadership* philosophy of engaged management. His greatest successes came as a result of hands-on leadership during his first term in office, when he was consummately involved in the details of his legislation, those responsible for voting it through Congress, and its daily progress toward becoming law. During his second term, as personal engagement gave way to hands-off delegation with little awareness of details surrounding his decisions or the individuals responsible for their execution, he paid the price for attempting to lead from "forty thousand feet."

Reagan eventually accepted responsibility for Iran-Contra, offering his explanation and heartfelt contrition: "I did not trade arms for hostages. My heart and my best intentions still tell me that's true, but the facts and the evidence tell me it's not" (Address to the Nation on the Iran-Contra Controversy, November 2, 1986). Americans forgave him, but the scandal took a political toll unlike anything he'd ever experienced. What not even those closest to him could contemplate, however, was that Reagan's greatest success and presidential legacy lay just a few months away—a lasting nuclear weapons agreement and the ushering in of the destruction of Soviet communism and the "Evil Empire" that had sustained it for nearly seventy years.

As historians like Professor Kiron Skinner now point out, despite his rhetoric and the firm actions that backed it up, Reagan the idealist longed for conciliation with the Soviets and an end to the threat of nuclear war. At the same time Reagan the pragmatist understood that any perceived weakness shown by the United States would be counterproductive and that meaningful negotiations could only occur once the Soviet leadership respected U.S. military strength and resolve.

Reagan shared his view on U.S.-Soviet relations with journalist Marshall Loeb shortly after meeting Mikhail Gorbachev for the first time: "I came to office believing that in years past there had been a lack of realism in our approach to the Soviet Union. We were seeing them in a mirror image, thinking that if we'd smile and were kind and generous, they'd smile and be kind and generous . . . [Gorbachev] is the first Russian leader who has ever proposed eliminating weapons they already have. Now that's a great milestone. That says something about their economic problems. I think we can do business with him, but it's going to be on that realistic note."[45]

No fuzziness of ideology here; no equivocation, no hesitation. This was Reagan at his finest, totally absorbed, speaking with utter confidence on the most important topic of his generation—tethering, if not destroying, the totalitarian beast that, as he saw it, "stole a man's dreams." Moreover, after the rise to power and demise of three consecutive Soviet heads of state—Brezhnev, Andropov, and Chernenko—he saw the possibility, unimagined by others, of helping to secure world peace for generations to come.

There is a story about Reagan that tells us much about his innermost feelings about the Soviet Union and nuclear arms control. In July 1979 he fulfilled a lifelong ambition by touring NORAD (North American Aerospace Defense Command), the nerve center of U.S. nuclear weapons defense, set deep in the Cheyenne Mountains near Colorado Springs. Afterward, Reagan asked four-star General James Hill two thoughtful questions: "What if the Soviets launched a missile directly at this center?" "They'd blow us away," Hill answered. "What if that happened to one or several of our major cities?" "We'd have fifteen minutes to evacuate the populations," the general admitted. It was that exchange that set Reagan thinking about a way to protect the 150 million Americans that General Hill predicted would be lost—*if the United States won the war.*

He was left disquieted by that visit and the long-standing nuclear weapons strategy of the United States called MAD—mutually assured destruction. For him, "there had to be a better way." The better way, he decided, was SDI—Strategic Defense Initiative—a breakthrough idea in that for the first time Americans were looking at the other side of the nuclear equation: not how do we attack? but how can we defend?

The reaction that President Reagan received when he proposed SDI to cabinet members was at best mixed. Many military experts scoffed at the idea; many scientists, though intrigued, were skeptical of its chances for success; political adversaries labeled it a "fool's errand." Reagan, on the other hand, who in his life had seen the dawning of rocketry, the perfection of radar technologies, and a U.S. space initiative that landed a man on the moon, remained optimistic. "History," he argued, "suggests that it is possible."

The president had expected a skeptical response to his proposal. After all, SDI was a game-changing innovation that threatened to revolutionize the rules of the cold war and funding for conventional armies and weapons along with it. Reagan understood the dynamics of government, so he knew that his idea was bound to raise the hackles of defense and political bureaucrats. What he could not have anticipated was the nearly hysterical response of the Soviets.

From his first days in office Reagan had been an outspoken critic of the communists in the Kremlin. "The only morality they recognize is what will further their cause," he declared in a speech just twenty-eight days into his term, "meaning they reserve the right to commit any crime, to lie, to cheat, in order to attain their goals" (Address to the Nation on Strategic Arms Reduction, February 18, 1981). It's no wonder that when Gorbachev, the young and sophisticated Soviet general secretary, first met Reagan during their historic nuclear weapons summit in Geneva on November 1985, he viewed his as a "dinosaur." Reagan was twenty-one years older than Gorbachev, but on the chilling winter morning when they were introduced he came off as anything but prehistoric, bounding from out of the Fleur d'Eau chateau like an athlete to greet him, wearing just a black, tailored suit while the stout Russian appeared out-of-date and stodgy smothered in a heavy overcoat, fedora, and muffler.

Many observers believed that Reagan's robust appearance alone won the day as photographers snapped photos and cameras recorded footage for news programs broadcast to an expectant worldwide audience that night. The real triumph of Geneva, however, wasn't Reagan's bigger-than-life persona, but the give-and-take discussions that went on inside the twenty-one-room chateau.

No doubt Reagan and Gorbachev each had an early opinion of the other drawn from State Department and Politburo experts; in fact, there was already history between them. The Soviets, incensed by rumors of SDI, had put a stock of SS-20 nuclear missiles in Warsaw Pact countries aimed directly at U.S. allies in Western Europe. Reagan, who had seen the ineffectiveness of Nixon's détente and Carter's wheat embargoes, went nose to nose with the Soviets, vowing that if the missiles weren't removed he would, with NATO backing, send American Pershing II and cruise missiles to Western Europe and aim them at Moscow. Despite the fact that the Soviets had during the late 1970s and early 1980s engaged in the biggest military buildup in history, the world's response against the president was explosive. Reagan was branded a "warmonger" and demonstrations broke out across the United States and Europe. The Soviets walked out of the nuclear weapons talks going on at the time—and Reagan let them.

Still, in the end, his stand prevailed and the Soviets returned to the bargaining table, signaling something that Reagan had always believed about them: they responded to strength. And that's precisely what intrigued him about their vociferous response to SDI; the reason Star Wars threatened them so profoundly, he surmised, was because their true claim to superpower status came not from an economy the world envied (it was falling apart) or a political system the world wanted to emulate (people wanted freedom), but from their nuclear arsenal. Fear was the poker chip that the Soviet Union had bargained with for decades, but if SDI actually worked, their leverage went away and they'd be exposed for what Reagan believed they were: a failed political, economic, and social system bound for the "ash heap" of history.

It surprised no one to learn that behind closed doors in Geneva, the two engaged in a spirited debate about the two political systems, expansionism, human rights, and economic policies before the topic inevitably turned to SDI. "It is an offensive weapon system meant to give America a first strike capability against the Soviet Union," Gorbachev insisted. "No, it is the means of moving to the total abolition of nuclear weapons," Reagan argued, adding, "and I have to tell you that if it's an arms race, you must know it's one you can't win because we're not going to allow you to maintain this superiority over us."[46]

Yet, despite their differences, one essential element of their meeting was that they wanted not just to end the proliferation of nuclear weapons, but also to actually reduce their number. As important, Reagan and Gorbachev liked and respected each other almost immediately. "What a unique position we are in," Reagan told him at the conclusion of their discussions. "Here we are two men born in obscure rural hamlets in the middle of our respective countries, each of us from humble beginnings. And now we are the leaders of our countries, and now together we can forestall a World War III, and don't we owe this to mankind?"[47] Gorbachev, as clever and theatrical as the old master himself, agreed, nodding with a twinkle in his eye. The two would meet again, it was decided, and in the interim they would exchange letters and ideas about how they could work out the differences between them.

The correspondence began almost immediately. Gorbachev worried that as technological advances on SDI began to take shape, its mission would morph from a defensive to an offensive one, setting off an arms race in outer space. Reagan, intent on keeping the dialogue open, explained, "I can understand that there are matters that cannot be taken on faith"; therefore, he offered to "share with the Soviet Union and the world" the Star Wars technology. "I am sure that you personally could not have any such intentions [to use SDI offensively]," the secretary general assured him, "but intentions are only intentions." Eventually, Reagan proposed a joint Soviet-U.S. SDI meeting where scientists could identify areas of the program that might be threatening in order to prevent the development of questionable technologies, but nothing he did seemed to work.

In January 1986 the strength of their relationship was tested when Gorbachev made public a letter he'd written to Reagan before the president had received it, which carried a startling proposal: the Soviet Union would consider a reduction of intermediate nuclear weapons in Europe, a moratorium on nuclear testing, and the elimination all nuclear weapons by the end of the century . . . all of this for just one concession . . . *the United States would stop the development, testing, and deployment of SDI.*

Understanding that Gorbachev's public letter was done to create international pressure for him to cave on Star Wars, Reagan didn't chafe at his friend's proposal, but answered with an offer of his own: the United States proposed a reduction in long-range nuclear weapons (where the Soviets had an overwhelming edge) along with intermediates, proposed a reduction of all non-nuclear forces in Europe (where the Soviets also had an enormous advantage), and publicly challenged them *to participate in the development of SDI, which remained the most promising means to eliminate the threat of nuclear war.*

With the current proposals for broad-based weapons cuts of astonishing proportions, Reagan recognized that he was witnessing a cold war thawing unprecedented during the past three decades. He also believed that he understood Gorbachev's motives: the Soviet economy was cratering. They couldn't afford to begin a costly new arms race in space or anywhere else. This was the moment, he knew, of maximum opportunity. He'd seen windows like this open before—narrow and sometimes for only a matter of moments—during SAG negotiations with movie moguls, where he learned to stand firm and hold out for exactly what he wanted. This was the situation he faced now with the Soviet Union, he believed, understanding that the bargaining chip that had taken him this far was SDI.

The harbingers for possible reconciliation were abounding when, in mid-September 1986, it was announced that a second meeting on nuclear arms would be held in Reykjavik, Iceland. Unknown to most was the precarious precipice on which their meeting rested. Just two weeks before, an American reporter named Nicholas Daniloff had been seized by the KGB and imprisoned. When Reagan checked into the man's status, he was assured that the newsman had no CIA affiliations and that the KGB had made the move in retaliation for the arrest of Gennadi Zakharov, a Soviet spy working in the United States. Immediately following the incident, the Soviets demanded a swap: Daniloff, the reporter, for Zakharov, the spy. Reagan, infuriated by their chutzpah and convinced that the timing was an attempt to strong-arm him into the swap, flatly refused and threatened to expel from the United States the contingent of known KGB agents working at the United Nations if Daniloff was not released. Later that month, when the Soviets refused to release him, and as the summit at Reykjavik neared, Reagan delivered his final ultimatum. Unless Daniloff was released he would not attend the meeting. Then, unbelievably, just days before Reagan and Gorbachev were scheduled to board jets for their historic encounter, the Soviets conceded, and without fanfare Daniloff quietly walked from out of his Moscow prison cell.

The two world leaders met on October 11, 1986, at a waterfront home facing the Atlantic. Three agendas dominated the early going. The first was Reagan's and it resembled a basketball full-court press related to human rights, Soviet expansionism in Latin America, and their ongoing invasion of Afghanistan. The second was Gorbachev's and it was no less intensive, focusing almost exclusively on what he called America's "testing and deployment of space-station weapons"—in other words, SDI. But it was the third agenda that both came prepared to address, nuclear disarmament, and on that long cold winter day the advances they made were nothing short of breathtaking.

Throughout the meetings Reagan and Gorbachev agreed on a list of spectacular reductions and eliminations of entire classes of nuclear weapons. Reagan proposed a "zero-zero" option to eliminate nuclear missiles in Europe; Gorbachev agreed. Gorbachev proposed the elimination of all ballistic missiles by 1996; Reagan agreed. When they began discussing the remaining threat of alternate delivery systems, such as bombers, both men conceded that these, too, should be reduced and eliminated. What about tactical battlefield nuclear devices needed to protect Western Europe because of the ten-to-one superiority of Soviet conventional forces in the East? Reagan asked, stunned to hear Gorbachev vow a sweeping cut in Warsaw Pact armies to facilitate their elimination once parity was achieved.

To the president, this must have seemed something like a dream. Here was a man who had—like most of his oversized ambitions—kept to himself the overriding ambition of his life, which was to remove the specter of nuclear war from the world. Now not only had he moved SALT (Strategic Arms Limitation Treaties) to START (Strategic Arms Reduction Treaties), but in two thrilling days had, along with Mikhail Gorbachev, taken that significant accomplishment to an entirely new level: the total elimination, by the end of the century, of nuclear weapons and the missile delivery systems that could unleash their devastation. Heart swelling with the understanding that something genuinely momentous in the history of humankind was about to take place, Reagan's spirits were rising when Gorbachev sat back in his chair, smiled wanly, and said, "Of course all of this is contingent on you giving up SDI."

The president couldn't believe what he was hearing. Midway through their first day of discussions he'd proposed side-by-side development of the initiative without a word of protest from the Soviet secretary general. So, again, he sought to explain his motives for going ahead with his "defensive shield." Why not conduct the reductions and eliminations parallel with the joint creation of SDI. The time frames they had discussed, even if faithfully executed, couldn't be accomplished for ten to fifteen years. What if some madman, renegade nation, or terrorist group gained control of these weapons or if through some miscalculation they were mistakenly launched? the president argued, realizing after looking into Gorbachev's smiling face that this had been his strategy all along. Lure him with promises, issue optimistic statements to their staff and the media, and count on his fear of losing face to get him to concede the single issue that Gorbachev really wanted—a halt to the development of the Star Wars defense system.

In that instant of realization Reagan sat back, pursed his lips, and nodded slowly. "This meeting is ended," he told Gorbachev and walked out of the room. Later that day, when Reagan stood before flashing cameras and an anxious media, with the secretary general at his side, Gorbachev acted mystified. "What more could I have done?" he asked, obviously shaken. "You could have said 'yes,' Mr. Secretary General," the President angrily retorted before getting into his waiting limousine; indeed, the summit was over.[48]

Reagan's October 12 diary entry recounts the emotions he felt on that final day of the summit:

[On the] final day . . . our team had given us an agreement to eliminate entirely all nuc. devises over a 10 yr. period. We would research & develop SDI during 10 yrs. then deploy & I offered to share with Soviets the system. Then began the showdown. He wanted language that would have killed SDI. The price was high but I wouldn't sell & that's how the day ended . . . I was mad—he tried to act jovial but I acted mad & it showed . . . The ball was in his court and I'm convinced he'll come around when he sees how the world is reacting.[49]

Like most adversaries who sought to confront Ronald Reagan, Gorbachev had misread him. Gorbachev saw an actor and concluded that Reagan was vain, but he was not. To Reagan, accepting a failed meeting and public ridicule would always be the choice over feigned success and public adulation. Gorbachev saw a seventy-five-year-old man and believed he would be physically weak and mentally compliant, but Reagan was neither. The president's stamina was at least equal to his opponent's; his mind, if not as quick, was easily as discerning. Finally, Gorbachev saw a politician who used SDI as a bargaining chip that would be tossed aside once the pot grew large enough to make it worth his while. But again, the Soviet leader misapprehended the most salient element of Reagan, who was not a politician but a character-driven leader idealistic enough to believe that SDI could be America's "gift to the world"—or a means at least to remove for a time humankind's ability to destroy itself.

Reagan predicted that the Soviets would return to the bargaining table—and he was right, but the eight months between Reykjavik and June 12, 1987, when he stood beside the Berlin wall to make his "Mr. Gorbachev, tear down this wall!" speech was one of the chilliest periods of the cold war. Domestically, there seemed little he could do to please liberals, who felt that he should have capitulated on SDI; and right-wing conservatives, who believed that he had gone soft on the Soviets and had already given away far too much in negotiations.

For anyone who believed that the president had lost his fiery disdain for communist totalitarianism, or his ability to pressure an opponent with political savvy and a sense of high drama, Reagan may as well have been speaking to Gorbachev eyeball to eyeball when he angrily castigated the Soviet system of repression as symbolized by the Berlin wall: "We welcome change and openness, for we believe that freedom and security go together; that the advance of human liberty can only strengthen the cause of world peace. This is one sign the Soviets can make that would be unmistakable, that would advance dramatically the cause of freedom and peace. General Secretary Gorbachev, if you seek peace, if you seek prosperity for the Soviet Union and Eastern Europe, if you seek liberalization: Come here to the gate! Mr. Gorbachev, open this gate! Mr. Gorbachev, tear down this wall!" (Address at the Brandenburg Gate, June 12, 1987).

Perhaps this was the moment that Ronald Reagan had been born to live, the "rendezvous with destiny" he so often wrote about, or perhaps it only appeared that way to the 110,000 cheering people there that day and the hundreds of millions who would later experience it through radio and television. Whatever the case, the distinction meant nothing to the historical momentum that his impassioned plea catalyzed, because four months later Gorbachev asked for another summit. This one took place in Washington DC on December 7, 1987, and was followed by another held at the Spaso House in Moscow on May 29, 1988.

The following excerpts from Reagan's diary running from the period after the Moscow meeting to his final entry on January 20, 1989, capture the whirlwind set of achievements that swept through the globe and changed the world forever:

May–June 1988
2nd meeting with the Gen. Sec. Touched on other subjects—congratulated him for his courage in leaving Afghanistan. Then tried to show him how some of these things we're urging on him would actually help bring about his perestroika. There is no question in my mind but that a certain chemistry exists between us.

On to the 4th plenary meeting with Gorbachev . . . Then on to the signing of the [U.S. Senate] I.N.F. treaty ratification . . . What can I say except, "Thank the Lord."

Just informed Soviet support for Sandinistas had dropped by 60%.

September–November 1988
NSC Report came in about a Soviet proposal. They want a free standing agreement—an exchange of letters while we continue negotiating on START.

In keeping with I.N.F. treaty we've notified U.S.S.R. we'll be taking space photos of missiles in its garage. They are to open the doors so we can see it's not an SS 20 treaty lets us do this 6 times a year.

December 1988–January 1989
Trade deficit figures . . . We have highest level of exports in history & the deficit is lowest it's been in years.

NSC Report Soviets have stopped jamming radio broadcasts such as Radio Liberty & and all the others. They have also announced they are releasing 120 pol. prisoners.

We have information that Gorbachev will tell the UN he is reducing his military unilaterally . . . In it he declared he want mil. reduced by 500,000 men, 10,000 tanks, 8000 artillery pieces & 800 front line planes.

Good news, budget report I'm getting this afternoon will be showing a surplus by 1993.

NSC Report 450 Cubans are now leaving Angola. Soviets are stepping up their withdrawal from Afghanistan . . . Geo. B & I met Gorby . . . I think our meeting was a tremendous success. He sounded as if he saw us as partners making a better world.[50]

By the time he left the White House on January 20, 1989, every one of the crystal clear objectives he'd set for himself and his administration were either realized or on their way to being accomplished. The economy was turned around and growing at historic levels, Soviet support of the Sandinistas in Nicaragua was waning, troops in Afghanistan and around the world had been withdrawn, and the nuclear arsenals of both superpowers had been massively reduced or eliminated as prescribed by his START initiative. Still, more important to him was the unmistakable realization that through his leadership American's faith in the greatness of their country had been restored.

During his eight years as president, Ronald Reagan confronted some of the most complex and perilous times of any president in U.S. history. Through each crisis, he persevered, never wavered in his ideological beliefs, and accomplished his objectives one by one, as if checking each off a list that he had somehow anticipated decades before. Yet many historians and political adversaries still see Reagan as shallow and detached. "He was a president who presided during a time that history favored," they will say, or "He was, himself, only an adequate leader surrounded by extraordinary advisers," or "He was just plain lucky."

France's President François Mitterrand may have best captured the essence of Ronald Reagan and what made what he did appear so easy and yet so elegantly profound. "They call President Reagan the 'Great Communicator,'" Mitterrand once told Canada's Prime Minister Brian Mulroney, "but he is not. Reagan does not *communicate* with his people. He is one with them. He *embodies* his people and the spirit of America and that is the secret of his success."[51]

RONALD REAGAN'S LEADERSHIP LESSONS

The leadership characteristic I admire most about Ronald Reagan is his modesty. Unlike Jack Welch and many other so-called "great" leaders, Reagan's modesty was perhaps his most attractive feature and the salient advantage he carried with him into political campaigns, negotiations, and domestic and international contests. Like Teddy Roosevelt, Reagan had learned to "walk softly and carry a big stick," but with a sense of modesty and quiet strength that underlies each of his presidential lessons.

Lesson #1
"Feed the Right Dog"

Every man and woman has a battle going on inside them for control of who they are and what their future will be. As the wise man's metaphor instructs, one dog, if it prevails, will lead them to a life that is vital—capable of affecting others, the world around them, and their own destiny—and to a character-driven life's journey. The second dog, if it prevails in the fight, will lead them into the abyss—a life that is dark, destructive and without meaning.

The crossroads that young Ronnie Reagan faced was not forestalled and the battle between the two dogs was won early when he shunned the path of his father, Jack, and the possibility of alcoholism, and chose the path of his mother, Nelle, to become, "Dutch" Reagan, the idealized young student-athlete of his own creation.

Reagan's choice to create, and become, that idealized self as a young man, not unlike FDR's choice so much later in life, determined not only that he'd be a leader but the kind of leadership he would exercise throughout his life.

Understand that who you are is a choice that begins with "feeding the right dog." Feed your good habits and starve the bad ones.

Lesson #2
Create "Alternate Endings"

After the Bay of Pigs fiasco, JFK wondered aloud, "How could I have been so stupid? Why did I ever listen to these so-called experts? It was *not* listening to the experts that got me elected!" Reagan had learned the lesson of listening to his own "inner voice" long before he became president.

Most experts look at history—compare it to the rearview mirror of a car—in order to determine the best course of action in a crisis. The reason the windshield of a car is so much bigger than the rearview mirror is that people going forward must look to the future for their answers not the past.

Perhaps it was Reagan's childhood imaginings, or his work in film where endings are written and re-written with multiple conclusions that nurtured his ability to see possibilities far different from the ones obvious to most of the experts, but Reagan had the unique ability to collapse history, pooling the past and the present to anticipate the future.

Understand that the way it was is not the way it will, or needs, to be. Just as Kennedy created an "alternate" ending to the space race by putting a man on the moon, and Reagan created his Strategic Defense Initiative to create an "alternate" ending to the nuclear arms race with the Soviet Union, never put a barrier between yourself and the world of possibilities by listening to those who would tell you, "it can't be done."

Lesson #3
"Connect the Dots"

Reagan during his NORAD visit saw the futility of the United State's nuclear program based solely on "attack" versus his alternate concept of a defensive program that could save 150 million American lives and render nuclear missiles obsolete forever.

"Before World War II, the British were developing a new defense system called radar to identify incoming bombers and rockets to . . . shoot them down before they struck . . . without that ability," Reagan argued, "England may have lost the war." If what was essentially a "defense shield" could protect England from bombers and V2 rockets, he wondered, why couldn't the U.S. protect itself from nuclear missiles with a new defense system based on satellites with laser weapons that formed a shield over head ?

Reagan imagined the game-changing power of SDI as president in July 1979, but in truth he'd spent his entire life "connecting the dots:" putting dreams, observations, facts, and possibilities together in a construction that created imaginative solutions for nearly every challenge he faced.

Though not obvious, much like Washington, Reagan's was also a steady march toward success recognizing, even in his failures, a way forward. From Eureka College to radio, from radio to Hollywood, from Hollywood to television, from television to corporate America, from corporate America to state politics, from state politics to national politics.

The art of "connecting the dots" depends on the ability to define a clear objective, observe the environment around you, understand your current situation, and then—with resilience, creativity, and a well-honed survival instinct—to innovate a practical way forward to achieve that goal.

Great leaders, and leaders in the making—whether facing small challenges or large—learn how to "connect the dots."

Lesson #4
Great Leaders Are "Maze Smart"

Some leaders know how to "run through the maze" because they are resourceful but few know how to "come out of the briar patch without all of those briars on your pants." The reason is that there's a different set of skills involved in being "Maze Smart" like Reagan.

The most underrated skill set in a character-driven leader's ability to be "Maze Smart" is charm, diplomacy, and purity of motive.

Reagan used humor: To Walter Mondale, who during their debate promised not to play the age card, "I want you to know that I also will not make age an issue in this campaign. I am not going to exploit, for political purposes, my opponent's youth and inexperience." Reagan used humility: When asked to explain his administration's success, he answered, "Maybe part of it is described by a plaque on my desk that says, 'There's no limit to what we can do if you don't mind who gets the credit." Reagan used compromise, "I've never understood people who want me to hang in there for 100% of nothing. Why not take 70% or 80%, and then come back for the other 20% or 30%. Reagan used persuasive language that elevated his arguments and ennobled his ideas, "I do not believe in a fate that will fall on us no matter what we do. I do believe in a fate that will fall on us if we do nothing."

Throughout his life, Reagan demonstrated a purity of motive—the foundation of his ability to be "Maze Smart,"—that was never more evident than at the height of Hollywood's infamous "Red Scare." "In a time of malice he was not malicious; in a time of lies he did not falsify; in a time of great pressure he didn't break or bend; in a time of disingenuousness he was clear and candid about where he stood and why."

In the end, a leader's most satisfying victories come without a battle, Sun Tsu reminds us in his book *The Art of War*. Charm and diplomacy are the skills necessary to settle disputes before they deteriorate into confrontation. But if a battle must occur, purity of motive is the best assurance for a leader to survive unscathed because his or her followers understand that he or she is character-driven, deserves their respect, and leads with values that—win, lose, or draw—will always be revered.

Charm, diplomacy, and purity of motive, are all elements of the skill set great leaders, and leaders in-the-making, use to stay "Maze Smart."

Lesson #5
Prepare Yourself for the Long Haul

On the day he took office, Reagan inherited an economy with an $80 billion budget deficit, interest rates at 21%, and an inflation rate of 17%. Less than a month after he'd been shot, he plunged back into the fray, addressing Congress on April 28, 1981, with a successful plea to pass his Program for Economic Recovery. One year after the program passed the economic situation was still on a steady decline: unemployment topped 10%, the recession deepened, and Reagan's approval ratings dropped to 35%. Even David Stockman, his closest economic advisor, publicly questioned the validity of his programs, but Reagan stood tall, never losing faith, and after two torturous years the economy finally turned.

Great leaders like Reagan, Washington, TR, Lincoln and FDR are not dilettantes. Most possess legendary endurance and every one of them began their leadership journey prepared to hang in for the long haul. Like championship athletes, they eat right, exercise, get enough sleep, stay passionate about their life, and put the right actions with their dreams.

Understand up front that few good things come easy.

Like Reagan, in leading the country through the worst economic crisis in decades, prepare yourself physically and psychologically to lead, be resolute in your beliefs regardless of what detractors say, and stay focused on the prize.

Lesson #6
Learn to be Selfless

Each of the six presidents we've studied—regardless of whether they began that way—had, by the time they confronted their greatest challenge, learned to subjugate their own ego before they became "great." When Gorbachev set before Reagan a Faustian deal that offered personal triumph over his allegiance to what the president believed was his sworn responsibility to the American people, Reagan rejected it out of hand.

The Soviet leader made an understandable miscalculation. Before him he saw a 75 year old former actor whose vanity, ego, and eagerness for an historical legacy would certainly overcome whatever pangs of conscience his out-of-fashion principles might give him, but that is not what happened because somewhere along the way to becoming a character-driven leader, Reagan had also become "selfless."

Given the identical circumstance, in my opinion, every one of the great American presidents we have studied would have reacted the same way.

In your journey to achieving character-driven leadership you, too, will become "selfless."

Chapter VIII

The Transformation: From Fearful Manager to Indomitable Leader

The *Harvard Business Review* recently published a series of articles on executive leadership. Some of the advice that the articles emphasize should sound familiar:

> Waiting for heroes on horses to slash through your company's thorniest dilemmas? No need. Look away from the limelight—to your quiet leaders already hard at work.[1]
>
> Before they take tough stands or tackle tough problems, quiet leaders calculate how much political capital they are putting at risk and what they can expect in return.[2]
>
> If you want to push important cultural changes through your organization without damaging your career, step softly.[3]

Each of these pieces vaunting the value of the "quiet" leader moving his corporation forward day by day is interesting, but after studying the lives of our six great presidents and the lessons we can learn from them, it seems to me that each is flawed in its basic premise.

"Heroes" are exactly what America needs—in politics, in business, in global affairs, and in everyday life. Indeed, if there is anything immediately discernable from our study, it's that each of these presidents was, in their own way, a "hero" in that they dared to be exceptional in a world weighed down by convention. They did so to the best of their abilities and with the purest of motives. If, in fact, we wish to emulate their leadership—and the enduring impact each created—we too must transform ourselves from fearful managers of our lives and careers to heroes of our own lives and leaders within the careers we choose to pursue.

Three thousand years ago, Aristotle defined political greatness as "the ability to translate wisdom into action on behalf of the public good." To be able to do this, he argued, requires a combination of "moral virtue, practical wisdom, and public-spiritedness."[4] Not coincidentally, each of the presidents we've studied—regardless of whether they began that way—had, by the time they confronted their greatest challenge, learned to subjugate their own ego before they became "great." For example, Washington knew well the bitter taste of failure—both in his ego-driven pursuit of a British military commission, and in battle—before maturing into the superlative general and commanding leader that history remembers. His belief in himself and his cause never wavered, but his understanding of the larger mission he was destined to fulfill dwarfed notions of his own self-importance to the point where he freely surrendered his position as commander of the victorious American forces the moment the war ended.

The same was true of FDR, originally a smart-alecky rich kid concerned more about social standing than the people who put him in office. It was only after he himself contracted polio that the plight of indigent whites and blacks, immigrants, and the infirmed became visible to him. It was then, and only with the surrendering of ego, that Roosevelt became capable of greatness, whereby he attained the "no fear" attitude necessary to boldly act on plans to make the nation and its citizens more secure, regardless of personal consequences.

I "SEE" YOU

In a recent graduation address, former president Bill Clinton spoke about South African civil rights leader Nelson Mandela, who once told him that the greeting among members of his African tribe doesn't translate into the typical American greetings of "Hello" or "How are you?" Rather, the tribe's greeting translates into the simple acknowledgement "*I see you.*" What this meant to Mandela, and means to our examination of leadership, is that these six presidents—Lincoln, Kennedy, Washington, FDR, TR, Kennedy, and Reagan—only became great once they learned to take off the blinders and recognize those unlike them as "visible."

So it was that Teddy Roosevelt prowled the nighttime streets of New York City's ghettoes with newspaperman Jacob Riis in an attempt "to see" the poverty and injustice that those of his social class did not know or want to know. Lincoln, who dared "to see" ex-slave Frederick Douglass, was vehemently criticized by many in both the North and South, but through that exposure he came to understand the plight of African Americans, internalized it, and was forever changed by it. JFK, once the "television" candidate obsessive about his hair and tailor-made suits, had reconsidered by the end of his life all that he knew, or thought he knew. Small vanities riveted in self-absorption gave way to larger concepts, specifically racial equality, nuclear disarmament, and world peace. Reagan, too, after his sobering visit to NORAD and soul-searching discussions with Mikhail Gorbachev, allowed himself "to see" the Soviets not as implacable "enemies" but as citizens of the world.

Because situational leaders look at employees, peers, and those around them as chess pieces to be moved in whatever direction best serves their own self-interest—with no regard for moral virtue—they cannot "see." For character-driven leaders who espouse leadership founded on principles (moral virtue), hard-won experience (practical wisdom), and purity of motive (public spiritedness), greatness is always a possibility and should always be strived for because character-driven leaders are "born to see."

Some may question the phrase "born to see," but in the final analysis I believe that each of us—like the six presidents we've studied—was born to see. The reason is that there's nothing in Aristotle's definition that makes greatness inaccessible to any of us today, or precludes us from pursuing it as a very real objective in our lives. If we want it badly enough—and we're willing to exchange the extraneous trinkets of self-absorption and greed for the gold standard of continuous learning and commitment to the greater good— each of us can become the heroes of our own lives. Whether an executive, an athlete, a homemaker, or a brain surgeon, we can transform ourselves from someone else's chess piece to the protagonist in the epic story that is our life.

A TOTAL TRANSFORMATION

If we adopt this perspective, what were formerly inconsequential details soon become important to us. The corrosive power of one's "white lies" becomes anathema; the betrayal of trust between a friend, subordinate, or loved one suddenly produces nagging discomfort; a missed deadline or one cocktail too many is unacceptable; the arrogance shown by arriving at a meeting ten minutes late is something to be personally reckoned with. All have become internal setbacks that must be addressed and overcome because true "heroes" forever strive to achieve, and need to always hold, self-respect dear.

Similarly, formerly inconsequential acts well-done also loom large to us. Coming to the aid of a colleague struggling with a project; being the first to attend and the best prepared at a meeting; steering group dynamics bogged down in dissension onto a positive path; and being totally trustworthy in dealings with a friend, subordinate, or loved one—these are the virtuous acts of "heroes."

To others who are unaware of the transformation you've undergone, the life you live each day may appear ordinary, but you know better: each life is an "epic journey," and each person is an "epic hero." And that is, I'm convinced, the way each of our six presidents carried on with their lives during the periods of their greatest challenge and their greatest successes.

Interestingly, as with Washington, who saw himself as a great commander decades before he became one; Teddy Roosevelt, who willed himself out of an invalid's bed to become the adventurer he'd imagined; Lincoln, the "uneducated rube" who dreamed of becoming president; FDR, who, even as a victim of polio, believed he could lead America's military forces; Kennedy, who, sickly and perhaps dying, believed that he could navigate the nation through the Cuban Missile Crisis; and Reagan, who dared to take on the awesome power of the Soviet Union, you can be the leader you imagine simply by working each day to become that person.

The first, and most important, step on the road to great leadership—or leadership of any kind—is the willingness to change. Unless you believe you can do better and continuously improve yourself as a human being, you will never be capable of achieving character-driven leadership.

Character-driven leaders aren't born. They are self-developed. Like the "corporate athlete" Jim Loehr and Tony Schwartz write about in "The Making of a Corporate Athlete," you must possess the will to continuously strengthen yourself for the challenges ahead; otherwise, your leadership talents, like unused muscles, will grow weak and eventually wither.[5]

Most will agree that there is no small portion of *belief* in the life of Washington, *principles* in the presidency of Lincoln, *action* in the adventures of Theodore Roosevelt, *creativity* in the policies of Franklin D. Roosevelt, *courage* in the deportment of John Kennedy during his thousand days as president, and *perseverance* demonstrated in the achievements of Reagan. Yet if there is one message that runs through all of their life stories, it's that they were leaders who deeply cared about the world around them, were not afraid to engage it, and tried their best to make it a better place.

BUILDING A BETTER SELF

One frequent objection to my ardent belief that leadership is a personal choice argues that many individuals lack the positional power or authority to lead. One middle manager, working for a *Fortune* 500 company, described feeling "powerless" to fulfill even the essential duties of his job description, "stuck," as he saw it, trying to escape from the "corporate box."[6] This complaint is not unique: Similar comments are often the first response to the ardent proposition that every person—in whatever field, and at whatever level—can lead.

If one takes a step back from the mythology that surrounds the six great presidents we've studied, there are many more likely to have become president. Few faced as many challenges as these men—ranging from abject poverty to physical debilitation, lack of education to chronic illness and near-fatal disease. Each passed through what Warren Bennis and Robert Thomas call the "crucible of leadership": nearly insurmountable challenges that forced them "to question who they were and what was important to them."[7] Yet they tried, failed, endured, and ultimately prevailed. Why is this? The reasons vary, but one undeniable fact is that they learned from every failure and internalized those lessons to "build a better self."

Perhaps, then, escaping from a "corporate box," or box of any description, has much to do with having goals, learning from experiences—good and bad—and never giving up. "Good things happen to guys that don't quit," observed Massachusetts boxer "Irish" Micky Ward, who, at the age of thirty-seven, achieved his lifelong dream of becoming middleweight champion of the world. Far from the most skilled boxer, definitely past his prime, and probably a better philosopher than fighter, Micky Ward accomplished his goal simply by refusing to abandon it.

Today, our families, our country, and the world face massive challenges, some of which are traditional (war, genocide, the spread of weapons of mass destruction) others that are non-traditional and, perhaps, even self-imposed (global recession, unstable financial systems, lack of faith in our institutions). Clearly, these times and our history call out to us for change, but it is not forward change so much as it is internal transformation, away from situational leadership with its quick-fix and quick-gains and on to the kind of character-driven leadership demonstrated by these six Presidents whose values and principles history has recorded for us to study and emulate.

We waste so much of our time, money, energy, and ambition on things that are fundamentally nonessential to us—car, clothes, the club that we belong to. How much time do we spend building a "better self"? How many hours, or minutes, each day? And if such ruminations do swirl through our heads, even on a weekly basis, *what do we do about it?*

If answers to these questions don't generate a blaring affirmative, perhaps we are in kind of a box, or in the midst of our own wilderness period—or, perhaps, we've never left the wilderness at all. Ultimately, then, great leadership begins with gathering the will to rise above one's own limitations because, in the end, there's something absurd about the fact that what there is to escape from is often actually, and ingeniously, a box constructed by ourselves.

The true lesson to be learned from the study of our American presidents is that great leadership in business, and in life, is up to each of us, just as it was up to Washington, Lincoln, TR, Franklin Roosevelt, Kennedy, and Reagan.

That's why I'm so optimistic about America and its future, despite today's challenging environment. The reason is that never in the history of the world has there been a nation or a people so innovative, so resilient, and so determined to succeed as the United States of America during the presidencies of these men and now.

Notes

INTRODUCTION

1. Musashi, *The Book of Five Rings*, p. 15.

CHAPTER I

1. Hay Acquisition Company I Inc., *Inventory of Leadership Styles*, 1.
2. Hay Acquisition Company I Inc., *Emotional Capacity Index*, 3.
3. Hay Acquisition Company I Inc., *Emotional Intelligence Competence Model*, 5.
4. Interview with "H. G.," August 17, 2005.
5. Hay Acquisition Company I, *Leadership Development*.
6. Welch, *Jack: Straight from the Gut*, 157–58.
7. Ibid., 393.
8. Ibid., 158.
9. Bianco, "Jack Welch: The Fall of an Icon."
10. Nixon, *Leaders*, 1.
11. Collins, *Good to Great*, 35.
12. Ibid.
13. Collins, pp Ibid., 32-33.
14. Interview with "B. O.," December 12, 2005.
15. Collins, *Good to Great*, 41.
16. Boy Scouts of America, *Boy Scouts Handbook*, 9.
17. Musashi, *The Book of Five Rings*, p. 27.

CHAPTER II

1. Zogby International, "Greatest Presidents Poll," 2008.
2. Goodwin, "The Master of the Game."

3. Shenk, "The True Lincoln."
4. Shenk, "The True Lincoln."
5. Carwardine, *Lincoln*, pp. 98-99.
6. Goodwin, "The Master of the Game."
7. Covey, *The Seven Habits of Highly Effective People*, 47.
8. Goodwin, *Team of Rivals*, 728–29.
9. John Stauffer, "Across the Great Divide."
10. Ibid.
11. Shenk, "The True Lincoln."
12. Wilson.
13. Carwardine, *Lincoln*, 81.
14. Ibid., 73.
15. Ibid., 35.
16. Ibid., 37.
17. Stauffer, "Across the Great Divide."
18. Carwardine, *Lincoln*, 121.
19. Ibid.
20. Ibid.
21. Carwardine, *Lincoln*, 52.
22. Ibid., 97.
23. Ibid., 117.
24. Ibid.
25. Ibid.
26. Ibid.
27. Ibid, 226–227.
28. Stauffer, "Across the Great Divide."
29. Ibid.
30. Goodwin, 464.
31. Ibid., 463.
32. Ibid., 459-472.
33. Ibid., 468.
34. Ibid.
35. Stauffer, "Across the Great Divide."
36. Ibid.
37. Ibid.
38. Ibid.
39. Goodwin, 480.
40. Ibid., 482–483.
41. Ibid.
42. Ibid.
43. Stauffer, "Across the Great Divide."
44. Dowd, "What Manager Reagan Can Teach Managers."

CHAPTER III

1. Reeves, *A Question of Character*, 153.
2. Dallek and Golway, p. 79.
3. *JFK: A Presidency Revealed.*
4. Reeves, *A Question of Character*, 189.
5. Ibid.
6. *JFK: A Presidency Revealed*
7. Reeves, *A Question of Character*, 97.
8. *JFK: A Presidency Revealed*
9. Dallek and Golway, 2.
10. Ibid
11. Reeves, *A Question of Character*, 122.
12. *JFK: A Presidency Revealed.*
13. Ibid.
14. Schlesinger, *A Thousand Days*, 9.
15. Reeves, *A Question of Character*, 169.
16. Interview with Gallagher, June 1999.
17. Ibid.
18. Halberstam, *The Best and the Brightest.*
19. Churchill, *The Gathering Storm*, 137.
20. Dallek, *Let Every Nation Know*, 43.
21. *New York Times*, November 5, 1960.
22. *JFK: A Presidency Revealed.*
23. Halberstam, *The Best and the Brightest*, 67.
24. *JFK: A Presidency Revealed.*
25. Ibid.
26. Ibid
27. *JFK: A Presidency Revealed.*
28. Dallek and Golway, 131.
29. *JFK: A Presidency Revealed.*
30. Dallek and Golway, 131.
31. Ibid.
32. *JFK: A Presidency Revealed.*
33. Dallek and Golway, 138.
34. *JFK: A Presidency Revealed.*
35. Dallek and Golway, 113.
36. Ibid., 149.
37. Ibid., 151.
38. Ibid., 169.
39. Schlesinger, *A Thousand Days*, 811.
40. *JFK: A Presidency Revealed.*

41. Ibid.
42. Dallek, "The Medical Ordeals of JFK."
43. Dallek and Golway, 178.
44. Ibid.
45. Ibid., 183.
46. Ibid.
47. May and Zelikow, *Kennedy Tapes*, 347–605.
48. *JFK: A Presidency Revealed.*
49. Ibid.
50. Dallek and Golway, 196.
51. Ibid.
52. Ibid., 199.
53. Ibid., 200.
54. Ibid., 201.
55. Ibid., 203.
56. Ibid., 213.
57. Ibid., 161.
58. *JFK: A Presidency Revealed*

CHAPTER IV

1. Ellis, *His Excellency*, 39.
2. Flexner, *Washington*, 32.
3. Ibid., 4.
4. Ibid.
5. Ibid., 6.
6. Ellis, *His Excellency*, 31.
7. Leckie, *George Washington's War*, 130–31.
8. Ellis, *His Excellency*, 14.
9. Jackson, *The Diaries of George Washington*, 1:26–34.
10. Leckie, *George Washington's War*, 132.
11. Flexner, *Washington*, 18.
12. Ellis, *His Excellency*, 4.
13. Ibid., 6.
14. Flexner, *Washington*, 18.
15. Ibid., 19.
16. Ibid., 27.
17. Ibid., 31.
18. Ibid., 32.
19. Ellis, *His Excellency*, 35.
20. Ibid., 146.

CHAPTER V

1. *FDR: A Presidency Revealed.*
2. Ibid.
3. Black, *Franklin Delano Roosevelt*, 20.
4. Ibid., 23.
5. Ibid., 42.
6. Ibid., 25.
7. Ibid., 30.
8. Ibid., 32.
9. Ibid, 36.
10. *FDR: A Presidency Revealed.*
11. Ibid.
12. Ibid.
13. Ibid.
14. Ibid.
15. *FDR: A Presidency Revealed.*
16. Bennis and Thomas, "Crucibles of Leadership."
17. *FDR: A Presidency Revealed.*
18. Ibid.
19. Ibid.
20. Davis, *FDR*, 288.
21. *FDR: A Presidency Revealed.*
22. *FDR: A Presidency Revealed.*
23. Musashi, *The Book of Five Rings*, 15.
24. *FDR: A Presidency Revealed.*
25. Ibid.
26. Ibid.
27. Goodwin, *No Ordinary Time*, 37.
28. Black, *Franklin Delano Roosevelt*, 183.
29. *FDR: A Presidency Revealed.*
30. Kennedy, *Freedom from Fear*, 303.
31. Goodwin, *No Ordinary Time*, 193.
32. Ibid., 68.
33. Ibid., 47.
34. *Atlantic Monthly*, February 2002, 62.
35. Kennedy, *Freedom from Fear*, 856.
36. Goodwin, *No Ordinary Time*, 318–19.
37. Ibid., 42.
38. Emert, *World War II*, 29.
39. Ibid., 29.
40. Ibid., 36.

41. Goodwin, *No Ordinary Time*, 391.
42. *FDR: A Presidency Revealed.*

CHAPTER VI

1. Churchill, *The Gathering Storm*, 97.
2. *Biography.*
3. Dalton, *Theodore Roosevelt*, 27.
4. Ibid., 431.
5. *Biography.*
6. Roosevelt, *Diaries of Boyhood and Youth*, 43.
7. Dalton, *Theodore Roosevelt*, 72.
8. *Biography.*
9. Roosevelt, *The Autobiography of Theodore Roosevelt*, 127.
10. *Biography.*
11. Roosevelt, 132.
12. Morris, *Theodore Rex*, 118.
13. Zacks, "The Police Commish."
14. Ibid.
15. Lacyo, "The Making of America."
16. Dalton, *Theodore Roosevelt*, 173.
17. Ibid., 174.
18. Ibid., 174.
19. Ibid., 179.
20. Ibid., 184.
21. Ibid., 357.
22. *Biography.*
23. Kasson, *Houdini, Tarzan, and the Perfect White Male Body*, 11.
24. Ibid., 12.
25. Ibid.
26. Morris, *Theodore Rex*, 159.
27. Ibid., 160.
28. Ibid., 169.
29. Leonard, "Theodore Roosevelt's Broad Powers."
30. Morris, *Theodore Rex*, 87.
31. Ibid., 94.
32. Leonard, "Theodore Roosevelt's Broad Powers."
33. *Biography.*
34. Ibid.
35. Ibid.
36. Dalton, *Theodore Roosevelt*, 404.
37. Ibid., 406.
38. Ibid.

CHAPTER VII

1. Reeves, *President Reagan*, xv11.
2. "Manager Reagan," *Fortune*, September, 15, 1986.
3. Noonan, *When Character Was King*, 317.
4. Ibid., 229.
5. Reagan, *Where's the Rest of Me?* 24–26.
6. Noonan, *When Character Was King*, 26.
7. Ibid, 20.
8. Reagan, *Where's the Rest of Me?* 18.
9. *Reagan: A Presidency Revealed.*
10. Hayward, *Greatness*, 88.
11. *Reagan: A Presidency Revealed.*
12. Noonan, *When Character Was King*, 21–22.
13. *Reagan: A Presidency Revealed.*
14. Noonan, *When Character Was King*, 43.
15. Hayward, *Greatness*, 33.
16. Reeves, *President Reagan*, 155.
17. Hayward, *Greatness*, 33.
18. Noonan, *When Character Was King*, 52.
19. *Reagan: A Presidency Revealed.*
20. Noonan, *When Character Was King*, 61.
21. Ibid., 65.
22. *Reagan: A Presidency Revealed.*
23. Reagan, *I Love You, Ronnie*, 45.
24. Noonan, *When Character Was King*, 68.
25. Hayward, *Greatness*, 108–9.
26. *Fortune*, September 15, 1986.
27. Ibid.
28. Ibid.
29. Ibid.
30. Reagan, *The Reagan Diaries*, xii.
31. *Reagan: A Presidency Revealed.*
32. Ibid.
33. Reeves, *President Reagan*, 22–23.
34. Ibid.
35. *Reagan: A Presidency Revealed.*
36. *Reagan: A Presidency Revealed.*
37. *Fortune.*
38. *Reagan: A Presidency Revealed.*
39. Ibid.
40. Ibid.
41. Ibid.
42. *Fortune.*

43. *Reagan: A Presidency Revealed.*
44. Ibid.
45. *Fortune.*
46. Noonan, *When Character Was King*, 290–91.
47. Ibid.
48. Ibid., 290–92.
49. Reagan, *The Reagan Diaries.*
50. Reagan, *The Reagan Diaries.*
51. *Reagan: A Presidency Revealed.*

CHAPTER VIII

1. Badaracco, "We Don't Need Another Hero."
2. Meyerson, "Radical Change, The Quiet Way."
3. Collins, "Level 5 Leadership."
4. Hayward, *Greatness*, 17.
5. Loehr and Schwartz, "The Making of a Corporate Athlete."
6. "H.G." Personal Interview, August 17, 2005.
7. Bennis and Thomas, "Crucibles of Leadership."

Bibliography

Badaracco, Joseph, Jr. "We Don't Need Another Hero." *Harvard Business Review*, 2001, p. 7.

Basler, Roy. P., ed. *Abraham Lincoln: His Speeches and Writings*. Cleveland: World, 1946.

Benchley, William. "Saboteurs." *Atlantic Monthly*, February 2002, p. 76.

Bennis, Warren, and Robert Thomas. "Crucibles of Leadership." *Harvard Business Review*, 2002, pp. 151–52.

Bianco, Anthony. "Jack Welch: The Fall of an Icon." *Business Week*, September 23, 2002, 53–54.

Biography [Theodore Roosevelt]. A&E Television, 1995.

Black, Conrad. *Franklin Delano Roosevelt: Champion of Freedom*. New York: Public Affairs, 2003.

"B. O." Personal interview. December 12, 2005.

Boy Scouts of America. *Boy Scouts Handbook*. Irving, TX: 1998.

Carwardine, Richard. *Lincoln: A Life of Purpose and Power*. New York: Knopf, 2006.

Chu, Jeff. "Loathing Abe Lincoln." *Time*, June 26, 2005, pp. 17–18.

Collins, Jim. *Good to Great*. New York: HarperCollins, 2001.

———. "Level 5 Leadership." *Harvard Business Review*, 2001.

Covey, Stephen. *The Seven Habits of Highly Effective People*. New York: Summit, 1991.

Clinton, Bill. Commencement Address, Rochester Institute of Technology, June 6, 2006.

Dallek, Robert. *Let Every Nation Know*. Naperville, IL: Sourcebooks, 2006.

———. "The Medical Ordeals of JFK." *Atlantic Monthly*, December 2002, pp. 57–58.

Dalton, Kathleen. *Theodore Roosevelt: A Strenuous Life*. New York: Vintage, 2002.

———. "The Self-made Man." *Time*, July 3, 2006, p. 37.

Davis, Kenneth S. *FDR: The War President*. New York: Random House, 2000.

Dole, Bob. *Great Presidential Wit*. New York: Scribner's, 2001.

Dowd, Ann. "What Managers Can Learn from Manager Reagan." *Fortune*, September 15, 1986, pp. 37-44.

Ellis, Joseph J. *His Excellency: George Washington.* New York: Vintage, 2004.

Emert, Phyllis Raybin. *World War II: On the Homefront.* New York: Discovery Enterprises Ltd., 1996.

FDR: A Presidency Revealed. A&E Television, 2005.

Fleming, Thomas. *The New Dealers' War: F.D.R. and the War Within World War II.* New York: Basic Books, 2001.

Flexner, James Thomas. *Washington: The Indispensable Man.* New York: Little, Brown, 1969.

Fornieri, Joseph R. *Abraham Lincoln's Political Faith.* DeKalb: Northern Illinois University Press, 2003.

Gallagher, Cornelius. Personal interviews. December 29, 1998, and June 12, 1999.

Goodwin, Doris Kearns. *No Ordinary Time: Franklin and Eleanor Roosevelt: The Home Front in World War II.* New York: Simon and Schuster, 1995.

———. *Team of Rivals: The Political Genius of Abraham Lincoln.* New York: Simon & Schuster, 2005.

———. "The Master of the Game." *Time*, June 26, 2005, pp. 67–69.

Halberstam, David. *The Best and the Brightest.* New York: Fawcett, 1969.

Hay Acquisition Company I, Inc. *Emotional Capacity Index; Emotional Intelligence Competence Model; Inventory of Leadership Styles; Leadership Development.* Frankfurt, Germany: Hay Group, 2002.

Hayward, Steven F. *Greatness: Reagan, Churchill, and the Making of Extraordinary Leaders.* New York: Three Rivers, 2006.

"H. G." Personal interview. August 17, 2005.

Jackson, Donald, ed. *The Diaries of George Washington.* 6 vols. Charlottesville: 1976.

JFK: A Presidency Revealed. A&E Television, 2001.

Kasson, John F. *Houdini, Tarzan, and the Perfect White Male Body.* New York: Hill and Wang, 2001.

Kennedy, David M. *Freedom from Fear.* New York: Oxford University Press, 1999.

Lacayo, Richard. "The Making of America." *Time*, July 3, 2006, p. 23.

Leckie, Robert. *George Washington's War.* New York: Harper Perennial, 1992.

Leonard, Erin Ruth. "Theodore Roosevelt's Broad Powers." University of Groningen, Netherlands, 2006, p. 3.

Loehr, Jim, and Tony Schwartz. "The Making of a Corporate Athlete." *Harvard Business Review*, 2002, pp. 144–46.

Maxwell, John C. *The 360 Degree Leader.* Nashville, TN: Thomas Nelson, 2005.

May, Ernest R., and Philip D. Zelikow. *The Kennedy Tapes.* Cambridge, MA: Harvard University Press, 1997.

Meyerson, Debra. "Radical Change, the Quiet Way." *Harvard Business Review*, 2001, p. 33.

Morris, Edmund. *Theodore Rex.* New York: Modern Library, 2001.

Musashi, Miyamoto. *The Book of Five Rings.* Riverside: Overlook, 1989.

Nixon, Richard M. *Leaders.* New York: Warner, 1982.

Noonan, Peggy. *When Character Was King.* New York: Penguin, 2002.

Phillips, Donald T. *Lincoln on Leadership*. New York: Warner, 1992.

Reagan, Nancy. *I Love You, Ronnie*. New York: Random House, 2002.

Reagan: A Presidency Revealed. A&E Television, 2005.

Reagan, Ronald. *Where's the Rest of Me?* New York: Karz, 1981.

———. *The Reagan Diaries*, ed. Douglas Brinkley. New York: HarperCollins, 2007.

Rees, James C. *George Washington's Leadership Lessons*. Hoboken, NJ: Wiley, 2007.

Reeves, Richard. *President Reagan: The Triumph of Imagination*. New York: Simon and Schuster, 2005.

Reeves, Thomas. *A Question of Character: The Life of John F. Kennedy*. New York: Macmillan, 1991.

Roosevelt, Theodore. *Diaries of Boyhood and Youth*. New York: Scribner's, 1928.

———. *The Autobiography of Theodore Roosevelt*. New York: Scribner's, 1958.

Schlesinger, Arthur M., Jr. *A Thousand Days*. New York: Mariner, 1965.

Shenk, Joshua Wolf. "The True Lincoln." *Time*, June 26, 2005.

Stauffer, John. "Across the Great Divide." *Time*, June 26, 2005.

Welch, Jack. *Jack: Straight from the Gut*. New York: Warner, 2001.

Zacks, Richard. "The Police Commish." *Time*, July 3, 2006.

Zogby International. "Greatest Presidents Poll." 2006.

Index

217

21625705R00135

Made in the USA
Lexington, KY
21 March 2013